MR BROWN'S
WAR

To Margaret Brown who trusted me with her father's diaries and answered my endless questions with great patience I dedicate this book. Sadly she died just a few months before publication.

MR BROWN'S
WAR

*A Diary of the
Second World War*

Edited by

HELEN D. MILLGATE

SUTTON PUBLISHING

This book was first published in 1998 by
Sutton Publishing Limited · Phoenix Mill
Thrupp · Stroud · Gloucestershire · GL5 2BU

This new paperback edition first published in 2003

British Library Cataloguing in Publication Data
A catalogue record for this book is available from the British Library

ISBN 0 7509 3170 1

Typeset in 10/11.5pt Plantin.
Typesetting and origination by
Sutton Publishing Limited.
Printed and bound in Great Britain by
J.H. Haynes & Co. Ltd, Sparkford.

Contents

Maps

Abbreviations

AA	Anti-aircraft
AG	Anti-gas
AMI. Mech. E	Associate Member of the Institute of Mechanical Engineers
AP	Anti-personnel
ARP	Air Raid Precautions
ATC	Air Training Corps
BLA	Browning Light Automatic
CD	Civil Defence
CMB	Coastal Motor Boat
CW	Chemical Warfare
DO	Draughtsmen's (Drawing) Office
DR	Dispatch Rider
EADT	*East Anglian Daily Times*
EAM	Greek National Liberation Front
ELAS	Greek Popular Liberation Army
FAP	First Aid Post
FFI	Free French Forces
FG	Fire Guard
FIDO	Fog Intensive Dispersal Operation
GOC	General Officer Commanding
HE	High Explosive
HG	Home Guard
IB	Incendiary Bomb
KR	Kingsley Reavell
LAC	Leading Aircraftsman, RAF
LCI	Landing Craft Infantry
LCT	Landing Craft Tank
Magna	Mutual Aid Good Neighbours' Association
MG	Machine-gun

MOI	Ministry of Information
MTB	Motor Torpedo Boat
MV	Muzzle Velocity
NAAFI	Navy, Army and Air Force Institutes
NFS	National Fire Service
NWEF	Norwegian Expeditionary Force
OP	Observation Post
PO	Platoon Officer
PRU	Photo Reconnaissance Unit
RE	Royal Engineers
REME	Royal Electrical and Mechanical Engineers
SA	Small Arms
SHAEF	Supreme Headquarters Allied Expeditionary Force
SW	Senior Warden
TAF	Tactical Air Force
UNRRA	United Nations Relief and Rehabilitation Administration
USAAF	United States Army Air Force
UXB	Unexploded Bomb
WR	Sir William Reavell

Acknowledgements

First and foremost I must thank my husband for his constant support: practical, technical, professional and moral. His enthusiasm for this project has matched my own and he has helped me at every stage. I am also particularly grateful to Area Archivist David Jones of Suffolk Record Office whom I initially approached and who, amazingly and immediately, found me a publisher. Norman Howard an ex-colleague of Richard Brown has been very helpful with information about Reavell and Co., and I must also mention Robert Moss who was interested enough to read through all the original twelve diaries.

I apologise for any factual errors in the text; it has been very difficult fifty years on to check all data or to trace all those people mentioned, very often only by first name. I trust we have offended nobody.

Conversion Table

1d (penny)	=	0.4 new pence
6d (sixpence)	=	2½ new pence
1/- (one shilling)	=	5 new pence
2/6d (half a crown)	=	12½ new pence
10/-	=	50 new pence
20/ (one pound)	=	100 new pence

one guinea (one pound and one shilling)

Introduction

Richard Finn Brown, born in 1902, spent all his working life at Reavell and Co. in Ipswich, starting as an engineering apprentice and finally becoming Chief Designer. He met his wife Dora when she was a tracer in the same drawing office. At the outbreak of the war their daughter Margaret was five years old and son Godfrey eighteen months. Reavell's, manufacturers of compressors, were heavily engaged in war work and Mr Brown worked on the design of submarine dehumidifiers. From the outset of war, he became a faithful recorder of life on the Home Front and events around the world in twelve notebooks containing 400,000 handwritten words and several carefully drawn maps of the theatres of conflict.

His daughter first showed me the diaries at a time when certain revisionist historians were questioning the Allied conduct of the war, challenging the statistics, and particularly implying that the British public were often kept in ignorance of the bad news. I think these diaries entirely refute that argument. Richard Brown, a 'member of the public' if ever there was one, with no access to restricted or secret information, seems to have been remarkably well informed. When I started to check figures he quotes I found only a very few minor discrepancies with contemporary statistics. More importantly the disastrous news seems to have been released with startling rapidity, for example, the sinking of the *Hood* on 23 May 1941 was reported by the BBC the very next day and there was equal speed in coverage of the fall of Singapore, the infamous raid on Coventry, the loss of Bataan in the Philippines and heavy RAF bomber losses, to name but a few. Numbers of civilian casualties were not withheld, only the location of those casualties. Nor were shipping losses concealed, though sometimes published monthly instead of weekly.

Concurrently with his narrative of the progress of the war, the design engineer gives us a vibrant image of life in wartime Britain –

rationing, blackout restrictions, shortages, air raids, the uncertainties of evacuation and the enormous burdens placed upon the many civilians coping with a full-time job as well as an almost full-time commitment to Civil Defence.

Of equal interest is Mr Brown's attitude: he never doubted ultimate victory though he was frequently impatient and scathing of the conduct of the war, particularly during the first two years of defeats and 'strategic withdrawals'; he, like so many others, had enormous faith in Churchill's leadership; and he was as disgusted by the French capitulation as he was admiring of the Russians. He was also a well-informed man, more than capable of making his own judgements based on the news reports of events often in places that had barely appeared on the map before but now suddenly became strategically important household names. There were misconceptions and he was sometimes prey to unlikely rumour but, above all, these diaries reflect the moral and social attitudes of the period and will I am sure be of great interest to those of us who shared these wartime experiences and equally to those who did not.

Note: The other people who appear most frequently in the diaries are: Richard Brown's mother who lived with the family; Dora's sisters Muriel, Sylvia and Gladys; Mr Brown's sisters Aggie and Win; Win's son Dennis; Mr Brown's work colleagues Green, 'Aldy' and 'Ven'; and neighbours George and Nelly Rudd, Harry and Doris Weaver, Reginald Thrower and Arthur Mayhew.

*The War Diaries of
Richard Brown, 1939–46*

1939

Although war was actually declared on 3 September 1939 after the German invasion of Poland, preparations had been mounting since the Munich Crisis a year before. However, as Prime Minister Chamberlain's voice drifted from wirelesses bringing the news that the country had feared, activity reached fever pitch. The armed forces were mobilised and the Civil Defence organisation put onto a war footing. On 1 September 1.5 million schoolchildren, mothers with small children and accompanying teachers were evacuated from the big cities to safe areas. Unfortunately the efficiency of the transport operation was not always matched in the reception areas where countless muddles and mismatches added to the anxieties of youngsters torn from their homes.

Richard Brown was already an ARP warden when war broke out, as were hundreds of thousands of his fellow countrymen, and his readiness was to be tested that very first night albeit by a false alarm. From the outset he was clearly determined to record the detail not only of foreign operations in all the theatres of war but also of the dramatic changes on the Home Front. Coping with the blackout, patrolling the streets looking for illegally shining lights, fitting gas masks, all quickly became part of the daily routine. By 12 November he and most of the country had 'slipped very easily into war habits' in spite of early teething troubles although he felt very strongly that some of his fellow wardens were not taking their duties seriously enough.

Beyond the shores of Britain action began slowly in the first tentative and tense days of hostilities. A British Expeditionary Force (BEF) was dispatched to Northern France in much the same way as in 1914 but this time France was presumed to be protected from Germany by the Maginot Line so the BEF was assigned to the Franco-Belgian border. Nothing happened. The only fighting was in Poland where on 17 September, as the Poles were desperately trying to repel the Germans in the west, the Red Army crossed their eastern front and Poland was lost. Then the Russians turned on Finland but were fiercely resisted with much courage and skill. Slowly, very slowly, plans were formulated to come to Finland's aid.

Impatience at home at the slow start was tempered by the widespread opinion that it would all be over soon. Meanwhile in Ipswich, lulled by the lack of air activity, many evacuees were already drifting homeward. Fewer people bothered to carry their gas masks. This was still a 'phoney war' but Mr Brown was convinced it would not remain so. From the outset he estimated that hostilities would last 'five to six years'.

Only at sea did the action begin in earnest as the German U-boat packs wreaked havoc on Allied shipping. Naval losses are recorded throughout the diary with astonishing accuracy, as is illustrated by the account of the sinking of the Royal Oak. *However, in spite of the losses there was something to be glad about. The country was cheered and enlivened by the dramatic events in the South Atlantic in December. Captain Hans Langsdorff of the German cruiser* Graf Spee, *trapped in Montevideo harbour, chose to scuttle the ship rather than face internment. He then shot himself. The gallant captain's suicide was regretted but it was a forcible demonstration of the effective long arm of the Royal Navy.*

FRIDAY 15 SEPTEMBER

I don't know how far this good resolution will keep good, but, there being no harm in trying, let's try and keep it for the duration.

The war being nearly a fortnight old I had better hark back a bit.

On the Sunday morning 3 September tension was pretty great but it wasn't till we heard a grave voice tell us to wait for an important announcement at 11.15 that the full gravity struck us. Hitler had been given until 11.00 a.m. to clear out of Poland and, as I hadn't expected him to do that, there was only one way out; but somehow, when the time came, it came as a mild shock. Chamberlain sounded quite annoyed and, at the same time, sorrowful and I noted that he referred to 'Hitler' and not the usual diplomatic 'Herr Hitler'.

George and I worked like the Devil then on the dug-out. Fortunately we were fitting the doors and when that was done the place was at least habitable. We are now patting our own backs over that dug-out, and we certainly have the laugh over those who said it wasn't necessary. Poor old Ven is quite contrite over his lack of foresight and continual 'don't think it will come to anything'.

That night we had our first air-raid warning, at 2.35 Monday morning.I was pleased that I was on duty at the post at the time, with Ungless, and it was pleasing to see how quickly the wardens turned up, 100 per cent strong. Fortunately it was a false alarm and the all-clear soon followed, but I was a little proud that I had been on duty for the first alarm. Next warning came the next Wednesday morning at 6.45. I dressed quite rapidly, I thought, trousers and waistcoat over pyjamas, and was tenth at the post. Soon after reaching my beat we heard planes and gunfire, the first guns I had heard fired to kill, but am afraid I wasn't too impressed. Analysing my feelings I found I was immensely interested in wondering if they were coming over the town. It was misty at the time and it was possible that the mist had saved us. However, the official news said it was not the enemy but our own planes.

It's queer to note the effect this war has on different folks. Ma, bless her old heart, isn't upset in the least. Aldy's tummy is a bit rebellious again and I'm sure it is the cause of Wilson's bilious bother. Ven takes it in his stride and Dora, I was pleased to note, takes things quite well. She has procedure mapped out in case of a raid and, though quick, doesn't fluster.

I can honestly say I am merely very interested. Didn't do much work the first day, possibly due to the lack of sleep, but more probably suppressed excitement. On the day war was declared I had a peculiar feeling of intense patriotism, a determination to do whatever I could to help (swank) and in the evening when the King spoke to us am afraid I stood up to attention when they played 'The King'. Queer how we get moved out of our usual feelings at times, because though I am patriotic I wouldn't usually have stood at attention with only myself for company.

In the land-fighting poor little Poland is sticking it manfully. She is continually falling back but is giving a good account of herself. Warsaw is nearly surrounded and it seems my estimate of three months before being swamped will be an overestimate. Now the news seems to suggest that Russia will hit Poland in the back. She is talking of Poland oppressing her minorities, and she is certainly mobilising. If she starts in this little war what will be the end of it? Why are they chumming up with the Germans who have always called them the scum of the earth? Am afraid it means no good to us and probably Russia is after the Baltic States and Poland, as before the last war.

By the way I have estimated this affair will last five to six years. What a hell of a time. Five times 365 days each of which might produce some sort of frightfulness in the way of air raid or bad news. Anyway who cares?

MONDAY 18 SEPTEMBER
Well, well. Yesterday Russia marched into Poland on the thinnest
of excuses. She said it was to protect her White Russian nationals
because the Polish government does not now exist. The Poles are
still resisting the Germans and making a few successes but, poor
devils, they are no match really. I wonder what it means. Russia
says she will remain neutral but will take over the Poland she used
to have and leave Danzig and the corridor to Germany. Will she
come into the war more actively, I wonder? If so and she tackles
the French frontier with Germany, and then Italy and Spain decide
not to remain neutral any longer, we look like being up against it.
Even so things are not hopeless by any means.

Some sub sank the *Courageous* today. Reports say they think the
attendant destroyers sunk the sub, but I guess not or they would be
more definite about it. Plucky devil to tackle a thing like an
aircraft-carrier. Haven't seen any reliable news yet though.

THURSDAY 21 SEPTEMBER
More exciting news tonight. The Roumanian Premier has been
assassinated by a group of young men, probably Iron Guard Fascists.
Results may be anything. Russia is still the ambiguous quantity but
she has occupied the Polish border with Roumania, possibly
intending to cut off any chance Germany may have of stealing
Roumania with her oil and grain. That point seems to suggest that
Russia and Germany are not so friendly as might be. We listened
tonight to Roosevelt addressing Congress on the repeal of the
Neutrality Act. From the enthusiasm of Congress I guess it will be
repealed. Marvellous wireless. We heard it all with no fading at all.

Muriel came down for an hour or so today and has gone back to
Rotherhithe, St Olave's Hospital. What a place! If the raids start in
earnest she will see some excitement and casualties too. Had a
peculiar feeling of comradeship with her when shaking hands at
saying goodbye. After all we are both working together now,
though my share is so small in comparison.

WEDNESDAY 27 SEPTEMBER
Warsaw has surrendered, poor devils. Half of it in ruins. Wonder if
that allows Hitler to concentrate on the Western Front. There was
some fear that Russia was going to invade Roumania, but whether
for own gain or to prevent Germany doing so wasn't clear. Now we
may see. Ribbentrop, the Estonian Minister and Turkish are now

at Moscow, for what purpose can't be told. Russia is also annoyed with Estonia for letting a Polish sub leave an Estonian port after internment, and seems inclined to make trouble out of it.

The War Budget came out today. Drastic but this war must be paid for somehow. Income tax is 7s 6d in the £1, beer up 1d, sugar up 1d, baccy up 1½d, spirits up 10s a gallon. I expected petrol to go up still more. It is rationed now and therefore the yield is reduced. But it wasn't mentioned this time.

SUNDAY 1 OCTOBER
Last day of old duties. Now we start doing 4 hours at post per fortnight, on patrol from 8 to 11 p.m. Post duty to be as company for full-timers who do 24 hours per day.

Quite a bit to report today. Thursday morning it became known that Russia and Germany are to request peace now that the Polish question is 'liquidated'. If we refuse it will prove conclusively that France and Britain started the war and have no desire for peace!!! Clever, as usual with Hitler, but can't say I want peace under those conditions. If it were agreed upon it would only crop up again a few months hence when Hitler will undoubtedly discover an ill-treated minority in France or England and it will all come again but more favourably for him. Wonder what Dad would think to my warlike wishes? All the same I think it best for future peace of the world, and us particularly, to keep on and dust Hitler's pants if we can. Apparently the official terms will come from Hitler next Tuesday. Till then we can, at any rate, expect no air raids over here. I should have added that the statement said if we refuse the peace suggestions, Germany and Russia will collaborate further to decide what steps they will take. At first it seemed to mean that Russia will declare war on us, but am not so sure now.

Reports say that Germany is massing on the Belgian frontier. She has also solemnly assured Belgium and Holland that she will respect their neutrality which, from previous experience, means that she has every intention of invading them. Apparently Holland and Belgium think the same for the Dutch are reported to have already partly flooded their land and the Belgians are manning the frontier. By the same token I guess our peculiar silence and inaction is due to the fact that we are probably mobilising on the Franco-Belgian frontier, waiting to support if necessary, leaving the French at the German frontier.

The *Express* this morning is cussing the British Ministry of

Information for not releasing news. All pictures published are, so far, German. Ours are censored for some peculiar reason. Apparently it's making America suspicious and I don't blame them. It's all very silly and mysterious. Russia has also agreed with Estonia that in return for munitions Estonia is to allow her to establish naval bases and aerodromes. The thin end of the wedge? Latvia next? The *Bremen* is known to be at Murmansk. Pity. Still she must have had a cold journey. All the same, I'm annoyed, a little.

Last Friday night was National Registration Day, 29 September. All returns to include those who spent the night at the house. I cheated 'cos I spent 4 hours of it, 12 to 4, here at the post. Was on with Thrower and had a very interesting 4-hour chat. He showed me sides of his character which I certainly had not suspected. Fancy him liking Scott's poetry. Good bloke!

I must, if I can, start the finishing off of the dug-out. Now things are quiet (now, I suppose, the siren will blow) we ought to get things moving. Must see if I can get it painted and distempered this week. Poor old George is queerish this week with a cold on his chest, so must see what I can do.

We get a varied type of Bobby here on patrol calls. All of them are reserves or war reserves. Good lads but, in my conceited judgement, a little suet-puddingish.

SUNDAY 8 OCTOBER
Coo! A whole week. And in that week a fair amount of 'nerves' and little progress. Hitler made big proposals in a speech at the Reichstag on Friday. There was a lot of splutter about his famous Polish victory, and a queer sort of résumé of what war might mean and a suggestion of a world conference. So now we must wait till Tuesday or Wednesday when Chamberlain makes a reply. And then do we start the war in earnest? When we do presumably we wardens will have a little more to do. At the present, for the last week I have been going to bed quite confident of a good night's sleep. Will it be so for much longer, I wonder?

They are doing things well at Reavell's. The dug-outs are finished, fire-watchers' posts and control centre nearly so, and instructions have been issued to everyone on how to get to the dug-outs. Wardens will be given a job in dealing with gas, and seeing that the offices and works are properly evacuated. Can't see anyone wanting to stay unless raid warnings get frequent and are false alarms. Did my first night's light patrol[1] under the new scheme last night, and of course it rained. Still I did one round and then went home to hear the news and dry off. On the second round, about 10.15, it started raining again so I packed up, reported, and got home by 11.00.

TUESDAY 17 OCTOBER
Well, well, well. We move at last. To give events in correct order, last Friday certainly was unlucky for Germany. On that day we sank three submarines, the news coming on the radio something like this 'Here is an important Admiralty announcement, and you may care to listen carefully for it is good news. The Admiralty announces that two subs (later increased to three) have been sunk today. That is all', and then the blighters went and torpedoed the *Royal Oak*, with loss of about 800 men out of 1,200. We heard today (today <u>Tuesday</u> notice) that it was sunk while at anchor and Hamburg boasts that the sub which did it made its way into Scapa Flow harbour and then got away again. We may hear one day what the facts were.

Yesterday, Monday, there was an air raid over Rosyth Dockyard; fifteen men killed, twenty-five injured but no civilians. All casualties on ships. The *Southampton* had a 'glancing blow' which did no damage to the boats but splinters hit a few men. Fighters brought down three planes and AA one more which I think is lousy on the part of the AA, there being twelve to fourteen planes.

This morning coming home the placard said 'Air-Raid warning over Hull' and I expected something in this direction but not as soon as it came. We were having dinner at 1.30 when the sirens went and less than a minute after they finished I heard what I think were bombs followed by AA fire. A hectic rush to the post to report, then back and a tedious wait in the street, with two faint salvos of AA at intervals until the all-clear came at 2.05. That's about all it was. The ladies went down the dug-out because of the firing but I had to make Ma go down. Shan't bother any more as I hear she was a bit of a nuisance with rather misplaced remarks.

There was a rather unusual silence in the office for the first part of the afternoon as though most of us were a little thoughtful. Conditions were certainly favourable with clouds at all elevations. Wonder what's coming tonight? Went the length of Leopold Road last night trying to find evacuees with babies under four for respirators, but there weren't any. We are going to have baby masks issued next Thursday, from 12 till 2. Dora says she will be there at five past twelve 'cos you never know.

FRIDAY 20 OCTOBER

Dora fetched the mask and it seemed a real good job. The boy whimpered a bit when we put him in but it didn't seem to be a defiant cry and would probably settle down after a bit. Let's hope he will never wear it. All the same when Hitler really gets desperate I firmly believe he will use gas and we may fall unlucky here. Which reminds me (fearful grammar), I guess there will be as much danger of incendiary bombs, and it's time I decided just how to deal with them.

Went for a swim at St Matthew's Wednesday evening. We just managed a few minutes before they blacked out at 6 o'clock. It seemed a little eerie swimming in dark water. I hear today the baths may keep open all the winter. Cheers.

There must be more than a dozen air-raid shelters in the centre of the town. Direction signs are always being put up. Now they are putting up directions to first-aid posts, but I believe there is only one special one besides the hospital and that is in Currier's Lane.

Another air raid over Firth of Forth today but don't know any details yet. Won a bet (1*d* chocolate) from Ven on Wednesday. I said there would be an air raid somewhere in the country and there was! Jerry is certainly playing fair so far. He is attacking strictly military objects (except with subs and propaganda) and the bloke who crept into Scapa Flow and sunk the *Royal Oak* at 1.30 a.m. then got home safely certainly deserved his medal and Churchill's praise. Wonder if they will praise our blokes in their Reichstag?

Did lights last night with Mr Sullivan. Quite a companionable bloke. We have started our new post. It's about 8 ft square, including two recesses for AG clothing and enough room for four or five people to stand up in. Can't say how it will accommodate us when we report for a raid. The steps leading to it are only just wide enough to get down when dolled up in kit. Still we shall see, anyone can criticise.

MONDAY 23 OCTOBER

Quite a bit to report. Last Saturday, Trafalgar Day, twelve planes attacked a convoy off Lincolnshire, result being four shot down and no damage to the convoy. Good going but it was the fighter escort who did most of the stuff. Where is that marvellous accuracy we have heard of with regard to our Archies?[2] Of course it was probably a try-out but I can't see much good in Jerry only using 12 planes; 120 would be more sensible. Perhaps he will next time.

Mr Thrower came round this evening to say he is to be notified of yellow warnings and will knock up us lesser fry. A good idea and will at any rate get us ready for the siren, which certainly does make one's ticker and tummy work overtime. Its wail is a little terrifying though I wouldn't have it otherwise. So now we can look forward to more disturbed nights, but who cares? Perhaps it will be 'yellow' and then 'red' tonight. Am on duty tonight 0000 hr to 0400 hr tomorrow morning, my first in the new post.

Talking of dug-outs we decorated ours over the weekend, biscuit distemper inside, grey doors and stained seat. Looks quite posh but expect the creosote from the sleepers will work out later and spoil it all. By the way, Dora thinks I am doing German when I sit down and write this. Dear me.

MONDAY 6 NOVEMBER
Not much action news. In fact the radio gave up altogether yesterday. At the 4 o'clock news it just said there was nothing and played records instead. Rather queer, all this. After all we had been led to believe that this would be a lightning war with huge air raids; it's nothing but a flop. Perhaps each side is waiting for the other to begin and then it can't be accused of 'air aggression'. Coo that's a good phrase!

We were told last week to be prepared to be rationed on butter and bacon in December. Probable amounts are ¼ lb per head per week of each, margarine will be unlimited.

SUNDAY 12 NOVEMBER
Life is not much changed these days. We have slipped very easily into war habits. At sundown, and recently lighting-up times, we conscientiously black out, which means we have to feel our way about parts of the house in darkness. At work it means closing all windows and drawing blinds, the result being a darned hot, stuffy office. So far we have only had it for half an hour or so, and that overtime. What it will be like for two hours I don't like to think of. I haven't been in the town yet in real darkness but in the twilight it seems a bit eerie. I don't mind admitting to myself that I think it will be wisest to funk the town and go home by back roads.

There are a good many basement shelters and trenches about the town. Very frequently one sees the blue boards with white lettering giving directions to the nearest shelter. Now there are added white boards and red lettering for nearest first-aid posts and red boards

with white letters for fire stations. Added to that, one sometimes
sees white arrows on the pavement leading to the nearest shelter,
and here and there are huge piles of sandbags round important
buildings. There are not quite so many gas masks taken about
nowadays. People are getting a little contemptuous I guess. Can't
help thinking we are soon to be in for a real series of raids.

SATURDAY 18 NOVEMBER
After a week there is quite a lot I ought to enter. Perhaps I can. I
should have recorded last time that the submarine *Oxley* was
destroyed by an internal explosion, they said. A big boat,
1,380/1,850 tons, and not much about it in the papers. We weren't
told how it happened either; perhaps we'll know afterwards.

Last Sunday Churchill broadcast a speech and such a speech!
The tenor of it was 'Poor old Goering, you would like to bomb us
but you daren't, I dare you'. He even said the fleet had been
waiting for them all week in the Firth of Forth without a visit. Next
day Jerry sent four planes and bombed the Shetlands. He said it
was a crushing reply to Churchill, showing that they could come in
any weather, and claimed two seaplanes destroyed. We said there
was no damage except windows, and one rabbit killed. The
wireless comedians have made the most out of that rabbit.

Times of duty have been altered again. Now we do one night a
week, 8 to 12, pardon, 2000 hr to 2400 hr, three of us at a time,
one to man the post the other two to go on lights patrol. Also once
in eight weeks we are to do 0000 hr to 0400 hr post duty. Those
poor devils of full-timers are now condemned to 72 hours a week.
What a life, and all for £3 a week. I can see one of them going
when he can, and don't blame him, though it would mean longer
hours for us.

Heard today the Admiralty might take over the dehumidifiers we
are making for Turkish subs. Don't know if it means the boats as
well but it is probable. The boats won't be much good without
blowers.

MONDAY 27 NOVEMBER
More ships gone, mostly merchantmen. One of them the
Rawalpindi was an armed auxiliary cruiser.

Heard some interesting news this evening when talking to
Brother Thrower. We were yarning in his dug-out and he
quoted a naval pal of his who is on the *Greyhound*, a destroyer.

Of course all is second-hand rumour but interesting just the same. He says the *Rawalpindi* was out as a decoy to the *Deutschland* but unfortunately the German got her blow in first. Certainly that would account for the death toll, there being only 17 survivors out of 300 and there is no news of how, when or where she went down. Also he says that when the *Gypsy* went down she was due to go sub hunting with the *Greyhound* and slipped into Harwich to drop survivors of a mined tug. Sheer bad luck to have hit a mine herself, for *Greyhound*, probably with others, found eleven subs in the Thames estuary, probably laying mines, four of them were bagged. Again, his opinion is this is essentially a naval war.

These nights are beautiful. It was a full moon yesterday and tonight the sky is cloudless and glorious. I came home tonight by the bypass and the sky was glorious. It was fairly dark, the moon just rising, and the clouds were breaking up and dispersing with the result that great rifts were in the clouds showing an infinitely deep purple, spotted with stars. The edge of the rift was jagged, torn yet fleecy clouds, lit by the moon and standing out like silver fluff yet mingling with the black rain banks. A little way off was Jupiter like a great lamp. Really it was indescribable, so I won't try any more. There is a good side to this blackout, somehow one could never get such beauty before.

THURSDAY 30 NOVEMBER
The rumour about the *Rawalpindi* is correct. Poor old gal, she went down fighting but Germany had the cheek to claim control of the sea as a result. Poor fools.

Haven't heard the report myself but Russia, blast her, has bombed Helsinki. Seems almost unbelievable that in these otherwise sane days any country can barefacedly trump up charges, as Russia did against Finland, and then accuse her of piracy, conduct a fierce propaganda war and then march in. Wonder if the USA will do anything active? Roosevelt offered to mediate yesterday but Stalin obviously wouldn't have anything come between him and his plunder. I go on duty tonight at 0000 hr so may hear the news then.

THURSDAY 7 DECEMBER
Russia is still lamming Finland, or trying to. She has repeatedly bombed Helsinki and other towns but, if reports are to be trusted, she is not having it all her own way. The Russians tried the stunt of dropping troops behind the Finn lines by parachute, but possibly

they weren't far enough behind 'cos they were picked off and it ended in failure.

We had a few minutes meeting in the canteen this evening, Hartley giving us wardens a much needed enlightenment on our duties. Tomorrow I am due to receive my equipment for use down at the Works which will save the necessity for taking the regulation stuff about with me. I must say Reavell's are doing things well. All we need now is an alarm to see how things really work and to buck up a few of the critics and sluggards.

WEDNESDAY 13 DECEMBER
Finland is still going it with a will. Chiefly in the Karelian Isthmus. There are now 1½ million Russians massing there, with 1,000 planes. Also the *Express* on Sunday reckoned this business shows the Russian giant to have feet of clay and the *Chronicle* is fairly smacking her for her previousness in saying so. It must be fearful fighting in those conditions and reports say the Russians are not well clothed to meet it. The Finns fight on skis and in white uniforms and everyone praises their pluck.

I should have reported some weeks back that the *Belfast* was damaged by mine or torpedo. Not much news was given about it except that it was in the Firth of Forth. Estimates put the bag of submarines at about forty. Five were sunk last week.

SATURDAY 16 DECEMBER
Chief item is the *Graf Spee*. On Wednesday she came across the *Ajax* which opened fire at 12 miles. All this is mere report, which accounts for some of the facts being a little peculiar. I can't see how 6 in guns can carry 12 miles and score a hit with the second round, but perhaps I'm too doubting. Anyway then the *Exeter* and *Achilles* arrived and, after several hours' action, *Graf Spee* bolted into Montevideo, damaged, with thirty-six dead and sixty injured.

Position now is that she has been given 72 hours' notice to quit and outside our ships are waiting. Poor devils. They were sports, treated the crews they had captured very well, who, when liberated, attended the funeral of the thirty-six, and it seems plucky to try to get out. Perhaps they won't but will prefer internment. Reports say the *Renown*, *Ark Royal* and *Dunkerque* have reinforced the *Ajax* and *Achilles*. Still war is war. Free she would be a menace, and must be stopped.

Tried to get a flash-lamp battery today. Only a casual request, as

I know one might as well ask for the moon. One can't get batteries for love or money. With petrol restrictions, cars are laid up and owners are cycling which requires two batteries, and with the blackout, torches are everywhere. Heaven knows when the manufacturers will get on top of it. Walking out at night, the streets are pretty black at times and most people use torches. One sees them flashing everywhere. I shouldn't have thought it was so easy to hit the railings or step off the path, but it certainly is easy. Cycling home the other night I couldn't find Leopold Road after a car had passed me with lights on.

WEDNESDAY 20 DECEMBER

There certainly is more news to record and lots of it. The *Graf Spee* incident has straightened itself out. Now it seems that the *Exeter* was first to come across the German, who opened fire at 12½ miles, the fifth salvo being a hit. In fact she concentrated her fire on *Exeter* and gave her a heck of a time, until hits in the boiler-room slowed her down till she couldn't make much steam. Also, only one gun was left in action and that hand-operated. Poor devils. Casualties were sixty-two killed, twenty-five injured and at the end the captain was giving orders by chains of sailors to the helmsman and others. All this gave *Ajax* and *Achilles* time to do 'summat' which they did, keeping to landward of *Graf Spee*. Commander Harwood is made Rear Admiral and KCB and well he deserves it. He must have done really well to force such a large boat to harbour, and with extensive damage too. Good old Nelson. Your spirit was there alright. Lord Haw-Haw[3], or rather old Goebbels, claimed it a German victory, poor fools, which seems rather strange in view of the following days. The Uruguayans inspected the boat and gave 72 hours' grace. Germany howled that this was not nearly enough, forgetting that they had claimed a victory, and Hitler personally gave orders to the captain to scuttle his boat. This he did. He took on 2,000 tons of fuel oil, steamed out at the appointed time, stopped 5 miles out, anchored, then blew her up. The Uruguayans are real annoyed about it. Also, I'll bet, so was the German skipper, for it transpires that the only boats waiting for them were the *Achilles*, the damaged *Ajax* and *Cumberland*, a sister ship to *Exeter*.

Later. Just heard that the captain of the *Graf Spee* has committed suicide. I can appreciate the poor devil's feelings and can sympathise. It was not a very glorious end to sink his ship but, as a man, he was no worse for doing what he was ordered to do.

The news also said that this evening aircraft appeared over the east coast. Wonder if it was over this district? Coming home I saw searchlights and twice saw peculiar lights which I took to be landing flares or star-shells.

TUESDAY 26 DECEMBER

Am writing on duty at the post. To my secret surprise we have passed through Christmas (so far, touch wood) without a visit from Hitler's air force. Have now made a set of blackout wood and paper frames for the front room. Only our bedroom and the kiddies' remain now. Must tackle the kiddies' room next.

There are notices now that the 'yellow' will be sent out to people like Wambach who will use his judgement about whom to pass it on to. I don't see the fun of being awakened very frequently for a 'yellow' though shouldn't mind now and then. There is also a notice asking for wardens to sign who can get time off from their employment on news of a red warning. We are getting a little more shipshape now in our organisation. Am just a little perturbed about the way some chaps are treating the patrol duty. Some don't do it and the last time I was on we all three stayed in and played shove-ha'penny. Hope I'm not a prig but it doesn't seem the right thing to do, but I can't push against the stream on my own. Must see what happens. After all we didn't join up just for the pleasure of meeting here and playing games. Still there are sure to be sources of friction, and backing out here and there.

NOTES

[1] Wardens patrolled the streets to check the efficiency of household blackout procedures.

[2] 'Archie' was the nickname given to anti-aircraft fire during the First World War.

[3] Name given to William Joyce, then member of the British Union of Fascists, who broadcast from Hamburg throughout the war.

1940

The hiatus, known as the Phoney War, continued. Rationing of butter, bacon and sugar began and the main topic of interest early in the year was the prolonged period of freezing temperatures. Allied activity was still predominantly naval, the highlight being the daring raid in Norwegian waters by HMS Cossack to free British seamen held prisoner on the auxiliary ship Altmark. By March Russia had overwhelmed Finland, the British aid then en route serving only to precipitate Hitler's audacious attack on Norway and Denmark on 9 April. Denmark was overrun in a single day but the Norwegian campaign lasted long enough for a British Expeditionary Force to land and assist, only to be evacuated three weeks later in spite of massive naval support.

The disastrous Norwegian campaign was the catalyst for the downfall of the Chamberlain government and Winston Churchill, the First Lord of the Admiralty, was appointed Prime Minister; the popular, if not political, choice. That very day, 10 May, the Germans swept into the Low Countries. The Dutch capitulated four days later and the Belgians on 28 May, leaving the BEF on the Belgian front stranded. The invader's tanks ignoring both the Maginot Line and the supposedly impenetrable Ardennes forest to the south raced to the French coast and squeezed the Allied forces into the Dunkirk salient. The miraculous evacuation at Dunkirk and Churchill's brilliant rhetoric raised everyone's spirits even after the astounding French collapse in June.

In common with most of the population at this period Richard Brown was very apprehensive and feared that the British Isles would be next on the list. He did however have great faith in Churchill and never entertained the thought of defeat. Ipswich was bombed for the first time on 18 June and Brown debates whether or not to send his family away. He was also very anxious to do more, notably hold a gun with the newly formed Local Defence Volunteers, known as the 'Parashots', and renamed Home Guard in August. He sent an idea for combating the magnetic mine to the Admiralty, but it was not taken further.

The Battle of Britain, Goering's attempt to destroy the RAF preparatory to an invasion, was unleashed in August and probably would have succeeded if Goering had not switched his bombers to London on 7 September. 'Civilisation was saved by a thousand British boys' (Denis Richards). As the Blitz began it was announced that Ipswich was to be voluntarily evacuated and Richard Brown moved his family to Northampton. The family returned in October in spite of continued air raids on Ipswich and the threat of invasion, as far as they knew, unabated. Meanwhile London was being pounded nightly and gradually Londoners were learning to cope with the great damage and disruption to their daily lives. 'We can take it' became their byword. On 14 November the infamous raid on Coventry took place and this was followed by a series of heavy raids on other large provincial cities.

In June Italy joined the Axis as expected and in August her troops marched into Somaliland. Then on 13 September five divisions crossed the Libyan border into Eygpt. Although initially successful they were to be driven back to their starting point by the year's end; this first allied land victory being greeted with wild enthusiasm. The Italians also invaded Greece in late October but didn't have much luck there either.

WEDNESDAY 3 JANUARY

The New Year. I suppose I ought to indulge in fogs of reminiscence but I don't pretend to be a model journalist so I won't. This whole darn thing is supposed to be a summary. Heaven knows there is plenty I could enter but can't find time or opportunity.

There has been another encounter with the Messerschmitt 110, the twin-engined long-range fighter. Three of our bombers encountered twelve near the German coast and shot down three, losing two of ours. I should have recorded that we are continually making reconnaissance flights over Germany. Seems we can do pretty much as we like.

We went in Harry's car to Felixstowe last Sunday, the last day of the year, and saw the balloon barrage, eighteen of them. The clouds cleared off leaving a perfect sky, showing them up very clearly. We are now in a frosty spell, about a fortnight old, and the roads were icy then, and we were unfortunate enough to encounter an accident. An RAF lorry was in a hurry and skidded round Langer Road bend hitting the kerb, a stationary car, a small tree and then us. Thank heaven Dora and the kids were not hurt. All

the same the RAF chap told me a warning had been received so
my first thought was to get the ladies home, so we put them on a
bus and I then had a lousy few minutes wishing I had gone too in
case they ran into a warning in Ipswich. However, no sirens were
sounded and all was well, that is, except with Harry's car. On the
way home I had the comforting feeling that we were passing close
to AA guns and searchlights, but nary a one did we see.

The Finns are still holding out, whacking at the Russians. Three
cheers. Various reports show that they can lay traps and the poor
Red Army falls into them quite cheerfully. There was that incident
of enticing them on a frozen lake and then bombing the lake. They
have also induced the Russians to fight each other. Clever large-
scale guerrilla tactics. Now, reports say, Stalin is asking for
German technicians to help him out.

I see the *Tacoma*, the boat which fuelled the *Graf Spee* has been
interned. She was coming out of harbour, saw a British ship
waiting, and chose internment instead.

MONDAY 8 JANUARY
Well, well, well. There are changes in the cabinet. Hore-Belisha[1]
resigned Friday, reason unstated. Naturally most papers, *Telegraph*
excepted, are indignant, calling for explanations, Parliament to
meet, etc. For myself I think that Chamberlain knows what he is
doing, has reasons for doing it, knows more about it than I do, and
I have every confidence in him. If he says that Hore-Belisha should
go, there is a damn good reason for it. It is significant I think, that
it comes after the King, Chamberlain and Churchill, etc., have
paid visits to France and rumour says it's because the Army is too
comfortable and democratic.

Summer time will probably begin on 14 February nice and early.
Then we might be able to buy dry batteries. I have been surprised
to find the nights not dark so often as I expected. Actually very few
have been really black though lots are dark. After being out for a
few minutes one can usually see fairly well.

Rationing starts today for butter, sugar and bacon – 4 oz butter,
12 oz sugar and 4 oz bacon and ham. We shall have to cut down a
little more on sugar, but not much. We ought to manage on 3¾lb a
week and as for butter, I like margarine just as well. Morrison[2]
explained it was to conserve cargo space for munitions and to save
foreign currency.

FRIDAY 12 JANUARY

Am afraid I told Dora the other day that I am running this diary. A weak moment. Still, one ought not to have secrets from one's dear wife, Richard, and one can still talk to oneself.

The first dehumidifiers were tested today, quite OK thank goodness, and in a heck of a rush. A great improvement, the monobloc, on the old type. Let's hope, and touch wood, on the smaller sets going together properly.

MONDAY 15 JANUARY

On duty again. The others haven't turned up, both unavoidably delayed. Next Wednesday there will be 'paper' incidents, being practice in making out reports and using the phone. Attendance optional if not detailed off. Haven't been detailed yet so will consider it.

Chief news is unsettled conditions in Holland and Belgium. Both countries are mobilising and our BEF leave was stopped yesterday. They fear something and in a way I hope Germany will be rash enough to invade. It will definitely put them in the wrong and give us an opportunity to use the Army. Let's hope (the wireless is just playing the 'Clock' symphony. Lovely) my faith in the Army is justified. It hasn't been proved yet. Reports tonight say the situation in Holland and Belgium is much easier. Incidentally, partly the scare was caused by a captured German airman having certain papers on him.

Have just found some drops of water coming in the corners of the post. The frost shows signs of ending, can't remember one lasting so long. It must have been here for three weeks with only two days' respite.

The Finns are being subjected to fierce air raids now the severe weather has eased. The *Telegraph* this morning was saying they will be in a poor position in March when the clear weather comes for they have no air force to speak of and the Russian aircraft will have everything just their own way. Poor devils. I can't imagine us doing anything in time, being England, and USA is talking and talking about help. The Finns have done wonders on land, seemingly surrounding whole divisions of Russians and annihilating them, which will make the Russians all the keener on finishing the job with aircraft. What will be the outcome?

MONDAY 22 JANUARY

On duty last night, 2000 hr to 2400 hr as usual, with Day and Roper. Nice fellows, but none of us any intention, I'm afraid, of light patrolling in this snow. Still I heard a rumour that light patrols are being tightened up (about time too) and the night shift 0000 hr to 0400 hr abolished altogether for part-timers. Really this weather is the limit. <u>Still</u> it freezes, and snows on and off most of the day. The roads are foul. No attempt to clear them at all, except in the town, and no wonder with the shortage of staff. This morning when I went to work the Cornhill and Princes Street top were well clear and then the snow fell again. Too disheartening to have to start all over again. Last Wednesday Gilbert said he measured 19 degrees of frost, and Corunna in Spain has had snow for the first time since 1800. What a winter. It has kept to the eleven-year cycle again – 1917, 1928 and 1939. All the same I don't think we have ever had a frost to last a month with only two days' break.

The chappie in the barber's went for medical exam today and passed A1. It's when an actual case comes to your notice that the damnableness of the whole business shows up. It's pretty rotten to be hoiked out of one's job and made to fight, even admitting all the arguments for patriotism.

FRIDAY 26 JANUARY

Principally weather this time. Still the damn frost continues. Have been staying to dinner at work all the week and today, with a slight sign of thaw, it darn well snowed like hell this evening. When will it end? Probably not till June. Twice the wind has boxed the compass; rather peculiar that.

This week the hood became compulsory for car headlights. Good things those. In a slight mist it looks like a large fan spread before the car, yet there is no glare and no light at all above 4 ft. The trams have them. They seem a little ghostly rushing about with two dim sidelights, hooded headlamp and dim blue lights inside. They still stop about 7.30 at night. Bikes may now be wheeled on the nearside without lamps. Shops, too, have a concession. They may have one light per 10 ft of window consisting of a 15-w lamp inside a box with a slit 6 in by ¼ in covered with tissue paper. Surprising what a light they give.

SUNDAY 4 FEBRUARY

Talking meteorologically, last night was a wonder. It thawed. The first frost was a few days before Christmas and it has kept it up since, except for two days. The snow outside has been there for almost three weeks. Phyl says the road to Felixstowe has been made possible by cutting a path through the snow for a single line of traffic with passing recesses. Trains are held up and people are short of coal. Factories are running short and it's all a helluva mix-up.

Ma is highly disgusted just now. She's bought a Rollo and found two short, can't be convinced it's quite fair either. If that's the worst discomfort, we shall do well.

Reverting, I wonder if there really is any offensive nature in those squads of masts round the coast, e.g. at Bawdsey. Certainly they are secret, these erections, and there is yet time to prove or disprove the popular theory that they can cut out a plane's electrical gear. When massed raids have been attempted, then we shall know.

Have just been listening to a radio item showing how German propaganda is intended to undermine our beliefs in our own country and government. An excellently portrayed picture. They finished by showing how the Jerry stories of a *Graf Spee* victory were disproved by the facts themselves. Apparently we have a monitoring service constantly listening to foreign news broadcast in all languages, 500,000 words daily, eight novel lengths, all sifted, mostly recorded and studied. A service we hear nothing about. In this week's *Engineer* they quote the Bremen newspaper saying we have lost twenty-four tankers since war began and giving the names. Five of them are still afloat and haven't been attacked, three others are not tankers at all and, in one case, the tonnage was given as 7,060 tons, actually it was 706. Our convoy shipping losses continue to be 1 in 500; 7,000 ships were convoyed up to 17 January and 14 were lost.

SATURDAY 10 FEBRUARY

Had a brainwave yesterday. Magnetic mines this time. The idea was a torpedo-shaped object propelled by air-jet and magnetised, moving in advance of its sweeper on the end of its pipeline. Being magnetised it might affect the mines enough to explode them in advance of the ship and, there being no working parts at all, it should be indestructible even if blown out of the water and the pipeline should be flexible enough. Trouble is I don't know enough about juice and magnetism to say if the field could be made strong enough for the job. It would be rather fun to see a boat oozing along with explosions in front of it. Must see if George knows anything about fields.

Bought a piece of deal today for the front fence, 4 in × 4 in × 5 ft 6 in and cost 2s 6d. Christmas! Still it's wartime.

Went on duty last Wednesday. The other two made no attempt to do light patrol and I, as post warden, was told by the full-timer that the part-timer usually clears off at 2300 hr so I went. All the same I think it's a darn shame. There is no genuine enthusiasm, only a desire to dodge all they can with the excuse that we have no authority over people's lights. People don't carry respirators about nowadays. Hope it is not a false security they are feeling; still I should do the same I suppose if I hadn't got one at work and at home. Went to an auction sale and bought a bureau on Wednesday. My first sale. Cost was £3 10s; now I can have somewhere to do work and 'German' in peace. Perhaps.

THURSDAY 15 FEBRUARY

Those blasted Russians mean it this time. For sixteen days they have been hammering away at the Mannerheim Line, 300,000 troops on the sector giving the Finns no rest. Yesterday they pumped 300,000 shells into one town in the day. No wonder they have made gains and captured some outposts. I very much fear the Finns are cracking but hope very, very much that I am wrong. All the same, reverting to the Karelian Isthmus, the Russians have had fearful losses, one estimate saying 40,000 dead and 200 tanks destroyed. The latter gives an idea of the mechanisation. It is now possible for anyone in England, over twenty-seven, to enlist in the Finnish army.

We lost three big boats day before yesterday, but bagged two subs causing the trouble. Tonnages 6,000, 9,000 and 12,000. The largest, a meat boat, went in Bay of Biscay and the sub sinking it was disposed of in half an hour. Probably, being so large, they were all in convoy.

Saw WR[3] today about my minesweeper and, bless his heart, he encouraged me and asked me what I intended doing with it. I had the nerve to suggest he might like to pull strings for me at the Admiralty; he wasn't offended and said no, I ought to handle it myself. So now I must get out the drawing board and do some homework.

SUNDAY 18 FEBRUARY

Lots to report. Re: the last entry, was talking to George this morning who says he has been working, electrically, on some trawlers in the dock. I mentioned mines and he said quite quietly, confidently and definitely that we shall have no more trouble with magnetic mines. We can now deal with them quickly, effectively and cheaply. All the same I think I shall submit my idea if only for the experience in such matters.

Quite exciting things have been happening near Norway. The *Altmark*, the German prison ship, has been foully cheated and robbed of over 300 merchantmen prisoners by the awful British Navy, bless it. Apparently she was in attendance on the *Graf Spee* and took off the rankers of the captured ships while the *Spee* had the officers. The captain is a hard-bitten Nazi who didn't treat the captives at all lovingly and, making all allowances for wartime exaggeration, they seem to have had a rotten time of it. For instance on the way some managed to drop overboard a tin containing information. It was recaptured and the offenders given three days complete dark, bread and water and no sanitation.

Recently the *Altmark* reached Bergen and was duly examined by the Norwegian authorities who, amazingly, did not find the presence of over 300 prisoners who were making all the noise they could (though deck machinery was going), nor found the arms she is supposed to carry, and gave her permission to travel in territorial waters. While doing so she was overhauled by some of our Navy, a cruiser and a few destroyers, and took refuge in Josing Fjord. We had orders from London to enter neutral waters and examine her. On entering two Norwegian torpedo-boats protested but refused the offer to hold a joint examination. Accordingly we withdrew outside, held further wireless with London and, after nightfall the destroyer *Cossack* was told to go in again, which she did with searchlights. *Altmark* tried to ram her (incidentally she is approx. 10,000 tons) but couldn't (fancy the idiot thinking he could ram a handy boat like a destroyer) and finished up stern on the rocks. Our men boarded her with cutlasses, results being one of ours injured, and about twenty casualties on the Germans and the prisoners taken off. Reports are garbled. The *Express* says today the British captain jumped aboard while going alongside and personally heaved the telegraph to 'full astern', which grounded her, and a few lines further on spoke of boarding party boats. Rather inconsistent. Also reports say time bombs had been set to blow her up. All this has caused a rare outburst in the world's press. Germany is cussing our piracy but says nothing at all about the prisoners, making it appear pure piracy. Strictly speaking we had no right to conduct an action in neutral waters but, on the other hand, the Norwegians had muffed their duty and something had to be done.

Poor Finland. She is retreating at last on the Mannerheim Line. She says 'not far', a few outposts being taken but I wonder if things are more serious than that. The Finns' morale is amazing but it can't be superhuman.

WEDNESDAY 21 FEBRUARY

Excitement hasn't died down yet over the *Altmark* affair. Germany is awfully wild over it all, and French opinion says it is because Germany has been using Norwegian territorial waters quite a lot in sending boats with supplies to Pietarsaari, in Finland. The Norwegian Premier, Dr Koht, spoke in their Parliament and tried to tick us off over the affair and said it would be quite in order to allow German armed boats in her territorial waters and anyway a few prisoners didn't matter and prisoners were quite legal things to carry in said waters. Chamberlain replied yesterday in a strong tone and commented with surprise that though on three, possibly four, occasions the Norwegians contacted the *Altmark* there was no attempt to search her. He said it was a difficult position to understand even if Norway is afraid of Germany. That, of course, is the secret. She is scared of Germany. As Churchill said, she is hoping the crocodile will not eat her till last.

The Russian advance has slowed up and reports say it has been very costly. The Finns had mined the land and the advance was so disorderly that Russian airmen and artillery bombed and bombarded their own advanced troops. All that was on the Mannerheim Line. North of Lake Ladoga the Finns have just annihilated a Russian division of 18,000. They surrounded them, cut off supplies, and killed them off at leisure, and now two divisions which were sent to reinforce have themselves been cut off. The Finns' air force is also getting into its stride, while I see today the Russians bombed a Swedish village. Probably a mistake but they won't get much sympathy after publicly saying they won't help the Finns. And now snow is falling again there, and they say the worst comes in March. Heaven help the Russians then, or should I say hell.

SUNDAY 25 FEBRUARY

America is trying a peace move, not necessarily between the belligerents, but to stop the war spreading. She is sending an envoy, Mr Sumner Welles, to Europe and he arrived in Italy yesterday. It may be significant, but Chamberlain and Hitler both spoke yesterday. Our bloke emphasised that peace is only possible if the present German government ceases to exist and if Poland and Czecho-Slovakia are reinstated, and said the next move is up to Germany. Poor old Hitler again trotted out the Versailles romp and yelled nothing much else but abuse.

Summer time started today, after 100 days of winter time. I did some gardening yesterday, the first for just about ten weeks. The frost killed off all my greens except the spring cabbage, so am able to make a completely fresh start.

I sent off that minesweeping suggestion to the Admiralty last Thursday. Scarsline typed it for me and did it well. Wonder what will happen! I haven't enough faith in it to hope for much. In fact if WR hadn't seen it probably it wouldn't have gone after what George told me. By the way, George was at Harwich on Friday and had to take cover while Archie was trying to hit a German plane.

FRIDAY 1 MARCH

On duty last night, on lights. The first time, for one reason or another, I've actually patrolled. Day and I were on and I must say the lights were none too good and we reported five.

The Finns are retreating a lot now, poor devils; 175,000 Russians are against them in the Karelian Isthmus and this morning they were almost in Viborg. The town has been absolutely evacuated and is almost completely demolished. They are also retreating in the Petsamo district. I see 3,000 British volunteers have left for there. Seems that we can spare them.

The twenty-threes registered 17 February and now the twenty-fours do so 9 March and there is talk of the twenty-fives. We were speculating when our turn will come. Early next year I guess.

We have made another flight over Berlin and dropped flares and leaflets without let or hindrance. The *Express* says it is 'cos they don't want to show their defences for the sake of a few harmless leaflet-droppers and that's probably correct. We shan't go over so easily when, and if, bomb-dropping boys arrive.

We have started a National Savings group at work; tomorrow will be the third week.

MONDAY 4 MARCH

We've done it again, we've done it again. We've been and gone and shot down one of our own bombers, over the Thames Estuary this time. It happened yesterday and the poor devils came down in flames, though I can't say how they fared. Killed probably, poor things. Suppose I ought not to have referred to it so flippantly, but something is wrong somewhere; probably her wireless was out of order.

Had a reply today from the Admiralty saying the business was being investigated and I should hear further. George was saying on Saturday that a talk on the wireless said they have already been using coils to detect mines so they won't think much of my scheme, most likely. He also said that they have some system now of marking the position with buoys. Somebody has just been decorated who thoroughly deserves the decoration. He's a bloke who first investigated a magnetic. Apparently in November a seaplane was seen to drop something with a parachute into the sea near Shoeburyness. It was decided it was a magnetic and somehow beached, and this bloke had the guts to dismantle the thing for examination. First of all they went off to it and took paper rubbings of externals to know what spanners to make. Must have been exciting.

Mr Sumner Welles saw Hitler on Saturday. The only reliable news concerning the visit is that he came away looking very grave. One report says Hitler went over all his old rantings about sloshing England, etc. and wouldn't hear much of whatever it was Welles wanted to say. Now Welles goes to Paris, then London.

MONDAY 11 MARCH

Rather a momentous statement in the House this afternoon. The Premier said that we and France have guaranteed help to Finland if she wants it and by that he meant all the help in our power. The complication is that Finland is now in conference with Russia at Moscow on peace terms. On 22 February Russia asked us to mediate peace terms but they were so bad we would have nothing to do with them and they then approached Sweden who had fewer scruples. She advanced the terms and that's how the peace conference started. All this was revealed tonight. Finland says a result will be announced today or tomorrow. The point is, is this offer of concrete help big enough to sway Finland to chuck the peace conference or had it already been considered?

Sumner Welles is in London. He has been to France and will return to Rome before going back to the USA. He seems well able to take care of himself with reporters and won't say anything about why he is here beyond that he is observing conditions.

WEDNESDAY 13 MARCH

Russia has got away with it and the Finns have signed the agreement. Finland loses the whole Karelian Isthmus, the land around Lake Ladoga, land in central Finland and some up north. What a pity she didn't ask for help. I can't see that too much blame should rest on us 'cos we can't force her to accept help and it was offered some time ago. It seems blasted Sweden deserves most censure. According to the *Express* she said she would blow up her railways if we attempted to send help. May she be the next to be pinched and have the beloved German attention such has been given to Poland.

Comment is strong from most countries. America is strong in condemnation but it would have looked more convincing if she had offered a little worthwhile help. And now where will the ruddy war develop, I wonder?

SUNDAY 17 MARCH

Well, it's happened. The first civilian has been killed by a bomb. Last night, don't know the time, fourteen planes attacked Scapa Flow. Many bombs dropped, a warship hit with seven injured, bombs on land hit five houses, killed a man and injured seven others. It is interesting to note they were injured while watching the fun and that's what is going to happen here in the first raids. Jerry says he hit several battleships and attacked aerodromes. He would. Actually they were mostly HE on land and a few incendiaries.

Seeing as it happened at night I suppose the shooting wasn't too bad, but I do wonder what the percentage hits will be. Possibly the suggested gloom is 'cos I bought a shovel for incendiary bombs yesterday and often I find an immediate need for things freshly acquired and it may be auto-suggestion. I seemed to realise the dangers a little more today. Dora and I were talking about incendiaries and when one thinks of it, seeing the probability of raids is in daylight, she will probably have to rely on herself quite a bit; but I fancy I can trust her.

Twenty-fives and twenty-sixes are to register soon, probably in April. Butter ration has been doubled and now stands at 8 oz per head. We probably shan't use it as we manage quite well with the present allowance together with margarine. We are even doing quite well on 12 oz sugar per head though it would be OK if it were increased a little, enough to go back to extravagance on seconds at dinner. Bacon doesn't bother us a bit. It was doubled a few weeks ago but even that didn't tempt us. We still have it about once in a blue moon.

Mussolini is in the picture. He has gone to Brenner Pass to see Hitler probably tomorrow. What is he up to? Rome papers say there are peace moves on and in fact Sumner Welles is delaying his departure on account of it all. More breathless suspense, oh yeah.

Have just heard the first of the 'Moonlight'. Not bad but I still prefer the version of Marlene Dietrich in *Dishonoured* though it was unconventional and ten years ago.

WEDNESDAY 20 MARCH
Quite a bit to report if I don't forget half of it. The most outstanding event on everyone's lips today is an air raid. We've been and bombed the Isle of Sylt in sheer devilry, as a reprisal for the Scapa raid on Saturday. It happened last night, from 8 to 3 this morning, seven hours of sustained raiding, not of heavy armadas but one or two planes at a time, about 30- or 15-minute intervals. The bombs were decent size, each plane only dropping two or four, there being about thirty planes and a report of 108 bombs. Damage amounted to two hangars ablaze, workshops and slipways damaged, also railway line to the mainland on the Hindenburg Dam. Losses, agreed by Jerry and us, were one plane down in flames. Today at 9 a.m. we sent two planes to photo the damage.

I've reported at length because it's the first so far. Everyone is naturally delighted specially as there was a dramatic turn when Chamberlain announced in the House last night that the raid was on while it was actually in progress. I hope though that this blinking war will not develop into a reprisal campaign. To be on the safe side I've put the lamp in the dug-out tonight. It's beautifully moonlit again, and one never knows. I wonder if in a few years' time I shall be able to regard these raids as dispassionately as at the moment. There is still a detached, ringside seat atmosphere about it all. We haven't come in contact with the war yet and it may be these raids which will supply the deficiency. Certainly Saturday and yesterday have brought realisation a little nearer. How shall we, and I, stand up to it when it comes, I wonder? I've mentioned and hinted at this many times already. It may sound windy and, if I trouble to read this later on, I hope I shall laugh at it. At the moment it is simply that one doesn't know what the future holds. It may be even worse than the terrible pictures the press has been giving us these past years and it may be just negligible. Anyway it turns out the chief thing, to my mind, is the way in which we conduct ourselves.

We are to build thirty-seven more munitions factories to be in production by next year, bringing total up to fifty-four. Some expansion. Doesn't look much like peace terms.

WEDNESDAY 27 MARCH
Saw quite a sight this afternoon. A Blenheim pancaked on the marsh at the back of Reavell's, presumably having had engine trouble. If so, the pilot deserved a medal. It was high tide, extra high, and the marsh was flooded and he chose about the only reasonable place within miles. It was flooded yet not deep so that he was able to make a softish landing and guard against fire as much as poss. Reports say he had two big bombs aboard and I saw them unloading what they could at 5.30. There were eight drums of ammunition, parachutes, an inflatable raft and incidentally the bottle looked about 4 in dia. by 12 in long. Soldiers with fixed bayonets prevented any of us going further than the railway line. The crew, three of them, were able to walk out, though cut about, and eventually taken to hospital.

The *Ark Royal* has been home to Plymouth and is at sea again. She had been out five months and scouted 5 million square miles. Naturally we made the most of it in view of Lord Haw-Haw's continued 'Where is the *Ark Royal*?' The bloke who said he sunk her was decorated with the Iron Cross One and Two. He must be feeling a mutt. He dropped a 1,000-lb bomb but it missed by 15 ft. A close thing but not close enough.

SUNDAY 31 MARCH
Reg Thrower has been round with instructions for the respirator census and examination. It must be done by Friday night. He was mentioned on the wireless tonight. The lady next door was expecting a baby and he happened to hear its first cry. He grabbed a baby hood and rushed round with it, handing it in in 40 secs. Said he did it for a joke. Bowden of the *EADT* got hold of it, a *Daily Mirror* man called today and it was mentioned on the

wireless that an Ipswich warden had made a record. Good old boy. He's put Ipswich on the map once again.

Re: again the respirator census and exam. If they are damaged, repairs are free but, after this, they must be paid for. A complete respirator costs 2s 6d. Wonder if I can get one as a filter for the circulating system for the dug-out? Must see.

They are taking the Blenheim away from the marshes. They had to cut the fuselage and wings away and do it in bits. They are certainly [well] made and all metal. The bombs were still there on Saturday. Reports say one was thrown forward and they don't know if the fuse cap is safe so careful handling is indicated.

Ought to have said before that I had a regret from the Admiralty, that considering the methods they have in use they see no prospect of adopting my idea. Never mind, as KR said, I've had my fun.

FRIDAY 5 APRIL
Have had a busy week doing respirator drill and examination. Did this side of Leopold Road 10 to 76, and saw 109 respirators. Mostly OK but found 2 with no valves, 4 defective face-pieces and 8 worn boxes. Several had the band in a wrong position. I was examining rather perfunctorily I'm afraid and just pulling the face-pieces in a sort of important way, not expecting to find defects, and when a hole showed up I sort of, kinda jumped with surprise.

There are very few respirators to be seen in the streets these days. People have simply decided it's a waste of time I fancy. So it is, till the time he uses gas. Indeed, except for a few soldiers about the streets, the Cornhill periodically blocked about 1 o'clock by those 6-in howitzers behind their lorries on the way to the Drill Hall, and a few planes, one can see no difference from peacetime. Certainly there are planes about. In reasonable weather they are fairly continuous and in bad weather still fairly common. They moon across the sky in threes mostly, sometimes singly, sometimes in sixes or twelves. We just look up and say 'Hurricanes', 'Spitfires' or 'Blenheims' and qualify the last as to short or long nose then get on with what we are doing. There are very few others around here. At night we see a few searchlights but we can't hear those so there is less incentive to go out and look.

Am pleased to note we are adopting a stronger attitude with Japan. I see that we have insisted that we shall maintain our rights as a belligerent in searching ships in Japanese waters. Incidentally, it's a decent blockade to reach that far.

SATURDAY 6 APRIL

Street traffic lamps are to be altered. At the moment they are blacked out except for a + in the top half. They are almost invisible in sunlight yet can be seen literally for a mile in the dark. Now they are to be black bottom half, clear top half, brighter by day and reduced by night.

New £1 and 10s notes are to be issued. They are printed the same but different colours and incorporated in the paper runs a thread which will be difficult to forge. Object being that Jerry has been trying to plant quantities of forged notes. A good idea on his part but dangerous for us.

Went to Felixstowe with Harry, Doris and Dora this afternoon. There are twenty-one balloons up which is surprising 'cos we had a storm this week and several came down in flames. We went to Miller's for a cup of tea. A wartime atmosphere insofar as the way the other patrons looked. Soldiers, girls in blue, military and girls in khaki uniforms. Was glad to take off my coat and display my ARP badge. Not much but 'twas all I had and showed willing. Possibly though I am doing as much for this blinking war as any others there.

Saw a whacking great plane this afternoon. It had the 'target' so was an RAF plane, probably a bomber, had four engines, was a mid-wing monoplane, single rudder and only doing 100 to 150 mph. Wonder if it was very heavily fortified? Possibly a convoy protection plane, slow and heavily armed.

TUESDAY 9 APRIL

Faster and faster. Things are moving so quickly now that I can't hope to record everything. Yesterday there was an air raid on Scapa again, Jerry losing two or probably three planes, yet other news was so plentiful and important that the *Telegraph* put that item at the bottom right-hand corner of the front page.

Last night came the startling, comforting and apprehensive news that we had sunk, by submarine, a German troop-ship containing 500 men and horses, a 12,000-ton tanker – their largest – and a 2,000-ton ship in the Kattegat, just off the Norwegian coast. Couldn't understand what a troop-ship was doing there, though I could have made a good guess, and this morning it was clear. Also two German subs sank one of our boats, a destroyer of ours took this as an unfriendly act and sank one sub.

Then this morning, 8 o'clock news, came the strong rumour from America that Germany had invaded Denmark and that Norway was at war with Germany. This was confirmed later. Also news that a large mixed German fleet was advancing to the North Sea.

It is difficult, impossible perhaps, to record the thrill underlying everything today. A tenseness, a strong confidence, a wondering, only modified by the chocolate which Green gave me in settlement of one of our little bets. Certainly a major event has happened. I cleared off early and raced home to hear the 1 o'clock news, when all the above was confirmed.

Briefly, things at the moment stand that all Denmark is occupied. That, in less than a day, is itself an achievement, though there was no resistance. Also landings have been made in Norway, Oslo has been bombarded by four warships and raided by air. The government has moved inland and we have promised Norway full aid. A strong force is on its way there, possibly the diverted Finnish aid, and a battle is proceeding off the Norwegian coast hampered by a heavy storm. Pray that we give them a good beating, though the North Sea is so fickle with her storms and mists that they may escape. I may have news after the 9 o'clock news. As I write there is a continuous, rather ominous, murmuring from Martlesham. I hope it is a show getting ready. As I see it, it is now our opportunity to raid Germany like hell from the air. Or should I admit that the Air Ministry know more of their job than I do, and let them do it?

A humorous, but deadly dangerous, aspect of it all is that today the Huns told Norway and Denmark that they are being protected from the aggression of the democracies and that Germany must make them a protectorate of the Reich.

After 9 o'clock . . . Norway claims to have sunk the *Gneisenau*, the Hun battleship, by shore batteries. Oslo is taken but the Norwegians are forming a defence line in front of their new capital. Germany has told Sweden that she may either accept Germany's protection or take the consequences. Italy is loud in supporting Germany's action and that means that I shall probably win that other 6*d* of chocolate. The naval battle is proceeding but no news is through because no wireless is allowed but Mr Chamberlain says that we have two strong fleets at sea. And – very ominous – Germany has had the blasted cheek to say that Britain and France are contemplating invasion of Holland and Belgium and that Germany may conceive it necessary to protect them. Beat that if anyone can. We know what that means.

Well, well, this blinking war has started at last. Now we may expect things to happen. In the meantime we must go to bed with what patience we may to wait for the 8 o'clock news tomorrow.

WEDNESDAY 10 APRIL

Well, well. We actually made a start. Bombers last night attacked
two German cruisers (*Kolns*) and two destroyers off Bergen, one
cruiser badly damaged, others slightly. A 7,000-ton supply ship has
been torpedoed off Sweden, also a cruiser. Good old subs. We must
have a little something the Huns haven't got in our submarines.
They seem to do pretty well. Also the 'Great Naval Battle', as the
placards shrieked, was probably an action which occurred off
Narvik. I'll give details later when I hear them, but *Hunter* was sunk
and *Hardy* run aground, both destroyers, and the enemy suffered
too. Poor old *Hunter*. She was mined, I remember, in the Spanish
'do'⁴ and managed to reach port under her own steam. There was
also an air raid on our fleets off Norway. Jerry claims the usual two
battleships almost sunk and we say only two cruisers slightly
damaged. They can't use wireless when at sea so we shan't have
definite news till later. Jerry admits loss of two cruisers *Blucher* and
Karlsruhe, both in shore battery actions and by mine, so if the other
losses are in addition he has suffered some.

Can't see how it was done but somehow he has a force of 2,000
at Narvik, according to reports. Even if he has I can't see them
making a success of it, all that way from Germany. At first came
reports that Norway was considering negotiating but now they are
denied.

Now Winston, what are you going to do? Don't disappoint us
please.

After 9 o'clock. Good old Navy! Darned good work. There are
lots of rumours but the sum of it seems to be 2 German cruisers
sunk, 2 damaged, 2 destroyers sunk, 3 damaged, 7 supply ships
sunk, 2 troop-ships reported sunk, in fact disorganisation of troop-
ship services. Our losses 2 destroyers and 2 damaged. Also
reported *Bremen* has been torpedoed with 1,300 on board. There
is still naval fighting going on at the mouth of the Skagerrak and
our planes have been bombing cruiser fleets again. I <u>enjoyed</u> the
news tonight. Nearly forgot we also shot down two Heinkels on
NE coast and another probably down at mouth of Channel.

Yes, I enjoyed it, and specially must I report the Narvik affair.

Apparently five destroyers went in and attacked six Jerries of
slightly heavier type. As I said *Hunter* was sunk, *Hardy* a wreck
on shore; *Hotspur* and *Hostile* were damaged and *Havoc* got
away undamaged. Jerry lost 1 destroyer sunk, 3 on fire, 6 supply
ships sunk. Just to help things along, on the way out as we retired

and withdrew, we met the *Rauenfels*, an ammunition supply ship, and blew her up. Good old Winston. The Nelson touch is back again, indeed it smells very like Roger Keyes.[5] All power to his energetic elbow.

Seems incredible but Blenheims were in action over Oslo today. Quick work. Hitler has introduced supervision and control in Copenhagen and Denmark in general. Newspapers are controlled and censorship by Nazi officials installed.

THURSDAY 11 APRIL
And still it goes on. The major action may be finished now but it was still in progress this morning. All the time rumours, reports and rumours. Some of it substantiated later and some of it modified. Seems, though, that the naval action has penetrated to the Kattegat and reports are persistent that Germany is continually losing cruisers and troop-ships. Also we have occupied Bergen and possibly Narvik.

At home everything is suppressed excitement. Papers are rushed out, with special editions almost as soon as the others are out. Paper boys are doing a roaring trade. At the office the excitement is there also. We nibble at what little work we have then discuss the pros and cons. And there, popping up now and then, comes the astounding realisation that only the day before yesterday it was all undreamed of. All due to the wonderful news service we have I fancy. We get it at 8, I leave off at 20 mins to 1 to hear the 1 o'clock, listen avidly then wait, with what patience we may, till 6 and 9 o'clock.

WEDNESDAY 17 APRIL
We have, at last, officially landed troops in Norway 'at several points' they say. All we know of is Narvik where there is fighting going on. Of course we ought to realise that wireless is a mixed blessing, insofar as the whole affair is only eight days old and we get our news so quickly and voluminously that we are apt to get impatient. All the same, Jerry seems to be still getting troops into Norway, by air chiefly, in the old slow 200-mph Junkers guarded by fighters. Of course we haven't any Spitfires there so they are pretty safe – till we get an aerodrome worth having. Jerry is drawing a line across Norway from Trondheim, whatever that may mean, but the Norwegians are holding out in other places. Apparently Oslo was taken very easily because of the presence of

Nazi sympathisers in high places. The papers say that Jerry knows more psychology than we give him credit for. He took Oslo with only 2,000 troops and paraded them about and played bands to make a show. In that case he deserved it.

Planes are buzzing again this evening. Went to Wambach's place last night for stirrup-pump drill. A bitterly cold evening, promise of a frost, and we had to lay on a groundsheet (a bit wet) on his lawn and use the pump hose. After that a lecture on incendiaries and their habits and I woke this morning with a stiff neck and a sore throat. That was of no account for it was all towards one in the eye for Hitler, but it does show how useless I should be in the Army. Sound like an old man, don't I?

Cadged a respirator filter from Wambach last night. It will do to fit on the door of the dug-out and save the cost and trouble of a 20-ft inlet pipe. Mentioned the idea to George tonight and he didn't seem too favourable but left it to me. I should feel much safer with it there, for I can't see us poor wardens hearing a gas bomb fall in the racket of planes, HE (possibly) and Archie. We don't even know what sound to listen for and if those women and kids are positively safe it will be a comfort. Also I would like to think out some scheme whereby if an incendiary penetrates the roof, a bell rings in the dug-out. I've got confidence in Dora's capabilities to deal with it but she must know before the house gets well alight.

SUNDAY 21 APRIL
Reports today say we have 50,000 men in Norway. Quite good if true. The news just now says we have men fighting in the Oslo district. Hope it is official.

Today has been a gloriously warm day, the first of summer it seems, and just such a day that we can say with relief 'This is what we were looking forward to when we used to put up the blackouts at 4.15'. George certainly has ideas. Today we were talking of juice and the Bawdsey masts were mentioned again. Supposing that there is something in the popular idea that they are for some cutting-out purpose. He opined that in that case it is possible that the light ships the Germans are so fond of bombing are not light ships, but similar stunts to the land masts.

SUNDAY 28 APRIL
News seems centred on Norway nowadays. A disquieting aspect of the business is that our press goes to some length to explain the

disadvantages at which the NWEF (name just given them) find themselves, the reason for this being that we are not having things all our own way out there. The situation at the moment seems like this. We landed a force at Narvik, or near it because of snowstorms and bad weather. We seem to have gone to sleep there for all the news we get. Reports say there are 4,500 Germans there and we are probably waiting for an adequately equipped force before doing anything definite. Lower down the coast we landed at Namsos, north of Trondheim and Andalsnes, south of Trondheim, and are making courageous but weakish attempts to take Trondheim. Jerry is sending reinforcements up two valleys, the only means of communication from Oslo, and we are trying to stop them joining. If they do establish contact and a good line of communication we can't do much about it besides resigning ourselves to a darned long business. We have a movement south from Namsos but Jerry has checked and held us and indeed forced a withdrawal which gave rise to reports in America we had been cut to pieces. The only line of advance for us there is beside a fjord in which are a Hun cruiser and four destroyers which enjoyed a little target practice on our troops as they advanced.

Goering is yet again threatening unrestricted aerial warfare because of alleged bombing on our part of open German towns. Well, suppose it might come some day. Am afraid my chief concern is how I shall show up in any emergency when it does come.

WEDNESDAY 1 MAY

A full dress practice last night for Clacton ARP services. A Heinkel was damaged by our fighters, about 2315 hr and after circling Clacton for 30 minutes eventually landed on Clacton. It had a mine or mines on board, magnetic ones, nice big ones with 700 lb TNT aboard, and after ploughing through houses the plane eventually blew up and the remains caught fire, killing 3 people, injuring 95, 27 seriously.

Later. Have just heard on the wireless the injured numbered 145. The plane ploughed through a house, killing 2 people inside, hit the ground, the mines exploded, threw the plane 30 yd against a building. Several houses demolished, fifty damaged. Reports praise the ARP services highly. I don't think it is merely meant for encouragement. People like the chump who said, 'If they want a uniform, why don't they join the Army' would be only too glad of the chance to criticise. Certainly they were ready, for the plane had been buzzing about, probably identified, and services were standing by, but rescue parties were operating in under five minutes. Incidentally, numbers here in Ipswich heard the explosion. I didn't though it only occurred a few minutes after I went to bed.

In Norway things seem approaching a deadlock. We are landing fresh troops and so is Jerry, chiefly by plane. Regret to record that *Sterlet* and *Tarpon* are overdue and must be considered lost. That makes total of seven subs, one of which, the *Oxley* was sunk by accident.

SATURDAY 4 MAY

Most people are feeling low-spirited. Can honestly say I'm not one of them but must admit there are reasons for a little disquiet. On Thursday came the Premier's statement on Norway – general and in particular the announcement that we had evacuated Andalsnes, our landing place south of Trondheim. Next day, yesterday, we heard that we have also evacuated Namsos, north of Trondheim. All very disturbing, but after all, when one examines the position, if we cannot hold the position it's far better to retire and save lives and equipment. Hitler has planned the whole business very well indeed and we may be sure that there is not a port or quay in Norway worth using which he didn't pinch. Lack of quays and aerodromes has been our chief source of embarrassment.

Well, there we are. The whole of Norway except the top narrow strip is now in German hands. I don't know where the evacuated troops went but can only hope they went to help at Narvik. We can't tell what is happening for there is no news, only a Swedish report – those pinnacles of truth – which says there has been a naval bombardment. If we can only force a victory there we shall save a little face with the neutrals, though they don't count much really. It's been a hectic three weeks and if we recognise that Jerry has the whip hand, well I can see no shame in admitting it and clearing out. Norway is not the only fighting sector. At the same time, when I paid up a 2d chocolate today to Aldy I thought that when we made the bet I little thought it would be the British who would not be left. I should have said the evacuation was made without losing a single man, but helped probably by the RAF pounding away at the chief aerodromes.

WEDNESDAY 8 MAY

A crisis has arisen in this little ole country of ours. Like this. There was a debate in Parliament yesterday on the Norwegian withdrawal and some strong criticism. A lot was from people who don't matter but 20 minutes came from Roger Keyes who accused the government of 'shocking ineptitude'. He said he spoke for many men in the Navy who were very unhappy over the business since they were not allowed to take the obvious active measures. He had gone to Whitehall with suggestions for sending a naval force to Trondheim and Bergen as we did at Narvik, but he was snubbed and told that surely he didn't think the suggestion had not already been thought of and rejected. He offered to lead it himself and take old ships if they thought we couldn't risk good ones owing to Italy, but his offer was refused. That certainly wasn't the way to treat a hero of mine. I'm certain the Navy could have done it and so we should have been in control of Norway instead of Jerry.

Dora, I'm afraid, seems a little nervous and apprehensive tonight. Hope it will work off, and I think it will. The planes have been droning over all evening and there were others early this morning and yesterday. They must have an effect on nerves in time, I suppose. Still, I know she is not the sort to panic or fuss, bless her old heart.

THURSDAY 9 MAY
Crisis blowing over. Chamberlain scored 281 to 200, 132 being absent. Today there are rumours of him resigning but only rumours. Churchill said he had already a plan similar to Roger Keyes's and rejected it as unworkable and made the remarkable statement that we could not afford to lose, or risk, ships in view of affairs in other places. He finished by an equally remarkable statement 'At no time during the last war were we in greater peril than we are now.'

Another calling-up proclamation today, covering people up to thirty-six (i.e. from twenty-eight). The twenty-sevens register on 25 May so it won't be long before we get to thirty-six. They reckon on another 2½ million in those classes but I guess there will be many unfits and exempts amongst them.

Holland has yet again cancelled all leave and is standing ready. Of course, it may be required one day but the *Telegraph* mentions that they did it sixty-one times last year. Ven says (*Express* report) that Belgium says she will maintain neutrality if Holland is attacked. Sheer blithering dunderheaded idiocy or fifth column work?

FRIDAY 10 MAY 8.15 A.M.

Here's news hot from the announcer's mouth. Holland and
Belgium were invaded early this morning. At 5.30 I was awakened
by naval pursuits and kept awake by activity which seemed from
Nacton. No wonder. Good luck to the avenging hordes (I hope
there <u>are</u> hordes available). Holland and Belgium have asked Allied
aid and now there will be two more anthems to play on Sunday
evening before the news.

Jerry has kicked off with huge air raids of 25 to 100 planes at a
time, also landed parachute troops. At the moment 6 planes brought
down. Also we have 'invaded' and 'protected' Iceland purely as a
protective measure but all the same, I can't see the idea. Too thick-
headed I suppose. Anyway all this is a tribute to the Chamberlain
government and their foresight in withdrawing Norway troops.

2200 hr on duty . . . A day of real activity culminating in a really
fighting resignation speech of Neville Chamberlain upon his
resignation. Poor old chap. He has worked very hard and now to
have to resign after that damn silly uproar over Norway seems to
me to be upsetting for everyone. He said some beautiful things
about Hitler in a vigorous voice which seemed to belie any
suggestion that he couldn't carry on the war energetically enough.
Anyway he has resigned and Churchill is now Premier. We should
now have no cause for complaint about the speed of prosecution of
the war.

Jerry is not having all things his own way. Altogether he has lost
over 100 planes today, according to a wireless bulletin from an
observer in France; the Hurricanes have been enjoying themselves,
without losses too. The Dutch and Belgium forces are holding the
Germans and our troops are streaming into Belgium.

People here are mostly apprehensive and the other two wardens
have gone on lights patrol with increased fervour. Probably they
will bag a few. We need an example just now. We have lost Mr
Laverick as full-timer which means the post is closed at midnight.
If a 'yellow' comes after that the seniors are to be summoned by
phone to open the post.

There has been a feeling of tenseness at work today. At 10.30 we
sneaked into the canteen to hear the news and again at teatime we
heard it. Although the invasion only started at 3 this morning we
are so soaked with news that I felt offended at seeing the placards
at lunchtime with the statement 'Holland and Belgium invaded'. It
seemed so stale.

MONDAY 13 MAY

Also Whit Monday but nobody seems to mind working on a holiday. That's the spirit.

I found today that Dora has already some idea on evacuation. We discussed the pros and cons this dinner time. There are various solutions but I think the best is to wait and act on the government advice and go where they suggest. Aunt Katherine's or Sylvia's would be very little better than here, probably worse except for air raids.

Churchill has formed his new cabinet. Chamberlain is still in, as President of the Council, Alexander is First Lord of Admiralty and Kingsley Wood, Chancellor of the Exchequer, Eden is Secretary for War. An energetic lot and, I hope, not too foolhardy.

Regulations are being tightened up around the coast. We are expected to carry registration cards I fancy. You couldn't go into Felixstowe yesterday without them and there are barricades on all the principal roads. Aubrey Ward was stopped at Colchester last night and the car examined, attended by fixed bayonets and a nice little mat studded with spikes ready to pop under the wheels in case they bunked. There are also barbed wire barricades at Colchester, I hear, which are closed at 9 p.m. Armed guards are now on all the main road bridges. In addition this weekend there was a glorious round-up. All Germans and Austrians in the country have been interned no matter who they are, provided they are not naturalised, and all other foreigners are under control. Even Dutch, Belgians and sympathetic neutrals are to report each day, stay indoors between 8 p.m. and 6 a.m., and not drive a car or travel except by public conveyance.

Seal is overdue and presumed lost. Our submarine patrol must be very effective for our losses, though heavy, are relatively light considering they operate on Jerry's doorstep.

TUESDAY 14 MAY

Have just heard some news which has made me all excited. Anthony Eden has just announced a scheme called the LDV, Local Defence Volunteers. It's unpaid but volunteers get a uniform and a gun. Wouldn't I like to join. My knee feels better at the thought. Wonder what Dora would think of it? There's no denying it would be dangerous if used 'cos it's only intended against parachute landings and my rheumatism would be encouraged but who cares about that. Must think about it.

Jerry is pressing forward like blazes. The Dutch have retired behind their water defences which means half Holland has gone and quite a slice of Belgium too. A clash, and a terrific clash, is imminent now. Let's hope that if we have to retire, and I've a sneaking feeling to that effect, that losses won't be too bad. The curse of it will be that he will have those advanced air and sub bases. Why <u>are</u> his subs so quiet?

WEDNESDAY 15 MAY
Last night Holland gave up the struggle. Poor devils, they must be a little sorry that they told other nations to mind their own business and that they were to remain neutral. Still, one shouldn't talk like that now. They fought well, losing 100,000 men, an incredible figure. Some companies lost 80 per cent and it was humanitarian reasons which made Gen Winkelman give in. Actually the Zeeland islands are still fighting and, I believe, backed up by the Allies, and the Dutch navy has now joined ours. Queen Wilhelmina and Princess Juliana are now in England. The fifth-columnists and aircraft were chief reasons for collapse. An observer said he saw about forty parachutists drop from a plane. An Archie fired and they just didn't exist any more. At night it was more difficult and many thousands were landed. Another observer said the internal distrust and papers examination was fearful and like a civil war. Practically all the air force is lost.

Well, well, a terrible collapse and I didn't think it would happen so soon, though I expected it. Now the Belgium line will have to fall back and, incidentally, we certainly may expect raids now.

Wireless messages are again warning us what to do in case of a raid. They are expecting something, and soon, I am afraid. We have lost a destroyer, the *Valentine*, off Holland by air action. Wonder what part the Navy has been playing?

THURSDAY 16 MAY
The battle is developing in Belgium. There is no news except vaguely in outline. The aspect of it which I don't like is that they are forcing us on the defensive. It's Jerry who springs the tricks and we have to counter them. It's a bit disquieting to read between the lines when the authorities say they are 'confident', but I hope my fears have no foundation.

FRIDAY 17 MAY
Germany is thrusting like blazes in one sector, near Sedan, and has formed a bulge in the line. Churchill has described it as 'the battle of

the Bulge'. Again, I can't give details, it would take too long, but the losses on both sides must be huge. They have brought out a new tank, heavily armoured, and we are finding it a tough nut. Liège, though surrounded and hopeless, is still holding out. The King sent the garrison a message telling them to hold out till the end and they are doing it. Brave fellows. Opinion says this is the biggest battle ever fought. Naturally, aircraft are playing a big part, especially since the weather has been almost cloudless all the time. An official estimate puts German air losses at 1,000 planes, an unbelievable figure, with ours a small fraction. Naturally the offensive suffers most. We are bombing transports and last night made another raid inside Germany on transport and communications, not losing a single plane.

A terrific struggle and certainly like what we were led to expect by the popular press, before the war. The most outstanding point is that it is mostly open warfare.

More warnings of parachute troops. The LDV is still enlisting and, in the first day, totalled 250,000. Good work.

The Navy has been terrifically active over this Dutch affair, chiefly with destroyers and CMBs. The destroyer which took off Juliana and family was intercepted by a plane which dropped a magnetic mine 40 yd ahead. It exploded on contact with the sea so no damage was done. We also helped to destroy oil reserves, closed the lock gates at Rotterdam and wrecked the machinery, sank a 12,000-ton liner in the fairway, swept up mines and laid ours, sent motor torpedo-boats into the Zuiderzee, took a merchant back to Amsterdam and rescued several million pounds worth of diamonds etc., etc. Some crews were in action against aircraft from dawn to dusk.

SUNDAY 19 MAY

All the evacuees still in these districts were moved to Wales today, which is a sign of official perturbation. We saw some going up the road to the school for congregating this morning about 7 o'clock. Still, they had a glorious cloudless day for it and they are in a safer place.

We had our exercises this morning and had one of the biggest incidents at our points. Greenwood and I were at Salt's house and, when we arrived, found two chalk rings in Leopold Road and Sidegate Avenue and a crowd of Scouts and Girl Guides were hanging about. We knew we were to have an incident but all this looked a little fearful. About twenty-five to thirty 'casualties' were laid out on the waste ground and then a smoke flare went up. We approached the umpire and learnt two small HE bombs had fallen and caused forty casualties and two dead and damage to overhead cables. Wake and I tackled the casualties and found each one with a ticket ranging from sprained ankles to gunshot wounds in abdomen and broken limbs. I had a brainwave before going out and wrote out three tourniquet notices which I was able to pin on the three tourniquet cases we had. Stiff took the report and services began to arrive. The mortuary squad took away the sandbags (dead casualties) and not a smile was anywhere as they solemnly tramped away with one bag at a time on the stretcher. We are taking these exercises much more seriously now. I took the umpire round and explained what we had done to each case and when we arrived at a Potts fracture and I didn't know what it was, was relieved to find him burst into laughter. Disarming frankness paying, perhaps. Anyway he complimented us afterwards, so we weren't too bad.

Dora and I have been discussing the evacuation possibilities and probabilities. It's a fearful predicament. I think it is highly likely to come about and, though I don't think it would be justified in view of the light damage (touch wood like blazes) we are likely to sustain here in this port of Ipswich, there is that awful thought that I may be wrong and Ipswich might be absolutely flattened like Guernica. On the whole it might be best for them to go but I shall miss them terribly to say nothing of the complication due to Margaret not having her T and A [tonsils and adenoids] out and the dilapidation the house might suffer. At the back of it all is the feeling that I don't really mind what sacrifices of a monetary and property nature we are called on to make as long as we win this blinking war. That's the principal thing and, if I have to feed and see to myself for a few years, well what matters. I'm not china, nor starched lace.

10 o'clock. Heard Churchill tonight speaking as Premier in what was really a call to the nation for effort. He put the position very clearly showing that the battle still raging was the biggest the world has known and that we are dealing with it well and truly. After all, as he said, they can't wipe out an Army of 3 million in weeks or even months, and we have the best staying power. He warned us though to prepare for air attacks of a heavy nature. They all say it is coming so I suppose it will. Dora just thought she heard machine-gun fire so we sidled out so as not to disturb Ma but it was only practice. And it wasn't nerves which sent us out either.

We did hear, though, terrific activity at Martlesham. It sounds as though every plane there is about to take off. It's a glorious night, really full moon and the searchlights are hardly visible.

TUESDAY 21 MAY
Position grave today. The Germans are making another big push and have taken Arras and Amiens. The object seems to be to take the Channel ports and they seem like doing it.

M Reynaud[6] spoke today, a calm, matter-of-fact, serious speech which showed the gravity of the situation. He said the German attack on the Netherlands was met by the French wheeling on Sedan and advancing into Belgium. Germany struck at the hub-joint where the French troops were weakest, most untrained, and unfit to meet the attack. By a mistake 'which shall be punished', bridges across the Meuse were not blown up and Jerry walked across. The attack and advance necessitated the British withdrawal which is taking place. Jerry is trying for the Channel ports but our counter has not yet been made. The British and French army has not yet been properly in action and, when it has, perhaps the attack will be worthwhile. He paid good tribute to the RAF and asked all munitions services to work 24 hours a day.

Well, it's serious enough but I can't see it as the beginning of the end. Perhaps I'm wrong but somehow I've faith in the recuperative powers of the Allies. After all, we often only win the last battle and that's the one which counts. Churchill flew to France on Saturday for a lightning visit and on Monday Gamelin was superseded by Gen Weygand. Now everyone is acclaiming the new man. Perhaps it's understandable. Gamelin seems not to be the wonder at strategy and militarism he was cracked up to be at the beginning of the war. If Churchill has a hand in it, the counter should be worth seeing.

Dora says she thinks she won't go away if they evacuate. Hope it will be alright to stay. We'll both feel pretty sick if the kids get hurt but there are so many drawbacks to them going. Perhaps the problem will settle itself. Ven told me today he heard we have thirty-four Archie round Ipswich. Not bad, but what a row!

We've lost our first cruiser *Effingham* on an uncharted rock near Norway. Bad luck. All personnel saved. Also a minelayer, the *Victoria*, with several lost. She was mined but we don't know how and where. And only today I was remarking we hadn't lost a cruiser yet.

Made the dug-out bolts more workable this evening and am trying to rig up a periscope. It will make it much more convenient to be able to see the house and it's essential for quick dealing with incendiary bombs. Dora and Mrs Rudd should be able to use the pump.

FRIDAY 24 MAY

Empire Day, but not a very auspicious one for us. Never mind, perhaps the tide will turn. Jerry has been advancing again. He has captured Boulogne today and Abbeville yesterday. We have held and even advanced a little at Arras and the French are in the outskirts of Amiens. On the other hand the 'Arras gap' is only 25 miles wide and Jerry is pouring through in the direction of more Channel ports. Pray God he doesn't get any more. When <u>will</u> we counter? We must be content to wait, it is less than a week since Gamelin went and Weygand is reported as unruffled and preparing his plans.

Something is badly wrong over there. Even allowing the superiority of tanks we ought to have found a counter before this. As it is they can send forward a stream of armed motorcyclists who can spread such havoc that they can occupy a town. Mechanised warfare *à la excellence*. Can't we do <u>something</u> about it? How badly have the French let us down? Why hadn't they any guns capable of dealing with 80-ton tanks? Some day we shall know, perhaps.

TUESDAY 28 MAY

On duty this morning, midnight to 4 a.m. On occasions during this war there have been occurrences when we sit in the office holding discussions instead of working, just because we can't work, and race home to hear the latest news. Today was one of those occasions. Going home this dinner time I gasped when I heard what the paper boys were shouting – there are no placards now – which was 'Belgian Army Surrenders'!!! Sure enough King Leopold had ordered his own army to lay down their arms. Reynaud spoke very bitterly about it and recalled the instant way in which we had answered Leopold's call for help. Other Frenchmen spoke of 'treachery' at a time when the Allied armies were in a difficult but not desperate position. Leopold's name has been mud today, and I felt wild about it. There were all those beautiful brave blokes betrayed in their very awkward position and facing probable annihilation. So that was why Weygand flew to see Leopold. I started the Belgian anthem and broke off into a rude raspberry. Ven was appreciative and begged me to record it in the diary, so there you are Ven, it's in.

Tonight comes the welcome news that the Belgian government has repudiated the king and decided to carry on the war. So that's that. A storm in a teacup I hope, but we must wait to hear the news Duff Cooper[7] gives us tonight. The BEF is in a very bad position. Jerry is rolling along up towards Calais behind them and if Weygand doesn't soon counter, we can't say what will happen.

WEDNESDAY 29 MAY, 7.45 A.M.
Definitely not a storm in a teacup; 300,000 Belgians have packed up. A fearful position for our BEF. Duff Cooper last night spoke of withdrawal. Hope they can. I'd give lots for them to be able to break forward and join up with the French.

Later . . . The Belgians are furious with their 'felon king' as they call him. Demonstrations today in Paris before the statue of Leopold's father, which was adorned with black and wreaths and placards. In fact the only people who seem satisfied about it all are Leopold himself and possibly Jerry. His army was 800,000 at the beginning and now reduced to 300,000, so the poor devils have been having a tough time of it.

Our BEF are withdrawing to the coast. Whether they will attempt to hold it or evacuate entirely remains to be seen. Poor devils. What a prospect. Naturally they have been supported by the RAF but, even so, their position is very bad. I'd give lots for them to extricate themselves with a victory at the same time.

Noticed something today. They are mining the station bridge. Two Reavell portables were chugging away on the top this dinner time and still at it this evening. Presumably all the other main bridges are being mined as well. I should have recorded that they are barricading all the main roads. I haven't seen any but I hear Norwich Road bridge, Woodbridge Road, Felixstowe Road have all barbed wire and concrete barricades. What do they expect? Or is it merely precautionary in view of the surprises Hitler has sprung on us in other ways?

News today that the Works are to do seven days a week officially now. We shall follow soon, in fact WR is planning to speak to us tomorrow probably on the subject. There is also a rational suggestion for holidays this year. I'm all for it myself. It's the least we can do.

THURSDAY 30 MAY
The BEF are retreating to the coast and fighting a fierce battle on the coast. The Navy is helping with evacuation and bombardment

but has lost three destroyers, *Grafton*, *Wakeful* and another. An official statement says our main store depots were not at the ports captured and, although we have lost a lot of material, our main supplies are safe. Hope that's true.

More and more warnings of the horrors to come. The coast towns from Great Yarmouth to Folkestone to be evacuated on Sunday and now they are asking us to register our kiddies for evacuation. What shall we do? Margaret will be really terrified alone and so far away, and it doesn't seem that Godfrey is being catered for so Dora can go. It's going to be a horrid ordeal, deciding.

SATURDAY 1 JUNE

Most of the BEF are now out of the awful position they found themselves in last week. Lord Gort has arrived in England so there are not many troops left. The actual position is not yet revealed except that Dunkirk has been surrounded by water floodings and is being strongly held by the French. Soon perhaps we shall hear the full story. One report says Jerry has a million men in the district and the losses are very heavy. In the whole action of recent weeks it is estimated Hitler has lost 40 per cent of his mechanised forces and north France is now the biggest scrap heap of the world.

A vague feeling about the place today. Probably due to what we heard this morning. Green has been grabbed as a parashot and apparently everyone who volunteered has been enrolled. He has a beat round Stone Lodge Lane and shares a shotgun with another fellow, their total ammo being two cartridges. When the siren goes they run to their post and do their best to ambush any paratroops. The position is as bad as that – they expect a landing or invasion at any minute. I hear that even Sidegate Lane has been barricaded and manned by a machine-gun and that refers to every road out of town and, presumably, every town. All over the country signposts are pulled up and milestones are taken away and buried nearby. What a state for England to be in!! We can hardly realise it, and perhaps that's for the best. Green has apparently heard something for he says the invasion, or whatever it is, may come any minute but if it can be held off for three weeks we have no further worries. If that's so, and I know anything of Hitler, it will come well before three weeks and Italy will hit France in the back just to prevent any help in that direction. It all depends on time and we may bet Hitler knows that. If he can hit us well and often, it will pay him well. Let's hope something goes wrong with his plans. What shall I be reporting in a month's time? If reporting anything at all?

SUNDAY 2 JUNE
Today is my birthday. Hope I don't get a present, politically, from Italy. Our peacetime politicians seem to have made such a muddle of the supply question that we can't be in too good a position to take them on. Am beginning to lean towards the view that Chamberlain has a helluva lot to answer for.

Anthony Eden, the War Minister, spoke at 9 o'clock, being relayed to America. He described the marvellous way in which four-fifths of the BEF were withdrawn, and said we have lost vast stores in Flanders, and appealed for planes, tanks and munitions. Probably that's why he was relayed.

Last week we had a circular at work telling us that Sunday work would be paid for at 15 per cent for a day's work. The other DO, who had already been grumbling at working 2 hours for nothing, groused again and asked for at least full pay. WR, wily old dog, answered by saying the notice ought not to have gone to the DO and said we shouldn't be expected to work weekends. That cut the ground from under them and incidentally stopped any chance of earning extra money. Our office were not invited to grouse as well, which is just as well. We all felt that, with the BEF fighting like hell for their lives and ours, it was sordid and mean to talk of money, etc. at a time like that and I was deputed to tell the old chap so. He was pleased, I think, and said he was hurt by the other blokes. I shouldn't mind working every weekend for nowt if it would do any good towards the final issue, but am afraid Ven and I are in bad odour over it. Who cares? They are welcome to any blood money they can wangle. It's their consciences, not ours.

TUESDAY 5 JUNE
Dunkirk, the citadel of the last rearguard of the BEF, was evacuated yesterday. Our losses are put at 30,000 and material included 1,000 guns. It will take a time to replace all that. Jerry has started another big offensive in France today. So he has chosen to carry on with France and, for the moment, leave us alone. What will be the outcome? Another withdrawal? Hope not. I hope the forces will be so wild at our previous defeat that they will do better this time. We shall see and there will be just a little suspense nowadays until we hear the news.

Tonight twenty-three planes went eastwards again. We haven't seen those squadrons lately. Hope they will be back before I go to bed. We take a sort of personal interest in those raids and when we hear the hum of planes, when a squadron is due back, we all dash outside and when they come in sight anxiously start counting.

SATURDAY 8 JUNE

Saturday afternoon, a hectic ARP week and a chance of a sit down, so why not? Specially 'cos it gives a chance of diarising.

The German pressure in the new attack is terrific. They have pushed us back a bit on our left flank at the coast but otherwise the Allied line is reported to be holding. Pray that it does. Jerry lost 400 tanks on Thursday alone, and an estimate puts their total losses at 2,500 since Holland was invaded. Their tanks have penetrated the lines at a few places but the infantry couldn't follow and the tanks were polished off. They don't find wayside petrol stations to fill at in France like they did in Belgium.

America is finding ways and means of supplying arms without violating her own neutrality. She is sending batches of rifles and 75s left from the last war. They sound old but presumably will fire. Also more planes are coming from their own air force and Fleet Air Arm. Good.

We have announced a 3-mile limit round our coasts into which any boat which trespasses will be fired on if it is not in convoy. Sounds garbled but this isn't a grammar textbook. A step against invasion.

At 0015 hr Friday the siren went. I was delighted to find I took it calmly, no excessive heart action, no dry mouth, no tummy turning over. Poor old Dora wasn't so fortunate. It was one of the few nights when she hadn't put things ready, not even the kiddies' clothes. However, that was soon done; the bath half filled, gas turned off, dug-out opened and we were ready. I dashed to the post, the date was odd and my turn at the post. I accepted it with what grace I could because Margaret being queer made it awkward, but Booley turned up and offered to relieve me, an offer accepted very gratefully.

There were no big results of the raid. Twelve counties had the warning but these were only single planes, I fancy. We heard nothing.

Last night went to HE lecture. Sure enough at 2300 hr just as we had settled down, Wailing Winnie went again. We are getting used to her now. Again I rushed to the post, again Booley relieved me, and again I returned. The night was darker with a low mist and cloud. Nothing happened till just after midnight when there was a flash in the sky. I counted at once and 47 seconds later came the bang. I had before that dashed in and packed Ma and Godfrey down the dug-out, leaving instructions for Margaret to follow if it got worse. Soon a low drone and, damn me, there was that changing beat again. It came nearer so I got Dora ready to move. However, when it was about six miles away it died down slowly and we kept to the house. With Margaret infectious, it was best. And so the time drifted on, I got Godfrey back again and eventually at 12.50 a.m. the all-clear went.

On duty tonight, 2000 to 2400 hr. That makes Wednesday morning duty, evening lecture, Friday morning raid, evening lecture, night raid and tonight duty, plus raid??

MONDAY 10 JUNE
Italy has declared war at 0430 hr from tomorrow. We have completely evacuated Narvik, transferring our troops elsewhere and I'm not going to be so damn silly as to tempt Providence by recording naval losses any more – we've lost *Glorious*, two destroyers *Acasta* and *Ardent*, a supply ship and a tanker.

Rumour says the *Scharnhorst* and *Gneisenau* are loose in the North Sea. Probably they sunk the *Glorious*. If they get back safely I shall be disappointed, but I suppose we can't expect everything. King Haakon and the Norwegian government are now in England.

German pressure is still terrific on the Western Front. The French are giving a little ground but not yet retreating. Hope they don't.

FRIDAY 14 JUNE
Heavy news today and on a fitting Friday. Paris has fallen, the French evacuating to save it from damage and yesterday Reynaud broadcast to America telling her, for heaven's sake, to make haste. France was on her knees and that was the last time Reynaud would be able to appeal. Only the day before yesterday they [the Germans] were 40 miles away, at 6 o'clock only 30 miles and at the midnight news, 24 miles away. Only yesterday lunchtime came a ray of hope with the news that, in a counter-attack, the French had advanced 5 miles. Today's news is a terrific anti-climax to that.

We have lost another armed merchant cruiser, the *Scotsdown*, 1,700 tons, by U-boat. Also the Fleet Air Arm have bombed

Bergen harbour and found the *Scharnhorst* there and hit her once with a direct hit 'abaft the funnel'. That's all very fine but why the Hades should the *Scharnhorst* get there? Haven't we got command of the North Sea? Or have we?

SUNDAY 16 JUNE

Germany still forging ahead, and about twenty miles south of Paris. Must be heart-breaking for the French. Naturally some people are a bit gloomy and apprehensive and wonder if the French will capitulate and leave it all to us. It seems fairly certain now that Hitler will try invasion of this country and it means serious, grim work for blokes like us. Where he will attack cannot be foretold. The obvious place is the east or south-east but Hitler seems to have things so well worked out that he may not attack in the obvious way.

9.30 . . . Am on duty and have just heard the news. The French cabinet met this morning and again at 5 o'clock to consider Roosevelt's reply to Reynaud. It was then 9 o'clock and they wouldn't tell us the result. Is it what we fancy? Is France throwing in her hand? Hope not, but Jerry is throwing all he's got at her and last week he was using 120 divisions. Probably he is using the Wops as reinforcements.

Rumour says Hitler's programme is to be in London in August, the 21st I think, I wonder! Last night the chief of the LDV spoke and addressed the members telling them they were about to be tried, which sounded ominous to me. Now then, are those masts any good or not? We also appealed for 12-bore shotguns to be handed in for LDV use. They are intended to use ball cartridge which are effective over good distances.

TUESDAY 18 JUNE

Well, it happened after all. Yesterday, Monday, came the news that the previous day M Lebrun, the President, asked Reynaud to ask for an armistice. Reynaud refused, his cabinet resigned and at 10 o'clock Marshal Pétain, the doddering 83-year-old idiot, formed a cabinet with Weygand, of all people, in it which asked for the armistice. Today Hitler and Musso met in Munich and have now decided the terms which are being transmitted. In the meantime hostilities are continuing.

Damn and blast the ruddy French. The moaners who have, for the last month, been wagging their heads and saying, 'It's the

French you know and they may throw their hand in' were right after all.

Yesterday was a very unsettling day. The news was just mentioned at 1 o'clock and there was lots of uncertainty. Some people who listened didn't hear it, others did, and at 6 o'clock, everyone was at home to hear for himself. Then came confirmation and the awful gnawing fear – what will become of their fleet and air force? Will Hitler insist on it being handed over? The odds are he will and the odds also are the ruddy French will do so. Still, I ought not to be too bitter. They had a tough time and fought to a standstill almost and still are.

Churchill spoke in the Commons today and gave the same speech over the air at 9 o'clock. Bless him, he even joked. Referring to the Admiralty and any new moves the Germans might make, he said 'odd as it may seem the Admiralty have been giving some thought to it'. The gist of it all was – there is a tough time coming. We shall be bombed and they will attempt invasion but our arms are increasing and we have a Navy and Air Force which is superior to the Germans in quality and we shall beat them back. Out of 400,000 men we sent to France, we have brought 350,000 men back with huge stores of equipment. Altogether 1¼ million men are under arms in the country and ½ million LDV with few arms but this is being repaired. America is helping us with equipment and we also have two Dominion armies here. We are in for a tough time but we shall weather it.

THURSDAY 20 JUNE
3.40 a.m. On the 18th we had our first sight of Jerry. The blighter kept us up from 11 o'clock till ten to 4. It was a glorious cloudless night with a full moon and good for fighter work. They sent 100 planes over and we brought down 7 mostly in this district, and so many came over here that we know the sound of a Jerry plane by now. In fact I can hear one now, but blow him.

It all started with a bomb explosion about 11 just as we had gone to bed. Four more followed while we were dressing. I had opened up the dug-out and was looking round before the sirens went. Soon there was a tiny silver speck in the sky, the focus of lots of searchlights, and I had seen my first German aeroplane. He disappeared north followed by the lights, who handed him over to the west district and Archie. Hardly out of sight when another came on the same course. He was caught by twenty-three beams and looked wonderful. It seemed the height of folly to try to destroy such a beautiful shimmering thing slowly and disdainfully moving across the sky, the apex of all those tapering beams. Then one remembered what he was and it didn't seem folly. I guessed the height at about 30,000 ft. Many shells burst well short, but others nearer, only enhanced the picture by their flash instead of doing any damage. Later on, however, a plane immediately above our heads seemed hit by a direct hit. I'm certain bits flew off and we all shouted and I nearly hugged Reg Thrower in delight.

With each raider we took cover, at Mayhew's when we looked east and Thrower's when Jerry went west. Later we saw one 'go west'. I was looking up the road and just saw a spurt of MG tracers in the sky. They were orange and turned deep red. Then some more, as the fighter chased the raiders. It was most thrilling and satisfying. He kept it up, burst after burst until over Felixstowe the bomber turned into a yellow star, fell, twisted, spiralled, always falling till it disappeared and crashed, throwing up a semicircle of flash as it exploded. We cheered and shouted and said we didn't mind losing sleep after that. Then the sky seemed full of planes, three being caught in the beams. We watched one over the houses and dashed round to see it fall in flames. We were getting on. The night wasn't quite so long after that.

Altogether we heard and saw thirteen of them. The last, cheeky blighter, came inland from Woodbridge way, turned and went out over Harwich. Only the searchlights followed it till it reached the coast, then a stream of five red tracers reached up, a wait, and the shells bust well behind. Five more and closer, but high; six more then, which seemed to be direct hits, but that plane was charmed. Or was she? She may not have reached home.

Then came rumours of a third plane down and we certainly rejoiced. It made the remaining wait more bearable, and we didn't mind the cold. I'm afraid I broke the rule by getting the ladies to see some of the fun when it was safe. There certainly won't be such conditions so suitable for raider and fighter again.

Next night sirens went again at 11.55. It would be, the date being odd. The all-clear sounded at 0004 hr and another 'action' at 0006 hr. Someone had blundered but we cursed, and proceeded to wait once more till 0400 hr with nothing happening. We had heard Jerry at about 10 o'clock but went to bed. We must have slept. I went on duty at the post till 0330 hr then came home and started this entry.

Again 100 planes used, 3 'downed' and 3 badly damaged. Yesterday 12 killed, many injured, today 6 killed, 60 injured. Coming again tonight, probably, so Richard put this down and off to sleep. On duty anyway, at 0000 hr to 0400 hr.

SUNDAY 23 JUNE
What luck. We had an undisturbed night last night. Margaret says it's because she asked God not to send an air raid. George and I have been busy today widening the seats of the dug-out and adding two bunks. Now there should be available four beds for the kiddies and seating room for the grown-ups. Ventilation is a bother. We are attempting to get over it by a flap in George's door and using the periscope outlet in mine. It's promising to be another clear night so we may have an opportunity of trying it out. This evening we have packed a bag with a few clothing essentials so that we are ready for a move if the house gets demolished. What a state. Civilisation with the lid off.

We've also spent some time in covering the windows with Cellophane. It's not a satisfactory solution and one can't see out of the window so well but its one of those things we must put up with. We are now trying to get the householders to go to bed with a bucket of water at their front gates for our use. There is a tendency among the wardens to take cover rather thoroughly so I can't see fires being dealt with very promptly just yet. Perhaps I'm wrong.

The French have signed the armistice with Germany and are now negotiating with Italy. After signing these, hostilities will cease 6 hours later, i.e. 7 days after asking for it. Hitler's a vindictive old blighter. Now where's that French navy? Will it surrender? It will undoubtedly be demanded.

Sunday again and no bells. About ten days ago it was agreed to sound them on the occasion of a landing by air or paratroops being dropped. When we hear them I can imagine a sick feeling in the tummy. Queer how a thing like that can be filled with portent and convey so much by just a sound. Like the old days of the Armada when the beacons flashed their warnings. What are we in for?

THURSDAY 27 JUNE
0130 hr. Yes, another raid. The third running and three last week. I had to think to make sense of that, what with loss of sleep and plenty to do I literally have lost count of the raids and what happened when. The first raid we brought no planes down, indeed

they were flying so high it was pitiful and sad to watch the searchlights trying to pick them up and failing 'cos of the mist and cloud. Last night it was better, five being downed, the night being clearer. Casualties were three killed on Monday night, several injured yesterday and conjecture for tonight. No great damage has been done and I'm inclined to believe that. When they bombed us last week there were twelve unexploded bombs, probably dud, on the Henly Road district and others out Woodbridge way. Mysterious, that dud business but we must accept it as a fact.

I felt really depressed Monday evening. Felixstowe had warning evacuation notices posted during the weekend and we heard on Monday that they were to be ready at an hour's notice to leave. There is now an evacuation scheme to take kids to Canada and Australia and Doris said she would go to Australia if Dora went. That set us thinking. Naturally it would relieve me a lot to be relieved of the worry of their safety, but it's a long way. There's Margaret's op and I'm wondering if they will evacuate Australia when the Japs get pinching places. Tonight we have preferred Canada, but it's a lousy business altogether. I've got hopes, which I daren't even enter here, that it may be unnecessary, but it is a big risk to risk the kiddies' nerves and health. Invasion can be unpleasant.

I'm pleased to say that the French colonies show signs of fighting on but there are no indications yet that the fleet have as much guts as that. We shall see. Gen de Gaulle is organising the French colonial forces and those outside France. That Pétain government is going to stink in history.

There are queer reminders of the war in the town. All notices referring to Ipswich have the name of the town blocked out, even some vans running about have blotches on them. I saw one today which read '. . . Gas Company'. With the signposts and milestones gone, I hear it's a bit awkward getting about the country. Everywhere, I hear, there are barricades. I've seen a few and they are placed at every road into town. Cedric and John Day are starting their military training now, being taught to slope arms, etc. We are now sending all our important drawings to be photoed as a record, an E no. being reduced to postcard size and all job sheets are being copied. Wonder where they will store them? Bury them somewhere?

It's now 2.30. Jerry usually keeps us hanging round for 4 hours, so must wait till another hour. Dora and the kiddies are in the dug-out. We've just installed bunks for the kiddies, so now everyone can sleep if necessary. Sleep is now elevated to a position of national importance.

WEDNESDAY 3 JULY
Jerry has been busy again. Daylight raids yesterday over Tyneside, 12 killed, 123 injured, 1 plane down. Again last night and then today 3 daylight raids, 5 planes down, 2 killed, 16 injured. One raid over Ipswich. About 5 o'clock we heard gunfire but no warning. Two Jerries came over and dropped bombs over Severn Road, Wye Road and Claygate Lane. Several injured but our fighters went up and both those Jerries came down.

Margaret went into hospital yesterday, and was operated on today. Hope Jerry doesn't bomb the place. Poor little kid, wonder how she's feeling?

THURSDAY 5 JULY
Sad but inspiring news. We have taken over a big batch of French fleet but, unfortunately, a big concentration at Oran, in north Africa, would not play. We offered several alternatives including suggesting they should go to their colonies, or even USA, for internment, which after all would only enforce the armistice terms which 'guaranteed' the fleet would not be used against us. Their sense of duty, I suppose, so Somerville opened fire on them. There were *Strasbourg*, *Dunkerque*, two other battleships and supporting boats there. We damaged and drove ashore either *Strasbourg* or *Dunkerque*, sunk one other battleship, a seaplane carrier, some destroyers and damaged the other battleship.

Well, that's that. A period of suspense ended and evidence, I must say, that Alexander is not as spineless as I thought him. I lost a couple of small bets on the subject to Green and Aldy and, as they wouldn't take the money, I paid 1s 6d to the Sailors' Comforts Fund and never paid money so gladly though it's a pity we couldn't have had the whole fleet more willingly. By the way, the Bordeaux government, the rotten swine, released 400 Jerry airmen prisoners after Reynaud had given orders for their transfer to Britain. May they rue that kindly little deed.

Another grave warning, from Churchill this time, that we are on the eve of invasion. Can't we be spared that? The forces will do their darnedest I know, but invasion, even attempted, will be pretty bloody on the civilian population.

MONDAY 8 JULY

Another raid here today. Dora had just arrived at the hospital to fetch Margaret home when a Jerry came over, leisurely turned and dropped a line of bombs in dockland and in the dock. The amazing unbelievable part is that they didn't explode. Can't make it out unless it indicates sabotage somewhere, but it's all to our benefit. Anyway the Jerry didn't get home to spread the news and get someone shot for two Spitfires got him off Felixstowe.

The 1909s registered last Saturday, 310,000 of them. At that rate I shall be registering soon.

Well, if all reports are to be believed, zero hour is approaching. Hitler should start his attack on us tomorrow though I can't see why he should be obliging enough to tell us.

SATURDAY 13 JULY

Now for naval stuff. Last weekend our boats found the *Richelieu* at Dakar harbour, and then followed a brilliant piece of work. They sent in the 'four alternatives' by sloop but the Frenchie wouldn't allow it near and he had to signal. They rejected the proposals and we waited even longer than the allotted time, till nightfall in fact. Then a ship's boat laden with depth charges slipped over the boom defence, crept unobserved to the *Richelieu* and had the damned effrontery to drop the depth charges under her propellers. Making off immediately at full speed the ruddy engines broke down but they managed to get one going just as they were discovered and a Frenchman came out in pursuit. By another peculiar chance, our boat passed the net defences safely but the Frenchie got caught in it himself. Then our planes attacked and hit with five torpedoes, the result being next day in daylight the boat was settled by the stern and had a big list and the sea was covered in oil.

A neat way out of a difficulty and one which entailed little French loss of life and none of ours, besides being a totally unexpected method of doing the job. Shows a bit of initiative, the sort of thing we love to hear about. Damned good.

Soon after, Monday I think, our fleet contacted the Wops. They soon turned tail behind a smokescreen but we managed one hit on one of their battleships and a plane torpedoed a cruiser and no losses on our side. We chased them to Sicily where they took refuge behind shore defences and then claimed a victory in which the *Hood* was again declared to be on fire and the *Ark Royal* hit with two shells on the flight deck. This time they evidently thought it better not to claim to have sunk them as Jerry has done so often. We deny the claims and I'm certainly believing our report. At the same time a force in the western Mediterranean raced like the devil to cut them off but couldn't manage it.

THURSDAY 18 JULY
Queer how this war changes habits and creates demands. Dora finds that sleeping in corsets, a procedure which is necessary on account of time, rather tiring so she has fallen in line with the rest and bought pyjamas so she can pop on a pair of slacks and be ready to dash down with the kiddies quickly. Must say she looks smart in them.

The threat of invasion still covers us. Every so often comes the rumour 'Hitler has postponed it. It will be so-and-so'. The last was it was intended for tomorrow, full moon day, and now they say it's postponed. If true, all fifth-column work I guess. Still, the threat is there, like a shadow. Many people have the opinion that Jerry has nowhere near the air force he swanks about and that's why his bombers come over in small numbers, but somehow I can't agree. When he wants to he'll send the fleet of hundreds. I've enough faith in him to believe that, but I hope I'm wrong.

The LDV are making, and training for using, Molotov[8] cocktails. Cute things. They are simply beer bottles lined with a glass cutter to break easily and filled with a mixture of petrol and tar. Outside are stuck a few wax Vestas which are ignited by pulling a pull-match. The bottle is then flung on a tank which becomes covered with burning, smoking petrol and tar and possibly seeps inside. The Jerries have to come out and are popped off, at least in theory. Darn good idea. Apparently the Finns used them very successfully, hence the title.

WEDNESDAY 24 JULY
We were peacefully having tea today. It was raining heavily at the time but that didn't stop Jerry making two unpeaceful noises. At the first we were at the back door, listening, within 5 sec. We heard Jerry throbbing, then the second rumble. They sounded as though he had popped down under the clouds unloaded in two halves, then popped back again. Suppose some poor devils have copped something again, and there will be more outcries against there being no warning.

There was a third War Budget yesterday. Income tax up from 7s 6d to 8s 6d, surtax up, beer up 1d, tobacco up 1½d, entertainment tax up and new purchase tax introduced. Kingsley Wood reckoned he had £800 million deficit and only budgeted for £239 million in a full year. Seems funny finance to me, but it's his business, not mine. All the same I feel a little 'out of it'. I don't smoke, or drink, don't run a car and don't pay income tax so I don't pay any direct taxes at all and have to be satisfied with paying Ma's tax on her stout.

We are now finishing off our windows with Cellophane. Dora has now perfected a method of putting it on and makes an excellent job of it. Another of the benefits of civilisation. Don't be sardonic. Many people are sleeping downstairs nowadays. George, next door, has moved into the front room, living at the back, cleared the two main bedrooms and packed all excess furniture into the third bedroom so that an incendiary bomb, falling probably into one of the two bedrooms, can be easily dealt with. Good idea.

I ought to have reported before that a bill has been passed aiming at reducing defeatist talk. The result was that several people have been imprisoned and fined for saying too much. One man was fined for saying he thought Hitler would win. A certain amount of newspaper outcry has induced Churchill to order all sentences to be reviewed. I had an argument on the subject this morning saying that in this free country we ought to have what opinions we please and the bill was something we were fighting in Germany.

SATURDAY 28 JULY
I hear Harvey's Canadian relations sent him a parcel of food this week, the postage costing $3. They are so fed with propaganda over there from Germany that we are starving, that they actually believe it. Goebbels must have organised it all.

Did I record that cooking fat and tea are now rationed? From 22 July. The tea is ample, 2 oz per head and we don't use more than under half that. The softener helps. Cooking fat is 2 oz per week which isn't much. On the other hand, we shall be allowed another 2 lb sugar per head for jam for the plum crop. The last 2 lb for bought fruits, we used on blackcurrant, and Dora managed 40 lb of jam from our raspberries. They were good this year.

America has agreed to build us 3,000 planes a month, starting right away with the factories. We are paying both for the factories, and incidentally for putting America on a war footing aerially, but as she will be in the war fairly soon anyway, that's OK.

We've altered our duties again. We now man the post each evening 2000 to 2400 hr and all day Sunday. That means an evening duty once in twelve days and a Sunday duty each fortnight. Should be rather better, certainly better than the proposed scheme of night duties of once in twelve days of 2300 to 0600 hr. That would have been lousy. I don't like the 'relief warden' scheme though. One warden per week is to take the place of anyone who can't turn up. Sounds good but I'd rather know just what duties I have to do.

WEDNESDAY 31 JULY
The news has just told us we have brought down 240 planes in July, being certified figures. That means probably 600 crew lost and more crashes we don't know of.

We are now in a curfew area. Not actually the town but all the area from the Wash to Chelmsford, including east of the railway from Beccles to Chelmsford. The curfew is from one hour after sunset to one hour before sunrise, affecting everywhere except in towns and villages. When we heard it and imagined it included towns, we anticipated that in winter we should say bye-bye to our wives on Monday morning and camp out in the canteen till Saturday afternoon.

WEDNESDAY 7 AUGUST
This is a diary(!!) and something in which I can record just what I'm thinking so I see no harm in recording this. I'm feeling a wee bit shaky and yet since I've put it down in writing I darned well don't. That's funny. Will probably read disjointedly too: still this morning there was the canker just taking root. The Wops are attacking Somaliland in three columns and are preparing an attack on Egypt. Because the papers this morning go to the trouble of saying how Somaliland is the least valuable of our possessions, and that even if the Wops take large stretches of north Egypt it isn't worth having, I seem to take it that we are booked for a defeat in those places. With the backing out of France it's only possible it is so, but it is so galling to read between the lines as though we are a lot of kids. It only breeds doubt that our Mediterranean blockade has leaks in it and yet we know that our fleet is itching to pay back a few old scores on Italy, that there are no leaks of importance. Soon we shall hear of heroic resistance of a weak force against overwhelming odds, even though they are Wops, and there will be a muddle over reinforcements and, eventually, a withdrawal and praise for the

magnificent work our Air Force did and then we'll settle down to another blockade and starve them out.

At the same time we hear that Germans are practising landings (methodical blokes) in the Baltic, that all German army leave has been cancelled, that it is recognised the 'tip and run' air raids we are having are nothing to what we can expect, and soon, and that an invasion is certainly still very much a likely event. Then we sort of subconsciously realise that Jerry is so darned efficient that, if he has set his mind on an invasion, he must know what he is up against and has probably got a counter to our counter and, in short, we are booked for a real bloody struggle. I have always recognised that if he attacks he will land. What that proportion will be I can't say, however I fancy it will actually be a small force, say 10,000 or so, but what damage they can do! Once having a footing, can they keep it? Personally, I think 'No' but one never knows with Hitler. I fancy the next full moon, due in about ten days, may answer the question and that we wardens will have a definite testing time. The accompanying raids will be systematic, well-planned devastating raids, in which the plane losses will be high but not overpowering. With 1,800 being built a month he can afford the craft, and with the fanaticism of his army spreading to his pilots he can afford those too, and then it becomes a question of whether he can just hammer a path into the country. I don't think he will, but by heck, he'll try. As an aside, Pershing in America, is urging his government to sell us fifty old destroyers 'before it is too late to prevent the spread of the war to America'. Ah well.

SUNDAY 11 AUGUST
I don't feel at all happy about the situation in Africa. In Somaliland the Wops are advancing 'into our main defence positions'. I don't like the way in which we are saying that Aden is easily defendable. It is telling us that Somaliland will soon be the scene of another of those withdrawals for which we are getting too darn famous. Recently we were boasting of a South African army which had been sent to east Africa. What the blazes is it doing? It was a decent size, consisting of several divisions. Still I admit the ruddy French have left us badly in the cart and upset our defence arrangements. That's the worst of it. It's always ruddy well 'defence'. I don't believe we could organise an 'offence' in the first three years of a war to save ourselves, yet if we don't soon, it may be too late.

More serious is the Wop army of 250,000 waiting to attack Egypt. Reports say it is including Jerry shock troops with tanks to form the spearhead, and there again we may go off and explain how difficult they will find it to cross deserts. Musso may be a Wop but surely he has sense enough to make some provision for that, knowing the difficulties. If we're not careful I can see us losing Suez and the canal, which naturally includes Alexandria, and another 'masterly withdrawal'. Yet surely even our boneheads can see the dangers. How I hope there is a decent size army on the way out there already!

We've lost another submarine, the *Odin*. I didn't report the *Otway* a few days ago (should have done) which the Wops sunk. That makes about thirteen or fourteen which is fairly high but nowhere near the German and Italian totals.

We are bombing the Wop concentrations in Africa. Good old RAF, giving them blazes.

MONDAY 12 AUGUST
Saw some of the town defences last week. I went past Nacton aerodrome, found it lousy with Blenheims but not a gun in sight. I'll bet they were there though in fact, if Aldy is to be believed, there are dozens there. All the heath, between Nacton Road, Felixstowe Road and Bucklesham Road is intersected with double lines of poles about 3 ft 6 in high. They are about 20 ft apart and in between is a ditch 3 ft deep. An effective obstacle to aeroplanes landing. On the heath, too, near Crane's were two Archie. Nearby were two camouflaged tents and smoke from a campfire. They looked so self-contained, and probably a happy little party; I felt jealous.

SATURDAY 17 AUGUST
On duty and the colour is purple[9] after 4 min of yellow. There has been no report of any raid today so far, so we may expect them now perhaps. Jerry bombed Eastbourne yesterday so perhaps he has started total warfare and thinks night-time better. It's a perfect night with a full moon. Duff Cooper, the silly romantic nut, has just been broadcasting and been daring Hitler to come and invade. He pointed out that last Thursday was the day (the 11th) when Hitler had promised to enter London triumphantly. Instead it was our record air day. The bloke speaks so romantically and poetically it was a change to hear a real sound fact from him.

It was announced yesterday that, up to 4 August, we had lost forty-seven warships of all types including submarines. Not bad, touch wood. Jerry claims we have lost 269, and still he doesn't come out to try conclusions with what's left.

We have again been over Germany. It is still a nightly and daily occurrence. The outstanding part this time is that it was an oil refinery near Leipzig, 600 miles away. We have also paid another visit to Caprioni and Fiat works in Italy.

WEDNESDAY 21 AUGUST

Saw something today which I have hoped to see but never dared to expect. I saw a Dornier Flying Pencil come down and crash.

We have had four raid warnings here today, the last being from 4.35 to 7 o'clock. About 6.30 I went outside just to see if I could see anything. Over Wattisham way was a plane very high up about 12,000 to 15,000 ft. It turned towards Ipswich, then spouted smoke and two Jerries baled out. Then it turned away from the town aiming straight for me and Reavell's, and two more Jerries baled out. Then as I fancied R. & Co. would cop it well and truly, it turned away, gave me a full view of its belly, the starboard engine burst into straw-coloured flame, and it crashed just at the back of Gippeswyk Park. It was plainly a Jerry. The crosses were visible, the thin body and twin rudders ensured that. As it came down I saw the starboard prop stationary, the port one idly turning, rather sadly, as it crashed a huge cloud of black smoke went up. Then I saw the parachutists. Two of them came down in dockland, looking like black dolls under the white parachutes, the other two had vanished.

News says Jerry lost 8 yesterday, 10 today, we lost 2 each day with 1 pilot safe out of each. Also Jerry has lost 1,051 since 18 June and 802 since 8 August, we losing 198 in the same time, odds of 4 to 1 which is excellent.

Churchill said yesterday our total losses as yet are 92,000 killed, wounded and prisoners, that compared with 365,000 in the first year of the last war.

SATURDAY 24 AUGUST

Tension still exists between Italy and Greece. On Wednesday reports, later denied, said that Italy had delivered an ultimatum that if Greece did not renounce the pact with Britain, Italy would march. Today's paper even said that Greece was expecting invasion this weekend. Italian troops are on the Albanian border and Italian papers have discovered an ill-treated minority in Greece. We have a pact with Greece that we go to her aid if she is attacked so something may possibly move. Personally I hope the situation will develop. It will have the benefit of making Turkey active (I hope) and make Greece definite. No one will be neutral by the end of the war so she may as well come in now so we know where we are.

We are moving the doors of the dug-out into the entrance way to give more room. A new system re casualties. They are not being published after raids but published at the town hall of the district concerned next day so locals can satisfy themselves. It's as well to keep Jerry guessing, I suppose. Mass raids have started again. Just heard today's bag is 34 planes to 10 of ours with 1 pilot safe. Possibly it will be larger by the morning's news.

TUESDAY 3 SEPTEMBER

The war has been on a year, yesterday's bag was 50 for 20 of ours, 10 safe. There's been more over today and tonight we've just heard that America has released those 50 destroyers in exchange for rights to certain bases in our possessions near America.

On the Home Front we are well 'dug in'. Rations give us 8 oz sugar, 6 oz butter, 2 oz tea, 1s 10d worth of meat and 2 oz cooking fat. Paper and wood are very scarce but obtainable, there will be no cream available after 1 October, and we can't buy new cars or lorries. Salvage is organised to collect waste of most kinds – paper, metal, bones and pigs' food. We have mostly done something to protect our windows. Some people have gummed strips of paper across the panes, others have completely covered the glass with Cellophane, and there is a preparation available which can be painted on the glass to form a similar protective coating. Again some large shop windows have a bracing device each side of the pane to give support and stop shattering from blast. We all have our Anderson[10] as home-made dug-outs, most of which have been converted to allow sleeping during a raid. There is still the white dotted line down the centre of roadways and traffic lights are reduced to a semicircle in daylight and a small cross at night. The siren sounds on an average every alternate day and we obey the implied instruction and take cover without any fuss or panic. At work we troop to the shelters and nothing ever happens to justify our taking shelter. They are now talking of taking no notice of the sirens and working through it, but having a watcher who would give warning if the raiders came close, so as not to interfere too much with production.

Internationally we are doing our best to make Italy wish she had kept out of this business, and now trouble is brewing in Roumania. She was forced by the Axis to hand over a large chunk of Transylvania to Hungary and there are now demonstrations against it. Quite a few Frenchmen are disgusted with the Pétain government and have banded under Gen de Gaulle who is organising the French troops, air force and navy. Various French colonies are also dissatisfied and are coming back to us as Allies.

SUNDAY 8 SEPTEMBER
Last night London had two bad raids, from about 5 o'clock for some time then 8 o'clock till 5 this morning. Some damage was done, about 500 planes being used and lots penetrating to dockland and East End generally. Docks were damaged, wharves set afire, a 'utility service' probably a power station hit and put out of action, and an oil store down the river, probably Thameshaven or Shellhaven. There were 4,000 fire appliances in use collected even from Ipswich and Colchester. Casualties provisionally 400 killed, 1,300 to 1,400 seriously injured. As revenge they lost 99 planes, 21 by Archie, I'm pleased to note, ours 22, 9 safe. It was sufficiently serious to broadcast a special bulletin at 10.15 this morning and the paper came at midday.

Well, that's the first. We've been expecting it since last September and the evacuation scheme is justified. They'll come again tonight I'm sure and I suppose we'll be in the garden again watching the procession. It was damn shameful, to my mind, the way Jerry came straight over last night, not deigning even to change course while those searchlights probed, sometimes, without catching even one. We watched twenty-one go over, got fed up and went to bed at 11 and heard five more go with the same result. It was a clear night too, till 10.45.

Things seem to be moving in other directions. The Home Guard and military were out last night and Harry's been to King's Lynn and found the same there; Bill was called up at 11 till 4 this morning. Someone told me something interesting this evening. Also heard today that the two destroyers we lost last week, *Ivanhoe* and *Esk* were part of a task force of 160 ships sent to Holland where concentrations of troops were reported.

I tried to join the Home Guard for Works defence but now it seems my ARP commitment makes it impossible. Was issued with armlet today. Looks posh. Today was a national day of prayer. Churches were well attended. Ma came home with more reports of men called up all night.

THURSDAY 12 SEPTEMBER
A lot to report if only I had the time to do it. Jerry is continuing to bomb London, indiscriminately now, in fact one bomb hit Buckingham Palace. We replied with another raid on Berlin, about the tenth and hit the Reichstag. Jerry yesterday lost eighty-nine planes but today's weather has stopped much activity.

Churchill broadcast last night and gave another warning. Jerry is concentrating hundreds of flat-bottom barges and ships and masses of troops from Norway to Brest, chiefly in northern France. Well, it's coming I suppose, and the sooner the better.

Tuesday morning going to work I had a shock. Notices were proclaiming that Ipswich was to be voluntarily evacuated in view of the threat of invasion. By lunchtime we had agreed to send Dora and the kiddies and Doris and Hazel. Next morning we started for Northampton in Harry's car, came back the same day and that was that. It was all as quick as that. A lousy business but, I fancy, a wise decision. The noise would probably be bad for the kiddies apart from the actual threat to them. I hear Ipswich is to be a garrison town in which case we will probably be bombed well and truly.

I saw one or two interesting things on the road. We ran into an air raid at Bedford where there were an impressive number of wardens on duty, but there were no incidents.

FRIDAY 13 SEPTEMBER
Jerry is still plastering London and other places too. London gets it every night and daytime too sometimes, the night raids usually hanging on from 9 to about 5 or 6 in the mornings.

We've been smashing Berlin again but places like gasworks, railway stations and aerodromes. Invasion concentrations are also receiving their share of attention.

What is the secret of last Saturday's affair? New York now has rumours that Jerry corpses were being washed up on the Yarmouth beaches in quantities. Green says 30,000 of them, but I should have thought they'd be too weighty with equipment to do anything but sink.

SUNDAY 15 SEPTEMBER

On duty 10 to 12 a.m. Re that last entry. I'm beginning to think a real attempt was made, not a rehearsal. The American report concerns an attack from St Malo on the west coast of England. Harry says another was made on Scotland and it's pretty definite that bodies were washed up on these beaches. The papers today are suggesting the risk of invasion is diminishing, partly because the ports he will use are being hammered by the RAF and lots of barges are being smashed. On the other hand Maun has just been along with leaflets for us to distribute, bucking up the people, urging them to evacuate and he says if they don't respond it will become compulsory. Well, well, we shall see, but it takes such a darn long time for the days to pass.

Dora is not comfortable in her billet and I can't see her moving anybody to do anything for fear of giving trouble. I had thought that, if this moon passes uneventfully, I'd have her back next week but if it's going to be a case of compulsion, she'd only have to go back again. Blast Hitler and, if it's all just because they want billets for the military, blast the authorities. Mrs Rudd has gone, George living with relations, Harry is living alone but dinnering with us so we're pretty lonely.

A little excitement yesterday. Archie started up over Martlesham, a Heinkel came over at about 7,000 ft seen occasionally above broken cloud, wheeled over the town, dropped some stuff and came back our way, disappearing towards Martlesham again, no fighters about and no warning. Win, the fat-head, is in a stew because she listened to Lord Haw-Haw who said Ipswich was being made a garrison town therefore it would be bombed and specially mentioned the Mansion. I mention it to show how they try to put the wind up us and succeed with some people.

TUESDAY 24 SEPTEMBER

As an innovation Jerry started last week to drop magnetic mines. I read the notice at the post Friday evening and within about six hours two had dropped here in Ipswich. One at the Woodbridge Road tram terminus, the other in Cemetery Road. There's mystery about that one. I definitely saw an explosion and heard it but people say only the nose-cap exploded, which is ridiculous. Anyway they daren't move it, so built up sandbags and detonated it. The bang was huge, shook the house and brought out many windows in Woodbridge Road, Carr Street and even Tacket Street and Elm Street. A devilish idea. I suppose he found he had stocks of magnetics he couldn't use, being almost useless, so decided to use them this way. Naturally upon hitting the ground they detonate immediately, coming down slowly by parachute, and the blast from the 700 lb of explosive is almost horizontal.

It exploded at 8 Sunday night, 20 min later the siren went till 11.30 and again at 3.25 till 5.45. My night off so I slept most of the time. We had been to see Dora and the kiddies and had had only 2½ hours' sleep. Last night I was on and Jerry came again. We were having an ambulance refresher lecture (Wake and I demonstrating bandages) when the siren went at 8.20 till 2.20 a.m. then again 4.20 to 6.20. Again 2½ hours' sleep, but woke up quite fresh. I'm tired now though. Jerry came over singly but there were about twenty-five.

There has also been activity over French Indo-China. Japan wants a footing there, to attack China, and reports say they have been granted bases there. Also news from Dakar. Three French cruisers and three destroyers went there from Toulon and now de Gaulle tried to land there with a Free French force, backed by the British.

We moved Dora and Doris to Rothwell on Sunday, to much more comfy digs (I hope). Got up at 4.15, started away 5.45, reached home again at 7.25, having done 276 miles.

THURSDAY 26 SEPTEMBER
The Dakar incident is over, and we ought to be hiding our heads in shame, unless I don't know all the facts, which is quite likely.

As far as I know, de Gaulle had reason to believe that a strong section of Dakar was in sympathy with the Free French party and he decided to go and get their active support. At the same time three French cruisers and three destroyers left Toulon for Dakar, with our knowledge. We took the view we should not interfere with movements out of France to the colonies, and let them go. Later they left Dakar and tried to go south but to this we objected and made them turn back. De Gaulle arrived, sent a party to land under a white flag and tricolour but the Dakar forts opened fire on them and on our supporting fleet. We, like the kid glove gents we are, said 'we shall be compelled to return fire if you don't cease' to which they fired some more and we returned it. Hits were obtained on both sides and we sunk two out of three French submarines and then withdrew altogether. The reason was that de Gaulle was in charge, he decided only a major operation could take Dakar and, as he didn't want Frenchmen to fight Frenchmen, he came away.

And that's that. The USA call it a 'major blunder'. I call it something else. Spain is being edged into this business and a strong attitude might have tipped the balance against it. Besides that, de Gaulle can be certain that, if he doesn't want to fight Frenchmen, they certainly want to fight him. If we want to beat Hitler we must take off kid gloves. We are too damn good at retreat. We could at least have destroyed those three cruisers. We know now they had Germans on board who replaced the de Gaulle sympathisers before he arrived. Let's turn to other matters.

Jerry arrived last night again, the sirens lasting from 8.45 to 12.45. As usual the sky seemed full for two or three hours, and I thought it wisest to get down the dug-out twice. He lost 26 yesterday to our 4, 3 pilots being safe. My raid 'on' last night and rations came round. They are modified now to two Oxos, one packet biscuits and a 2d Bournville chocolate, the latter much to my taste.

FRIDAY 27 SEPTEMBER

As usual Jerry came over in quantity last night, but there were no sirens. His procedure this week has been the same most nights. He arrives about 8.15 or 8.30 and comes inland singly but with one or four planes in the sky at most times. This keeps on till about 10.30 or thereabouts, some coming overhead and hanging about seemingly, in which case Ma and I take cover in the dug-out, others going back again, but all flying very high and attended by three to sixteen searchlights groping about the wrong part of the sky. By 9 o'clock flashes occur, some brighter than others, but rarely followed by the sound of explosions and sometimes we see the barrage put up outside London flickering in the sky, with sometimes the actual flight of an exploding shell. By 11.30 things are usually quiet and, if Ma will go, I pack her off to bed and wish I could go too, if I'm on duty. Till early morning when the all-clear sounds things are sometimes quiet but sometimes a few planes are about. Usually, I'm afraid, we get the bombs nearest when there is no siren, but always there is the wonder, the apprehension, that the next plane may have a bomb, or one of those damnable mines, for just our neighbourhood. One day it will come, I suppose.

The nights are getting longer now, and cold, and it certainly helps to know we are being handed out with rations. Incidentally I keep two bags packed in the dug-out and, as a house precaution, keep both windows and doors open. A fine reflection on civilisation.

Up to 5 o'clock we brought down 98 Jerries today. Yesterday's

bag was 34 for about 3 of our pilots and 8 planes . . . but I fancy
they are doing quite a bit of damage. Still our raids into Germany
are very heavy. The list of places is too long to remember, and the
recital gets a bit boring, or would do if it were not interesting. We
visit Berlin almost nightly, last occasion being for five hours.

WEDNESDAY 9 OCTOBER
Things are getting serious with Japan. We take the line that, as we
closed the Burma Road as a gesture of goodwill to Japan and an
opportunity to start peace negotiations, and as Japan has done nowt
about settling the business, we are to reopen the road on 18 October
when the agreement expires. Japan has nothing to say, saying it is too
deep a question, but they have landed troops on an island which we
have leased from China. Americans are being advised to leave the
various ports of China and Japan, the American fleet is to be
brought up to full war strength immediately and Japan says she will
bomb the Burma Road inside China. She has the bases in French
Indo-China from which to operate. A pretty situation, no, an ugly
one. Still Japan did not enter this new agreement with the Axis for
nothing and it was bound to come. Can't yet see what Russia's
attitude will be but I fancy it will be neutral, or friendly to the Axis.

MONDAY 21 OCTOBER
I've been a little neglectful of this diary lately but hope to do better
now. Dora and the kiddies are back again, came home yesterday,
and now perhaps shall have a little more time.

Harry says he saw several 'big' guns up near Martlesham and
Waldringfield. Young says they are erecting 'field guns' as Archie
round here and Saturday, while we were away at Rothwell, I hear
there was a big barrage put up so I wondered if we have adequate
protection here, at last.

It's a treat to have Dora back again, lovely to see her cheery dial
about the place. Mild excitement here today – a Jerry came at
Erwarton last night (again in Shotley district, any connection?) and
the crew baled out, possibly being in the district. Harry says two
were seen on Barrack Corner this morning though don't know how
they were recognised.

MONDAY 28 OCTOBER
Italy today declared war and attacked Greece. At 3 a.m. an
ultimatum was handed to Gen Metaxas[11] demanding the right to

certain bases, timed to expire at 6 a.m. Metaxas regarded it as an act of war, mobilised and asked Britain for help. Italy attacked on the Albano-Greek frontier at 5 a.m. our time and has bombarded from the seas and attacked by air. The Greek army consists of fourteen divisions and one of cavalry plus reserve men. Their air force is small.

Well Richard, what next? Is it to be another wonderful withdrawal? I sincerely hope not. We just can't afford another reverse of that type and I shall grieve if it occurs. Our big hope is naturally the Navy, bless it. It was bombarding Sidi Barrâni on Saturday so we can't tell where it is now but I should say the Wop units bombarding Greece should be easy meat. We shall see, or shall we?

Am darn sorry to report the *Empress of Britain* is sunk. She was attacked by one solitary blinking bomber who hit first, returned later and scored again with an incendiary and she caught fire, blowing up after being taken in tow. Certainly that Jerry deserves all the credit he gets and someone here deserves all the kicks he gets, for weak defence.

Last night's raid was new – for Ipswich. After the Martlesham attack three Jerries came over and dropped small canister bombs and machine-gunned haphazardly. Aldy heard firing from the ships in the dock, went to the door, and saw a Jerry, only 100 ft up, firing blindly and spraying out these small canisters. He has three bullet holes in the roof and picked up some shrapnel from the bombs. Apparently they are filled with scrap metal as shrapnel and used against infantry concentrations. The police were examining an unexploded one up Aldy's way when it went off and killed one and injured others. One prize idiot, twenty years old, found one outside Ransome Rapiers, took it inside and pulled it to pieces. It exploded killing six or seven people. WR found one in his garden, but recognised it as a bomb.

SUNDAY 3 NOVEMBER

Another interesting Sunday, aerially. It's been a day of foul weather, cloudy morning with rain starting about 11 and still at it, therefore low clouds. Wailing Winnie moaned about 4.30 and I went out in the rain, and those of us who were out were telling each other with satisfaction that Jerry was over 10 min before. This palled and I went in to tea and dashed out again on hearing guns or bombs. Soon noises came nearer, over the town in fact, and soon I interpreted it as another plane on the same game as last Sunday. There was a

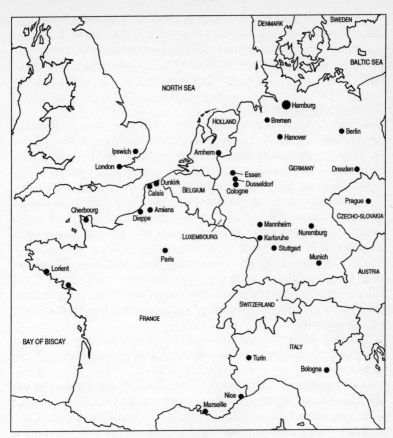

Western Europe

spluttering, uneven series of small explosions, MG fire and in the middle came a 'bump'. I reckon it was a Jerry dropping those small bombs and shooting up Ipswich. We then saw him coming over from Golden Key direction, very low, and decided to take cover under Arthur Mayhew's porch from where we saw him pass by. He looked like a Dornier 17 or 215, so low I could see his aerial masts. He disappeared and I saw tracer going up from the Rushmere Road district, so someone was having a pot at him.

That's the closest I've seen a Jerry flying, and quite enjoyed it. Can honestly say there was no fear present but was glad to find Dora and the kids had got under the table.

News today that we've troops in Greece. Can't say how I feel about it, as I don't see how we can stand up to Jerry out there with our lengthy communications, but suppose we must do some land action. I wonder if we've worked out the 'strategic withdrawal' plans from Greece. We're getting expert at that.

SUNDAY 11 NOVEMBER
Poor old Chamberlain died on Saturday, aged seventy-two. His passing is recorded in the papers but not as front-page news, partly because the news was released midday yesterday. He was a well-liked man, but we are war-minded now and all conscious of a huge desire to bang Jerry well and proper and it is to be feared that Chamberlain was not a wartime Premier. A good man, an honest, virtuous man and a typical Englishman, accepting rebuffs in the cause of peace but liable to be overcome by 'righteous indignation' when peace is overthrown.

The Greeks, so far, are doing really well. It is now official that they have completely routed a Wop division which, in its flight, took with it heavy reinforcements come up in support. A large amount of equipment has been captured and Italian losses are reported as heavy.

Molotov is up to some mischief. He is now visiting Berlin and the press promises a huge diplomatic defeat for us as a result. We shall see.

Had a yarn with Day from the Test House today. He says he saw the *King George V* still in dock a month ago and the *Prince of Wales* is not so far advanced. The *Duke of York* still had not all her engines aboard, so the newspaper guff about there being some in the Mediterranean was – guff. He, Day, took 48 hours to get to Scotland recently, with air raid slowings and changing at stations and general slow running. They are now raising the speed of trains during raids from 15 to 25 mph.

FRIDAY 15 NOVEMBER
Jerry carried out an intensive raid on Coventry last night. Haven't heard details yet except that Archie made him fly high, probably with the effect of missing worthwhile targets, but damage to property was considerable and casualties are expected to be 1,000. That's the first time we've mentioned the name of a town in communiqués so I suppose it was really severe. We had no warning here but Colchester had it from 8.45 to 4 a.m. and we heard Jerry

most of the night. There was lots of flak too, muttering away continuously but we couldn't locate the direction, due probably to a faint mistiness.

We are getting a fair amount of mist lately and sometimes fogs. Wonder if the new government orders are helping to cause it? Firms like ours, with a chimney, are asked to smoke so as to help make objects indistinguishable from the air.

Yesterday Jerry lost 21 planes, 14 to 1 squadron of Hurricanes, and we lost 2 with both pilots safe. He is using Junkers 87 dive-bombers again and for some reason or other we usually find them easy meat.

SATURDAY 23 NOVEMBER
A neglected diary, but not intentionally so. Chief item to report is that Koritsa has fallen to the Greeks. Naturally they, and we, are overjoyed and their tiny air force is harrying the retreating Wops. They smashed up a tank attack and used the captured tanks for pursuing the Italians. There is one small corner, down south-west, where the Wops are on Greek territory. Elsewhere the Greeks are at least five miles into Albania and mostly further than that.

An excellent state of affairs but I fancy it heralds a German support of Italy. Indeed Roumania has joined up with the Axis, so has Hungary, and Turkey is preparing for things to happen. She has declared a state of siege in the Straits and is to introduce military measures and precautions. Gen Metaxas, the Greek minister, is appealing strongly for 'planes and planes and planes', which suggests our aerial help is not as strong as it could be. I hope we are not too late again.

I went to Chatham on Wednesday for the test on *Torbay*. I'm afraid my interest in the job itself was very secondary to the anticipation of what I would see but what I saw, though very interesting, was not startling. HMS *London* was there, apparently having deck-hangars fitted, a cruiser was being built, there were a few destroyers and two small searchlight ships. I suppose I had expected to see half the ruddy Home Fleet. I was surprised at the size of *London*, she seemed to tower out of the water and appeared an easy target for gun, bomb or torpedo but, possibly, that isn't so. After all, a mile is point-blank range at sea.

Torbay was interesting. I've never seen so many men on one job before. The technique of progress aboard seems to be to shoulder one's way forward when the mass of bodies, quite automatically and as a matter of course, parts to let one through. I counted fourteen men on the plank between the main engines alone. Inside I found it surprisingly light, spacious and airy. That effect was mainly because of the white paint and plenty of light. The men there seemed to ooze chumminess, helpfulness and good nature. Nothing seemed too much trouble for anyone to take, sailorish in fact.

My first impression of Chatham was gained at the station when I realised I was in an important town. A bobby at the barrier wanted my identification card, nature of my business, proof of it and, when he saw my letter of introduction, allowed me through. It was a little more difficult to gain entry to the Dockyard, and I'm darned glad it is so.

We aimed to arrive at 1.40 on Wednesday. From 6 p.m. when we were at the cinema, to arriving home the next night, raids were continuous but nobody taking any notice at all. When in the cinema, the place shook to either bombs or gunfire but nobody bothered. We left by the 6.19 from Chatham, actually 6.40 and I walked in here at 2.10 next morning. All the way up to London Bridge gun flashes were brilliant and continuous, even till we reached Liverpool Street but, after that, things were quieter till I saw six flashes, bombs I believe, and two flares near Colchester. It took 4½ hours to come from Liverpool Street to Ipswich.

Last night we had a cinema lecture at Argyle Street on incendiaries and rescue party work. The latter was very interesting and I enjoyed it. I hear the full-timers are now going to do 24-hour day duties again.

MONDAY 25 NOVEMBER
The Greeks are still doing remarkably well. They have advanced beyond Koritsa and are now threatening three other important towns. An amazing performance but apparently other things have contributed. We had an air squadron there within 24 hours of the declaration of war and had raided 12 hours later. Valona had its jetty completely destroyed, Durazzo had its harbour badly damaged and, with attacks on Italian reserves and reinforcements, the Wops had nothing to bring up in support and no means of landing heavy stuff. I've just read that we've landed a big force of airmen and ground staff without any opposition from the Wops.

We had a War Weapons Week here in Ipswich last week. They asked for enough to buy a destroyer, say £350,000, or if possible, £500,000. To my amazement £339,000 was invested on the first day and by Friday night, £648,000. Can't say what the final was, but it's pretty good for Ipswich. Wonder where it came from? Nationally, the War Savings scheme is a year old today. They asked for £475 million and £463 million was realised.

FRIDAY 29 NOVEMBER
We had a long raid last night, 7.10 to 5.30 this morning. I guess the blokes were glad of the new scheme. When they had a similar raid when I was away last week they gave up at 5 o'clock in disgust. As it was I went on at midnight till 3 and enjoyed a night's rest. Liverpool was the object of attention; 200 or 300 planes being employed but we claim the barrage beat them off.

Mrs Rudd has the wind up I fancy. She came along this morning with the news that Haw-Haw last night promised to 'Coventrate' Ipswich. She says she doesn't believe it but I noticed she went and cleaned the dug-out out. I should have said 'It's promised for tonight' and the siren went at 6.30, so I know someone who is wondering. All the same I admit I'm not going to scoff at it though I can't see anyone giving away his plans beforehand, and there have been reconnaissance planes around here lately.

Milk is going up to 4½d next week and we are going to be asked to use less owing to the dry summer and small hay harvest. Rationing, too, is to be modified next year. Books after July will be for twelve months and coupons are not going to be cut out but stamped with a rubber stamp now. It's astonishing how it will effect savings. The latter measure will save handling 14,500 million coupons and save 15 million coupon envelopes, while the former saves 1,000 tons of paper and £90,000 for the postal delivery.

TUESDAY 3 DECEMBER
Pogradec fell on Saturday and the Italians are still retiring. In one action the Greeks have just captured 5,000 Wops, the biggest bag so far, and are continually taking equipment. Winter is starting in that district now, so the mountains are no picnic. Saw a picture of six Bren gun carriers in Greece today, so it seems we are landing a few troops there.

Jerry is still following his new dodge of concentrating on one town at a time. After Coventry it was Birmingham, Bristol and now Southampton has had two successive nights. Tactics seem to be to concentrate incendiaries and follow up with HE. The centre of the town is usually attacked, indiscriminately of course, and

damage is usually heavy. On the other hand casualties in
Southampton were peculiarly light, total 370 dead and seriously
injured in the two raids.

Ship losses were up last week or rather, the week before. Nineteen
of our ships, 75,000 tons and three Allied of 12,000 tons. I have an
idea that things are getting a little serious. Imports are being
restricted, no fruit except oranges, no tinned fruit, less meat; on the
other hand they've promised us 12 oz sugar and 4 oz tea for the week
before Christmas instead of 8 and 2, so that will help.

TUESDAY 10 DECEMBER
Yesterday came the grand news that we have advanced to the
attack in Egypt. We have taken the initiative and have smitten the
Wops at last and taken 1,000 prisoners in the first day. It's early yet
to say how things are going but it's certainly the time to do the
attacking. Badoglio has resigned the Albanian command, Vecci has
resigned the Dodecanese control, the chief naval bloke has also
resigned and reports say that Graziani tendered his resignation in
Egypt which was not accepted. The Greeks are still doing wonders,
bless them, it only being the foul weather which saved a complete
sector of Italians from annihilation. The rains are ending in
Abyssinia and there is a report of a revolt already started. In view
of all this we can now look forward to more development and take
a keen interest in our news bulletins. We are up against a big job
but I think we can manage it.

Our Wellingtons are now going out again. I just went outside
and was fortunate enough to see one in the moonlight. Jerry gave
the whole country a quiet night Saturday and last night but made
up for it on London on Sunday.

FRIDAY 13 DECEMBER
We are still playing havoc with poor old Musso's chance of getting
Egypt. Our troops are doing wonders. Today's bulletin isn't in yet
but yesterday's spoke of more than 20,000 prisoners with lots of
equipment and munitions. The operation has been to cut in
between Buq-Buq and Sidi Barrâni in which two divisions are
isolated and well defeated in Sidi Barrâni. The surprise was so
complete that we were able to capture the second in command of
the Italians, while his chief was killed, and supply columns actually
barged into our advanced troops. Now Buq-Buq is captured and
the Navy's shelling the road from Sollum into Libya. The only

road passes close to the coast and traverses two defiles which may well be, and I hope they are, a death trap to the retreating Italians. Poor devils, they are attacked by our unleashed chaps, bombarded by the Navy and attacked from on top as well. The RAF are doing a fine job. Right from the start they have kept the Wops down on the ground, bombed the aerodromes and fought them when they did get in the air and then machine-gunned troop concentrations. Their bag up to last night was forty-one for a few of ours. One significant item is that we've captured four more generals in the bag of prisoners which suggests unexpected defeat.

The Premier calls it a victory of the first magnitude and, insofar as it frees Egypt from all threat of invasion, it certainly is. The papers are even speaking of an Italian crack-up like that of France, but I don't see eye to eye with that. Graziani has 250,000 troops in Libya so he's not done yet. I only hope that we don't stop at the Libyan border but sweep on and tackle Bardia, and perhaps, Tobruk. That would be really important and perhaps decisive.

Am bound to admit that the fact that a war is on was evident this evening. I came home to a delicious smell of poached eggs on toast and realised that such things are for the kiddies but not for me. With the cutting off of the Norwegian and Dutch markets new-laid eggs, though obtainable, are scarce. Oranges, too, are now scarce for the first time. They are controlled at $5\frac{1}{2}d$ per lb, which may have something to do with the scarcity, and the fruiterers can only get a crate sometimes. If we have no worse than that to endure we can't grumble.

Musso lost still two more generals in a flying accident and we had the misfortune to lose a big Air Force administrative bloke who was flying to Egypt. He was forced down near Italy. The mighty are fallen.

SUNDAY 15 DECEMBER
A foggy day, no aerial activity and no small wonder. Am on 3 to 7 this week.

In Africa we have now entered Libya and are fighting on Italian soil. Although not stated it seems we must have taken Sollum and our scouts report streams leaving Bardia and Fort Capezzo, which is promising. Seeing that the campaign only opened last Monday we've made excellent progress and one comments that in Sir Archibald Wavell[12] we have at last found a strategist. The Italian press have now released most of the news and even admit the position is serious. Having got them on the run anything may happen if we keep it up.

Who knows what will happen? We await the 9 o'clock bulletins now with something like awe. We hear nothing of the subterranean workings but we can draw conclusions from the new facts. Each time nothing is said of any German help for Italy and we wonder 'Why?'. Let's hope it never arrives. We want to release our Mediterranean Fleet.

An important event which may have some bearing on the previous comments is that there is something of a crisis in France. Marshal Pétain has expelled Laval and replaced him with Flandin, another pro-Nazi. A report says the reason is that Laval was for allowing Hitler to pass through unoccupied France and was even in favour of war with us, but naturally nothing reliable is known.

The siren's just gone and I see the moon is up and the fog going. I thought we were to have a quiet night. Wonder if our aircraft will be grounded? Have just got my equipment and coats ready just in case. Went outside then and saw about ten shell bursts high up and here I am sitting down again. Truly we are blasé. Incidentally there were no searchlights. Shooting by detector I suppose.

SATURDAY 21 DECEMBER
The shortest day. Now, though we can look forward to freezing cold patrols, when even two coats, scarves, etc., etc. are inadequate, we can at least know that the blackout time is getting later and later. True we must wait till January before the same can be said about blackouts-down but it's on the way. On the whole the experiment of keeping the Daylight Saving Bill going all the year has been a success. There has only been one evening when it was a miserable ride home, generally there is enough light left in the sky till 6 o'clock for the journey home to be quite reasonable. At the other end I do have a job to wake up, even at 7.30, now it's dark. The latest blackouts-down will be about 8.38. We also make the most of the daylight. The only snag, but one I'm quite willing to put up with, is that I don't see those marvellous skies I saw last winter, coming up the Colchester Road.

A little excitement this evening. We were peacefully having tea when there were five clumps rather near. We popped the kids under the table and I went out. There was the remains of a ground flare in the direction of Nacton Road aerodrome and sounds of excitement from the neighbours, while I could hear a plane now and then. It was interesting when the searchlights found a vapour trail. They edged along it, showing it up like a silver streak, trying to find the plane. One could almost sense the keenness and excitement of the chase. The usual hard luck was there however, as after following it through about 90° they lost it in a high cloud bank.

We had two RAF warnings this morning, the first lasted about ten minutes and the second was over before I reached the shelters. The system worked OK. In case I haven't recorded it before, we get the six pips when the town siren goes and all who wish then go to the shelters where one of us wardens takes care of them and notes their names and checks numbers. When the raiders are within 15-mile radius we get the tip from RAF observers and the hooter hoots for 1 minute when all who are left drop everything and run to the shelters. When the Jerry goes over the 15-mile line we come out and the remainder come out at the town all-clear. Naturally if the raid doesn't justify a town siren we will sometimes get the RAF applying to all of us, as this morning.

MONDAY 23 DECEMBER
Bardia is still holding out. There are about 30,000 men besieged there so it won't be any picnic for us.

Churchill broadcasts tonight. Wonder what on? One always looks forward to these broadcasts with just a little apprehension.

Swordfish is overdue and presumed lost.

TUESDAY 24 DECEMBER
Churchill has a fine way of speaking which endears him to all of us just now. He spoke of our mild and decent treatment of Italy during the first eight months of the war and it was put down to fear and effeteness and a worn-out policy. Now we show it is not fear or effeteness. He said 'our armies are tearing and will tear your African empire to shreds and tatters' and the way he snarled 'will tear' was great.

Well, it's Christmas Eve. The predominant thought is 'will there be an invasion attempt this week' and not, I'm afraid, of a Christmas character. Nobody is scared about it, at least no one shows it, it's just a sign of curiosity and interest.

SATURDAY 28 DECEMBER
Jerry started it all again last night. The alert went at 7.45 till about 11. I was asleep at the time so can't say accurately. Am on 8–12

next week. Working the shifts backwards like that gives me a night off tonight, seeing that we change over at midnight on Saturday.

This afternoon Dora was in the kitchen making tea. I heard a thump on the door and opened it, expecting she had her arms full and knocked for us to open it. Actually she didn't, so I suppose it was a big explosion somewhere, most probably a mine off the coast. Perhaps some ship hit.

In Libya we are now sitting down outside Bardia and getting reinforcements for the siege. All that is excellent and our forces have done wonderfully well but it won't do to get too optimistic, for Bardia is only just over the border and Libya is a huge place. On the other hand Musso has lost a lot of men and equipment and his plans must be all upset and there are now more reports of revolt in Abyssinia. That Graziani cove can't have many who love him in Abyssinia, apparently he had a pleasant way of dropping unruly chiefs out of aircraft onto their own rocks. He's got something coming.

Tuesday 31 December

Have just been round the local ladies organising a fire-party to work during daytime. I don't think there is so much risk of day raids as night raids as Jerry seems to be using the fires as guides, but it will cover a blank spot.

Have made two 1s bets with Ven and Hattersley today. They say the war will be over by this time next year. Optimists they are. Can't see how it possibly can. We haven't touched Germany yet.

Have booked up an allotment today. Wonder what success I shall make of it?

Well, this is the end of 1940. Tomorrow starts a new year, but what it has in store is well in the lap of the gods. Will it bring invasion, heavier air raids, perhaps taking away some of our friends and relations? Or will it contain an attack by us on Germany, and an effective answer to the night bomber? The only certain thing is that it will be eventful and let us hope that in the main, the events will be to our advantage.

NOTES

[1]   Leslie Hore-Belisha, Secretary for War 1937–40.
[2]   Herbert Morrison, Minister for Home Security and Home Secretary 1940–5.

3   Sir William Reavell, 1866–1948, founder and chairman, Reavell &
    Co., Ltd.
4   Refers presumably to the Spanish Civil War, 1936–9.
5   Admiral of the Fleet Sir Roger Keyes, popular hero of First World War
    naval exploits, for example Zeebrugge.
6   Paul Reynaud replaced Daladier as French Premier, 20 March 1940.
7   Alfred Duff Cooper, Minister of Information 1940–1.
8   Named after V. M. Molotov, Russian Foreign Minister throughout the
    war.
9   A 'purple' came after a yellow warning, and meant that raiders were in
    the vicinity.
10 Anderson shelters, named after Sir John Anderson, then Home
    Secretary, had been distributed gratis to anyone who wanted one.
    They consisted of sections of curved corrugated iron, bolted together
    in an inverted 'U', embedded in a large hole and covered with soil.
    The Browns and their immediate neighbours the Rudds erected a joint
    shelter which straddled their adjoining gardens: however, this was not
    an Anderson, but built of timber and concrete.
11 Premier and virtual dictator of Greece, died January 1941.
12 Sir Archibald Wavell, Field Marshal who conducted the North African
    war against Italy 1940–1.

1941

The winter of 1940/1 was severe. Air activity on both sides was reduced during January but as the freeze retreated, raids began again in earnest. The Blitz on London continued until May and other industrial cities suffered severe attacks; the provinces were less organised than the capital and a large proportion of the citizenry took to 'trekking' into the countryside each night in fear for their lives. In February Richard Brown's ARP post was damaged; Ipswich got its first heavy raid in April and suffered constant alarms and regular loss of life in the months that followed.

The population also increasingly felt the pinch of rationing as 1941 progressed. On Whit Sunday clothes rationing was announced – food had been rationed since January 1940. It became fashionable to look shabby, not that the majority had much choice as hand-me-downs were remade, wool reknitted and precious clothing coupons bartered. The Ministry of Food, organised by the talented Lord Woolton, deluged the population with information and juggled the available supplies with skill. Nobody starved, communal feeding was widespread and it remained possible to eat well in a good restaurant – if you could afford it.

Mr Brown faithfully recorded developments on the Home Front but was preoccupied by the dramatic and decisive turns in the course of the war during 1941. In North Africa the year opened promisingly as Allied forces penetrated 500 miles into Libya and made incursions into Somaliland and Abyssinia. However, the situation was to change in February when General Erwin Rommel took command in North Africa and German troops entered the fray. The Germans also swept through the Balkans, subdued Yugoslavia and came to the aid of the Italians in Greece with serious consequences for the Allies.

By the end of April the Commonwealth forces, diverted from North Africa to aid the Greeks, were evacuated, some to Crete where they faced yet another German assault and defeat. At home the BEF was known as 'Back Every Fortnight'; Richard Brown shrewdly remarks 'this is possibly our last defeat'.

Before the news of the Greek defeat had sunk in there was even more startling news on 10 May when Rudolf Hess, Hitler's deputy, parachuted into Scotland – literally out of the blue – on a purported peace mission. The Hess incident was soon temporarily forgotten in the wake of what followed only a few days later. On 24 May the heavy British cruiser Hood *blew up after an opportune hit on her magazine from* Bismarck. *British revenge came quickly and was sweet. The* Bismarck *was herself sunk three days later. Within a month there was more good news: Abyssinia was liberated and hostilities avoided with Iraq and Iran.*

Then on 22 June Hitler turned to the Eastern Front and attacked Russia, an act which totally changed the nature and direction of the war. The Russians were overwhelmed but German attention was now diverted away from the British Isles. The population saw the threat of invasion recede as the situation grew increasingly grave in the east. Early in December the Germans were halted before Moscow, by the deadly combination of winter and General Zhukov's hundred reserve divisions; they penetrated no further.

Tension was mounting in the Pacific too. By December negotiations between America and Japan were on the verge of collapse. On the 7th decisive action came. Japan launched an attack on the American fleet in Pearl Harbor and did what diplomacy had failed to do: it pitched the United States of America into the war. This was followed by the appalling news that the Japanese had sunk the HMS Prince *of* Wales *and HMS* Repulse *which were en route to help defend Hong Kong. Then on Christmas Day Hong Kong surrendered to the Japanese.*

Mr Brown followed the international developments with his inimitable combination of healthy scepticism, pointed observation and belief in the Allies. But events much closer to home shaped life too. In fact 1941 turned out to be a year of tragedy for the Brown family. Richard, however, was finally satisfied that he was 'doing his share' when he was allowed to join the Home Guard in November.

FRIDAY 3 JANUARY

This winter seems now to promise to be as bad as last winter. Even my two coats, etc. and Balaclava were not warm enough. Jerry came again last evening, about 1900 hr till 2350 hr. It was alternately snowing and then displaying a perfect stormy sky with a procession of Jerry as a sound effect, both going in and then coming out, and a few vivid flashes and specks of light as some guns couldn't stand it any longer and banged away at them, so it wasn't an entirely dull evening. Everywhere is still snow-covered, with no sign of a thaw, darn it. Just now the darn siren went again and it's still snowing. Having walked all the way home from work I'm thundering tired so I wasn't at all pleased, and then I had just reached the post and signed on and the all-clear went.

Thunderbolt has covered herself in glory. She's torpedoed an Italian submarine, an excellent comeback. Let's hope it's the start of a glorious life.

The meat ration is being reduced to 1s 6d each on Monday and pork and offals are now included.

Last night certainly was eventful. I was on patrol and saw somebody who told me something interesting to the effect that invasion is considered imminent. The Home Guard is standing by and has orders to take 24 hours' rations when they get the orders. It may happen any moment and they have been told that the 9th Suffolks will certainly come in contact with the enemy. He will probably land air troops under cover of a smokescreen and dive-bombing.

I can honestly say I had reckoned this snowy weather would favour Jerry. Snowy conditions will help gliders to land, will show up hedges and help bombers to find our convoys of reinforcements on the road. Him being the attacker, he won't need heavy tanks, whereas we shall, and the snow and following slush won't help them. Our airfields and planes will show up as easy targets too – or will they? Am I showing myself to be a greenhorn? Now I see that heavy wintry conditions are settling on the continent so perhaps his air force will be grounded too and the whole affair come to nothing – as yet. On the other hand perhaps it won't.

MONDAY 6 JANUARY

Bardia is fallen. It capitulated after thirty-six hours' fighting which followed thirty hours' naval and air bombardment. Over 30,000 prisoners, including five generals, and lots of equipment have been taken and the Australians have covered themselves with glory. They managed to explore the tank traps and defences, bridged the traps under cover of a barrage, penetrated inside both lines of defence and tackled the main defences from the rear, defences which were built with no cover at the rear. It all confirms the oft-repeated saying that the Wops have no stomach for this war. Dimbleby, the BBC commentator, actually passed through hundreds of Italians, armed, who were looking for someone to surrender to. Now for Tobruk.

TUESDAY 7 JANUARY
Am deeply sorry to report Amy Johnson's[1] death. She was piloting a plane in the ferry service, somehow got over the Thames Estuary when the engines failed. At 200 ft she jumped, too low for the parachute to operate, and was approached by a motor boat. One of the crew dived after her, held her, but the cold overcame him and he let go. She is lost and he is hovering between life and death. The country has lost an outstanding personality. She was outstanding insofar as she was intelligent besides being a popular stunt flyer and did a lot for flying when it needed popularity. A great pity; she was still young and doing good service to the country too.

It's now revealed that HMS *Terror*, a monitor, has been doing good work at Bardia, firing 550 tons of 15-inchers in 3 weeks. The Navy is very versatile and is using all classes of ships. Talking Navy, it seems that the *King George V* and *Prince of Wales* are in commission, the other three being due this year.

A day of raids and crash warnings today. We had 3 crash warnings this morning and 2 this afternoon combined with 2 public warnings. The latter lasted from 2.05 till 5 o'clock and I had the extremely doubtful pleasure of officiating over the youngsters who are supposed to use the trenches in an alert. Naturally we get a few of the draughtsmen who like being different, and awkward, and delay getting to the trenches. I had to hang about for some and missed seeing a Jerry who passed over and later dropped a bomb, which did not explode, on Holywells Park. It was fortunate he didn't think Reavell's looked more exciting than the gasworks, or is it that our camouflage is really effective?

Had an argument with Green this morning, who considered it a waste of time to go to the trenches at a crash warning and offered as support the fact that the women in the houses opposite were getting on with their washing and not skulking in pits in the ground, so why should we? A queer intelligence. It may indicate bravery but is also short-sighted.

In Libya we are now approaching Tobruk.

WEDNESDAY 8 JANUARY
The total figures of shipping losses for 1940 published today say 3.6 million tons. A colossal figure when one interprets in terms of boats and the labour, thought and design which goes into the making of each. What a waste!

Another RAF warning this morning. The blighter bombed Landseer Road and Fletcher Road killing two people and injuring others. We saw two Hurricanes take up the chase but it was pretty hopeless in the cloud. By now Jerry must have a pretty good photographic record of this district and I don't suppose he wants it for nothing. Wonder when he will use it?

SATURDAY 18 JANUARY
What weather! Twelve degrees of frost yesterday and ten the day before and now an easterly gale is blowing and it's snowing like blazes. I've just been along the street; some places are almost clear then one stumbles into a 1 ft drift and there is every indication it will hang about for a fortnight. Never mind, gas will freeze in weather like this but it means the allotment must wait.

We had a successful meeting last night to discuss the fire patrol scheme. There were nearly 100 there, a good result. Mr Parker is leader of our block and seems keen. That missus of mine, too, is having some helpful thoughts and suggestions on the subject. Greenwood made a decent job of the meeting and everyone seemed keen and interested in the job of leader-choosing and duties. They are working in our block in pairs, there being seventeen volunteers to sixteen houses, and we are taking one night complete when the siren goes. There will probably be two white boards to be hung over the gate of those on duty so the wardens can contact the right people and wake them if they, possibly, oversleep and I'm putting my pump outside each night when going to bed. As a warden I'm taking no active part but I'm sure interested to see it go well.

Green was a little excitedly informative this morning, telling us to take our respirators nowadays, even going to the end of the street. He's heard now that invasion is imminent and that we're likely to get some round here. He says Jerry will use barges for gas spraying when the wind is right which will naturally give us a clue when to expect him. I was surprised to hear the Home Guard has had no gas lectures and, when he asked me to, I volunteered to go and give them a few tips about it all. I'd rather like that; it would really be doing something useful.

Jerry comes in all weathers. This afternoon with this snowstorm raging we were startled by a stick of four bombs no more than a mile away. I went out and heard Kesgrave siren going and a few more rumbles and, I think, MG fire. Nothing more occurred so I sought shelter from the storm.

George tells me a merchantman rammed an 800-ton coal boat outside our dock last week. She went down soon, all her crew were saved, but it's a loss all the same.

SATURDAY 25 JANUARY
Am now helping to eat a 2 oz Cadbury's milk chocolate at 2½d. Am afraid it's so much of an event that I can record it here as a real event. Chocolate is very scarce this last four or six months, the Services have bags of it but we don't. Poor old Orbell who used to have such a selection of sweets now has a very bare counter. Yesterday he charged me 7d for ¼ lb of toffees and no chocolate. Still we want the munitions from America so we can't spare the ships for both.

I staged a demonstration this afternoon in one of Harry's cart sheds, for the fire-watchers. It went off very well, most of them turning up and the ladies were keen enough not to mind lying down and extinguishing a fire with the pump. We provided a straw–paraffin fire for each one so now we are all experienced fire-fighters.

THURSDAY 30 JANUARY
Such goings-on today. We've had twelve RAF warnings since 11.45, including two during the lunch hour and, in most cases, we heard the Jerry concerned. Once quite a barrage went up, answered by MG fire just to enliven the proceedings, and then a Dornier was seen to amble over the town. Weather conditions were favourable, low Scotch-misty clouds, so perhaps it was the same tyke oozing round and round, just to retard our production. Miss Reynolds didn't want to go down at the first warning 'cos she was going home late and 'innocently' seemed not to know it mattered. I politely disillusioned her. Later, on the next warning, I had a peculiar attack of second sight when I found her office empty. I looked in her clothes cupboard and, sure enough, there she was and looked a little foolish. More arguments and she eventually went to shelter, upon which I thanked her most earnestly and politely, so she had the impression she was doing me a favour and we were both pleased.

Last night the spell was broken – by Wailing Winnie. Planes were droning over from 7 to 9.30 and they say London had a small-scale raid. No searchlights but frequent shots in the dark. Jerry doesn't seem to mind that but comes in over Harwich way with a perfect indifference to Archie. The raid lasted till 2 minutes past 10. Dora was on duty fire-watching so she had her first spell –

of 2 minutes. I wanted to be able to go to bed at midnight and order her to keep the post but was spared that pleasure. The fire-watching seems to have caught on. When on patrol, I found five out of nine cards already outside.

The new proclamation has been signed covering six age groups: 18 and 19, and 37 to 40. The nineteens sign up on 22 February, so Dennis signs on the dotted line. Hope for his sake he's lost his conchy tendency.

Drew rations last night which included a Horlicks. I'm saving it for iron rations. One never knows. I've also been able to get a 2*d* chocolate now and then and have three saved in my bureau. They'll be handy for the kids if we can't get any later on. Saw D. . . last night and I fancy he's not too sure of the result when Hitler invades. He imagines a gas barrage dropped inland to prevent troop reinforcements and a ferocious attack, with only the Home Guard to meet it and that, frankly, a partly trained force. All the same I'd love to be with them and I can still see myself pinching an overcoat and a rifle to do a little helping. It's going to be bloody round here Richard, but I hope it's not my kiddies' blood nor Dora's, and if only Ma would consent to wearing a respirator it would help one's peace of mind. Naturally it isn't all a black outlook. We're better than in June when the Home Guard only had shotguns – sometimes – and no cartridges except what the public surrendered.

We gave Wilhelmshaven its forty-second pasting last night and so we've both emerged from the shell.

FRIDAY 7 FEBRUARY
Wonderful news. Excellent news. Benghazi is fallen and in record time. Details are not issued yet but it was only about two days ago that we were told we were past Derna on the way to Benghazi and now we've taken it, apparently merely by blowing our trumpets outside. Thursday we heard the Navy had made another sweep and 'fulfilled an important mission' in the central Mediterranean. I wonder if they stormed the harbour, where a landing certainly would not be expected, and so demoralised the Italians? We shall know soon.

We're having amazing weather. Tuesday night was brilliant moonlight, not too cold. Then Wednesday night the wind was <u>south</u> and the coldest of the winter. Powdery snow blew like a blizzard and well we knew it, there being a Jerry visitation from 10 to midnight. By morning the snow was too deep for cycling but it

actually <u>thawed</u> with a north wind. It's going nicely now and our
Wellingtons are going over eastwards. They went out last night and
walloped the invasion ports, playing ducks and drakes with barges.

TUESDAY 11 FEBRUARY
Churchill gave a general war commentary, the best speech I have
heard for some time, but ended with a warning against
overconfidence re invasion, which is probably coming.

   Nearer and nearer. Jerry dropped ten bombs last night in a stick
from Rushmere Road to Northgate Schools, too near for being
pleasant. No. 48 Rushmere Road was demolished killing two
people, but all the others hit open ground or roads. One was just at
the side of our post and it's fortunate it has 13½-in walls. Even they
were cracked. The craters were about 15 ft in diameter, probably
50-kg bombs. We were at a bomb lecture at the time, heard the
whistling, fell flat without saying a word, much to my amusement,
then continued the lecture.

FRIDAY 21 FEBRUARY
I haven't written much about the Greek war, probably because the
weather being even fouler than it is over here, they have done
nothing vividly spectacular. All the same those splendid troops have
been pushing and pushing, hilltop after hilltop, until Musso must be
almost despairing. About a third of Albania is now in Greek hands.
A few weeks ago the Italians staged a counter-attack on a big scale
but the Greeks beat it back again and took yet more prisoners. Now,
with spring a possibility (though to have seen the snow this morning
a small hope at that) the Greeks are appealing to America for planes,
asking both us and America to waive our present claims in their
favour. The paper tonight reports that America is rushing planes to
the East in which case it looks as though those thousands of planes
promised us are again being postponed.

   Talking of planes I'm getting a bit interested in spotting. It's
rather a fascinating hobby but will be difficult to get reliable
silhouettes according to *Aeroplane Spotter*. It's a weekly which I've
just started taking. I've wondered about trying Argyle Street to see
if there's a class I can join but can't say what I shall be letting
myself in for with gardening demanding so much time soon. All
the same I've got a daft idea that the more useful I can make
myself to this old country, the more chance I might possibly find of
being some use. At the present I feel almost useless.

TUESDAY 25 FEBRUARY

More excitement locally last night. Several Jerries came over, those queer sounding engines like motorbikes, one dropping two bombs on Bloomfield Street. I was outside in the garden at the time and heard the whistling of the bombs but heard no explosion. Queer, but becoming a frequent occurrence. Wonder why? It was only half a mile away. He concentrated on East Anglia up till about midnight. I was on at midnight but went out about 11, getting up from bed to do it. I'm afraid that, just before I got up, I remarked to Dora 'that b. . . is diving'. Tut tut. Should be more careful. He is back again tonight. I've just been watching flashes over Woodbridge way. When it was all over a fighter arrived.

We were reckoning up today and came to the conclusion that bombs have been dropped on Ipswich on at least twenty-one occasions plus half a dozen or so just round about – Whepstead, Bealings, Culpho and so on. Didn't think it was quite so many.

Today went to see the bomb which fell on Holywells Park some weeks ago. It's on Christchurch Park now. A handy thing, 2 ft 6 in diameter and 11 ft 9 in overall, weighing 1¾ tons, and the usual German cylindrical design. I hear the method of disposal used is to drill holes and wash the explosive out with soap and steam or water. The nose was sharp and I expected to find it hardened of armour-piercing type but it was quite soft mild steel. I filed it with a nail file.

SATURDAY 1 MARCH

Bulgaria has today joined the Axis. Serve her darn well right. Now I suppose poor little Greece will be getting it in the neck or, rather, in the back. Hope Turkey does honour her agreements with us. I can't see just how it will benefit Bulgaria, unless it's a case of Hobson's Choice and I expect that's how it is really.

The RAF has been doing well in Albania. Altogether in two days it shot down thirty-five Italians with nine more probable for no loss to ourselves. An excellent performance and I hope it does the same to the Jerries.

THURSDAY 6 MARCH

Official details are now released of the raid the Germans reported we made on a Norwegian island. They said we sank a few fishing boats and that the raid was 'senseless and without military value'. So it was senseless, from their point of view. It was one of the

Lofoten Islands off Narvik and we destroyed the cod-liver oil producing plant, used for manufacturing glycerine for explosives, sank 11 ships in the harbour totalling 18,000 tons (one of 10,000 tons), and brought away 215 Germans, a few quislings and some Norwegian nationals. Into the bargain we left a stock of food and cigarettes for Norwegian consumption. That was a fine piece of propaganda. It both encouraged the Norwegians and showed them we are not, at the moment, short of food here. That's the second raid of its kind, the first being Costellorizo, or some such name, in the Dodecanese. May there be many more.

Ominous signs that the shipping losses are going to be severe again this year. One minister says we may hear our kiddies say they are hungry next winter. Well I suppose a huge submarine fleet can do something but so can a decent-sized corvette fleet I shouldn't wonder. I often think, though, of Rolfe's argument some months ago in the canteen saying we will be short of essential foods before the war is out.

MONDAY 10 MARCH

For the last few weeks the Americans have been debating the Lease and Lend Bill. Now it is passed and will become law on Wednesday. We should get a good deal of aid from that. I forgot the actual construction published at the beginning but it is to the effect that America is almost in the war, without making the declaration. She can supply us with ships, tanks, planes or guns, loaning them to us without pay and having them returned at the end of hostilities and, if repairs are necessary, pay the bill herself. Actually they are now advancing a £2,500 million bill of credit for us. There is also *Express* talk about a scheme whereby we swop 2 of our new battleships for (I think) 10 cruisers and 25 destroyers.

The South Africans who have pushed so well into Italian Somaliland are now marching into Abyssinia. Abyssinia seems doomed, I'm glad to say, and Keren in Eritrea, is being heavily besieged.

In Albania the Greeks are taking the offensive and mopping up the Italians, taking over 2,000 prisoners.

The RAF is very quiet now. Probably bogged, I suppose. Now the weather is improving a bit perhaps they can get away. I hear that Hurricanes are now being fitted with racks to take two bombs. Good idea, though we copied it from Jerry.

TUESDAY 25 MARCH
Jugo-Slavia has been and gone and done it. The silly mugs have
signed the Three Power Pact with Germany, Italy and Japan.
There is unrest in the country and several important people have
resigned over it but it hasn't made any difference. The pact
contains a few reassuring clauses ensuring that Jugo-Slavia can
remain peaceful but that's probably eye-wash. Now, I suppose,
poor little Greece can expect a packet. I think it is significant,
though, that Eden is still in Cairo.

Shipping losses for week ending 16 March were 72,000 tons.
Though above average they are less than the week before and less
than I had expected.

They say a lone Jerry was brought down near Martlesham this
morning; I think it is reliable.

THURSDAY 27 MARCH
Wonderful news. Jugo-Slavia had a mild revolution at 2 a.m. today
in which the premier and foreign minister were arrested, the
government dissolved and Prince Paul, the Prince Regent, has fled.
Prince Michael, the 17½-year-old heir to the throne, who would
have ascended in September in any case, has assumed the throne
and formed a new government, under the air minister, which has
repudiated the pact signed with Germany, etc. The army has gone
over too, and sworn allegiance to the new government. Churchill has
promised all the help we can give in the event of war and I'm hoping
the report of a week or so ago that Russia would help too is correct.

The news has run through the country like a tonic, if our Works
is really representative. People are discussing it with enjoyment and
shining faces, and it seems so encouraging after yesterday's
'another faint heart' feeling. There are now three countries with
backbone in Europe.

9 p.m. More good news. Keren and Harar are fallen.

FRIDAY 28 MARCH
The papers are jubilant today, owing to the Jugo-Slav volte-face
and the Keren capture. The Greeks seem to have taken the
opportunity too and smitten the Italians yet more, while our subs
have again been active, *Parthian* having sunk two transports.

All this has happened while Matsuoka, the Jap minister, has
been in Berlin visiting Hitler and it can't have impressed him
much. Hitler was to have made a speech last night but cancelled it.

If his plans are very much upset in the Balkans I wonder if he will consider the invasion of Britain more favourably still?

Meat ration next week is down to 1s per head, from 1s 2d, and cheese will soon be rationed to 1oz per week, country workers getting 8 oz which is only fair. Jam and syrup are 2 oz per week.

SUNDAY 6 APRIL
Well, it's happened. Germany declared war on Jugo-Slavia and Greece at dawn this morning and immediately attacked down the Struma Valley into Greece and bombed Belgrade and Salonika. Those reports come from Germany itself, no news having yet come at all from Jugo-Slavia and little from Greece. The excuse this time is the thinnest yet. The declaration against Greece is because of Greece's 'unneutral' attitude and against both countries as a means of striking against Britain. Naturally the usual documents have been found, showing that Britain has considered some aggression.

News, so far, is scarce but they have given some figures of Jugo-Slavia's strength which surprised me a little. I had always considered her as a weakish nation, big in courage since it embraced the Serbs and Montenegrins, but small in fighting forces. The army, fully mobilised, consists of 1 million men, mostly infantry, but very poor in mechanised forces, though the infantry is well equipped. The air force has about 900 planes but some are Furies though others are Hurricanes, Blenheims and Dornier 17s. The navy is one cruiser, a few destroyers and four submarines. In other words it is another Poland, but let's hope it will have a different fate. We have had a few weeks or months for preparation and surely even we have made full use of the time.

Wonder what our plans are? Hope our bombers are sufficiently numerous. Now, what will Turkey do? Shall I put two question marks? The obvious step is to come in now but I suppose we must trust the ones who know. Just to make things easier Iraq has suddenly turned pro-Nazi and, as she lies between Iran and the Mediterranean, I hope it won't lead to complications.

Glorious news from Abyssinia this afternoon. The bare fact came through that we have taken Addis Ababa. A wonderful feat and virtually the end of the East African campaign. What a circus the South African striking force have had! Up the coast to Mogadishu, inland to Harar, Hargeysa and Dire Dawa then down to Addis Ababa, all since 25 February.

I should have said that Italy is coming in against Jugo-Slavia too. May she enjoy it, but I've an idea she won't. She may not have realised that we have bases in the Adriatic.

TUESDAY 8 APRIL
Raids were prolonged last night. We heard the alert at the Spotters' meeting at 8.30, the all-clear sounding, to my surprise, at 5.40 a.m. We had personal attention, we Ipswichians, a Jerry dropping at least two bombs, some say four. One at the end of Sandhurst Avenue has caused a lot of damage. Another near, or on, the gasworks, damage unknown yet. Mother woke me at 12.30 for an aspirin so I heard the Jerry, blow him, dive and drop his bombs. It's a bit startling to hear the steady throb of his engines change to a snarling crescendo and then the whistle of the bombs, changing note as they come nearer. While the whistle is still running down the scale a flash comes and one confusedly wonders why it should, until the thump comes. All we heard was a noise like a wood shed falling over with no suggestion of an explosion yet, at a distance, the boom is heard distinctly enough to waken people.

A warden was killed, poor chap, at Sandhurst Avenue, and eight people injured. Jerry claims to have bombed Ipswich. There were two RAF warnings today so possibly he came over to photo the damage and the alert has just gone again so perhaps we shall have a return visit tonight. Queerly enough I saw George Young as I came home and he said, re the lack of activity, that he sometimes wished that just a little incendiary might drop in the middle of the road. Two hours later his boss, the warden, was killed.

Yesterday was Budget Day, coming as a complete surprise, the day being kept secret. The only tax was an increase in income tax to 10s and reducing allowances, but a proportion of the increase will be paid back after the war. A form of compulsory saving in fact. An excellent and fair budget on the whole.

SATURDAY 12 APRIL
We had our first definite raid here on Ipswich on Wednesday evening although it was the twenty-ninth occasion on which bombs have been dropped here. A Jerry arrived at 11 o'clock, made a practice run, dropped a ground flare round dockland then dropped incendiaries which set Gabriel's timber yard alight and then leisurely made three more runs dropping HE on the docks. Then he went off and a pal came along and made two more runs dropping

HE and cleared off at about 12.15. They made their runs over our district and we heard the plane diving and the bombs screaming but, peculiarly enough, heard very few bombs explode. In fact we thought they were mostly duds but from the amount of glass being swept up in Fore Street they probably were not. One man was killed by shrapnel in Constable Road and five injured in the bomb area.

It was interesting to see the MG barrage from the dock. They couldn't see the plane so put up a fan barrage through which he would have to pass. Actually, though, he came so low on one occasion the glare of the fire showed him up well.

The dirty tykes visited Coventry again two nights running, damage and casualties being heavy. Poor Coventry. Can't be much left by now.

Most nights, every night in fact this week, Jerry has been over and mostly we had the alert from 8.30 to 4 or 6 in the morning. Our fighters shot down about 8 or 10 each night, total I believe being 33, and 5 by AA. It's bright moonlight, except yesterday, which helped.

We've been raiding too, including a reasonably heavy one on Berlin, and been losing five to eight each night. Jerry's losses are estimated about 5 per cent and ours about 3 per cent, suggesting about 250 planes per night which is interesting.

Jerry is making progress in the Balkans. We heard, with much dismay, on Wednesday that Salonika had fallen, cutting off a Greek army to the east, but were slightly mollified to hear later that we hadn't intended to hold it anyway and Salonika had been pretty well blown up before evacuation by us. It was only yesterday we heard that British advance forces had been in action but there are no details yet. The RAF, however, have been pretty active, thank goodness. Is there no stopping the German panzer divisions? Let's hope there is and that it's our troops who will do it.

In Cyrenaica we appear to be making a stand at Tobruk, Jerry claims to have captured 2,000 men and 3 generals, which we admit half-heartedly, saying it's possible.

Yesterday was Good Friday and I spent the day, 8 till 8, fire-watching at Reavell's. There were no alarms and I really enjoyed it, having cleaned my bike and played lots of darts.

Was surprised to see today that the present tax on tobacco is 19s 6d per pound or 1s 2½d per ounce. All the same consumption has risen to 200 million lb per annum. A terrific tax.

MONDAY 14 APRIL

Let's talk about grub for a little. They've rationed milk this week, in a way. We are to be allowed six-sevenths of what we had for week beginning 2 March but hospitals, kiddies' milk at school and cheap milk are not to be reduced. The saving is to be used for cheese and renewing stocks of condensed and powdered milk. Meat is still at 1s worth per head which still doesn't affect us much, not being big meat-eaters and Dora makes soup twice a week. Sugar is still 8 oz per week and we actually save on it, about ¼ lb a week, for jam-making. Cheese is 2 oz and, though I thought I should miss my breakfast cheese, it doesn't after all seem inadequate. Things like dates, raisins, sultanas and figs are treasures from heaven, not rationed, but if Dora manages to buy some by some queer stroke of luck there are whoops in the house. Oranges are unobtainable, lemons too, while apples though obtainable are about 6d for cookers and up to 1s for eating. Damn robbery. Biscuits are a bit scarce and if they have chocolate ones at work, I get two per month for the kids. Sweets are scarce, naturally, and milk chocolate is not now manufactured, while the plain kind we can get is not plentiful. Hilda from the canteen rations us to one 2½d piece per ten days or so, and my newsagent smuggles my weekly ration of 6d of choc or ¼ lb of sweets across the counter when the other casual customers are not looking.

There's reason in all this. The expeditionary force overseas has to be fed and that cuts two ways because besides that food being an extra, ships are wanted to transport it, and they are also taken off the food trade for this country. America, too, is supplying us with munitions and equipment and it has to be brought here in ships. Also chocolate, for instance, is exported to provide currency abroad. The general effect on us is one of annoyance rather than going without.

Roosevelt is organising a plan to make Greenland a base, so that short- range planes may fly over here. Hitler objects, Greenland being Danish, but no one takes notice of that.

WEDNESDAY 16 APRIL

Rather serious news to report tonight I'm afraid. Jugo-Slavia's troops are 'now not serving under a unified command but resistance is expected to continue in the form of guerrilla war'. In other words it's all up with Jugo-Slavia. Quite a price to pay for the privilege of having their anthem included with the other Allies on

the Sunday evening broadcasts. All the same it's better than
subservience and there is still the chance of regaining it. That
means I suppose that forces will be increased against us in Greece
where, by the way, our line has been withdrawn to a line almost
horizontal. (Wailing Winnie interfered.)

THURSDAY 17 APRIL
The siren certainly did interfere. From the alert at 9.25 till all-clear
at about 5 a.m. there was a continuous drone of planes with only
very occasional intervals. It was awe-inspiring at first then it
became just commonplace as, I'm afraid, it was fairly clear that
London was probably the target. I don't mean that heartlessly but
the trepidation with which I heard the first two come over
disappeared.

London got it alright, poor devils, Jerry sending more bombers
than at any other raid. They said it was a reprisal for our raid on
Berlin, which suggests we did quite a bit of damage there. We
brought six down.

No huge battle has developed in Greece yet but Jerry has been
pushing tentatively to test our defences. Let's hope they prove
impregnable and later, offensive.

In North Africa Jerry has pulled a fast one over us. The
Express says he has 800 tanks there and 1,000 planes. There is a
minor mystery about how they got there, but the point is that
they are bypassing Tobruk and are at Sollum and Fort Capezzo.
Of course, it's not all bad, for instance we have repulsed two
heavy attacks on Tobruk and even sallied out to take prisoners,
also the Navy has shelled a park of tanks and cars near Sollum.
The crowning event though was the news today that our fleet
intercepted a convoy from Sicily and Tripoli of five merchant
ships and three destroyers and annihilated it, us losing a Tribal,
the *Mohawk*. Four were laden with mechanised equipment and
the other with munitions.

WEDNESDAY 23 APRIL
Rather disquieting news. The Greek army forming the left flank of
our line has capitulated. They surrendered at 10 p.m. yesterday to
the ruddy Wops. It's tough luck that they were able to beat them as
they did and now have to give up to them. The Greek king and
government have gone to Crete and made the usual vows of
fighting to the bitter end.

Things look black but I fancy they are not as black as all that. It might be though, being accustomed to this sort of thing, somehow I don't feel great alarm (touch wood like blazes). They say our defence lines, besides being much shorter, are much more capable of defence but Jerry has such a way of surmounting obstacles that one shouldn't bank too much on that. If we haven't improved our position in the next six months possibly we shall have to withdraw. I hope all arrangements are made for that.

We had a notice at work today saying that as a gas exercise we were to wear our respirators at the next RAF warning. It came at 2.15 and Jerry came over Ipswich to make things more interesting. I saw him in the distance, being late out as usual through delay action by draughtsmen and typists, but I hear he was an Messerschmitt 110. The alert has just gone. Wonder if he's been home and developed his photos?

MONDAY 28 APRIL
A little good news at last, such as it is. We have taken Dessaye in Abyssinia, the last Italian stronghold. That doesn't mean the war is over out there but it should help.

I think I reported our new bombs recently. From time to time they tell us a little about them and one pilot says of a raid on Hamburg that his bomb caused 'a huge heaving mass like a volcanic eruption which rose and settled down into a great red glow fully half a mile diameter'. Others say similarly. Some bombs!

Jubilation in the papers, 26,000 cases of oranges have arrived in the country from Spain. Should provide one orange per household.

Churchill gave a reasoned non-alarmist survey of the war situation last night revealing, by the way, that Wavell did all his stuff with two divisions, 30,000 men, and, by imputation, we had 40,000 in Greece. Amazingly, pitifully small but it's done its stuff. He also said that America is taking up the neutrality patrol, using 200 warships to do it.

Some time ago we had alterations at Reavell's. Barbed wire fences were erected all round. The Home Guard patrols every night, and all employees enter by one gate only, while periodically the police hold hold-ups to see if we have our passes. We have a receptionist to control all visitors as well. Now everyone is issued with a tin hat. A girl dropped hers and it dented but they should shield most blows likely to be encountered from flying bricks.

WEDNESDAY 30 APRIL

We have evacuated 45,000 of our troops in Greece, out of a total of 60,000. Although sad to lose 15,000 it is wonderful that the figure was not higher. We have lost our heavy equipment but Churchill said 'the enemy is not lacking in heavy equipment'. It is also revealed that the evacuation was made and the retreat started at the instigation of the Greeks who realised that they had no equipment with which to continue the struggle, so decided not to waste our men. A heroic nation that, deserving an eventual reconstruction.

A wonderful effort has just been revealed, worthy even of our wonderful Navy, bless it, and a piece of superlative cheek. It's this. Our ambassador in Jugo-Slavia has been missing so *Regent* calmly dodged two minefields and entered Cattaro [Kotor] harbour in search of him, flying her largest white ensign. She found the harbour in the possession of the Italian army but the CO went ashore and (wonder how?) took an Italian officer on the sub as hostage while he searched the town for our ambassador. For nine hours she lay waiting until two Italian dive-bombers eventually attacked and machine-gunned her, whereupon the sub submerged and proceeded to sea with the hostage still aboard, I'm afraid. If anyone ever deserved a medal, that chap does. While we've men like that it's surely going to take more than Hitler to beat us.

SUNDAY 4 MAY

Today we start a new experiment. At 2 a.m. the clocks went on another hour giving us two extra hours of sunlight and, at the same time, the blackout times are three-quarters of an hour after sunset and before sunrise. Sometime in June blackouts will be 11.19. I hear it won't be popular with some gardeners here because, sunset being so late, it gives them time to go back to the allotments and get thirsty again! All the same I think it's a splendid idea and just what we want.

More trouble has flared up, this time in Iraq. Rashid Ali, the pro-Axis bloke who recently seized power, allowed the first batch of troops of ours to land according to the Anglo-Iraq treaty, but objected to reinforcements following them until the first batch had crossed the country to the oilfields. We have a training (chiefly) air station at Habbaniyah near Baghdad and he had the darn cheek to forbid any air action there and, after exchange of pleasantries, the blighter opened fire with artillery and an action ensued. The outcome is obscure except that we have done some bombing of the artillery and we now have control of the power station and a few more places. News tonight says that the Iraq regent has appealed to the people to disown Rashid and, as Rashid has asked Berlin for military help on Friday, I guess Jerry will soon be there and be first.

TUESDAY 13 MAY
There can be only one topic of conversation in all the country today and that's the amazing, almost unbelievable, event of last Saturday, the 10th. At 6 p.m. that day, Rudolf Hess, the third man in Germany and Hitler's deputy, started from Augsburg in a Messerschmitt 110 and later landed in Scotland. It has now been established that he is here definitely as a refugee and the rumours which immediately sprang up, that he had brought peace proposals, are denied.

It all started yesterday with Berlin saying he was missing, was suffering from delusions, had been forbidden to fly by the great Hitler, had procured a plane and was then missing. We countered immediately with the news that he was here in Scotland, having baled out in the country breaking an ankle in the process, was taken by a ploughman and was then in hospital.

Naturally speculation is in everyone's mind as to why he came. Some say he was trying for Ireland as a step to America but he was too high up. I think it's just plain running away from what he knows will be coming, after some serious disagreement on policy and it's ironic that he chose the country with which he is at war as the only safe refuge. Of course it is the safest place, the freest place, in the world. Any other country would be full of Jerry agents waiting to bump him off.

Jerry has now published that he is in England. What the effect on the German people's morale will be can't be seen yet, but it certainly won't be an improvement. What's behind it all? Why did he leave? He intended it, as he had identity papers, no loaded guns on the plane and was willing to cooperate and be pleasant. Suppose we will know some day.

3.30 a.m. Have just done what most of us are liable to do. The alert went at 11.30 and neither Dora nor I heard the all-clear so, being awake at 3 o'clock and should have been on duty at 2.00, have just been round to the post to make sure. Fortunately the all-clear was at 1.14. Still, best to be on the safe side. I didn't want anyone having the laugh on me, reason being as follows.

Harold Greenwood has just been promoted to a job at Swansea, meaning we had to elect a new White Hat. Stiffy being the deputy naturally he had a claim but was surprised, but grateful, to find that little me was elected instead. That was only yesterday, Monday, and, as Stiffy now calls me at 2 o'clock, I was naturally perturbed at the possibility of him failing to wake me. Wonder how the job will suit? Hope I can hold it down alright. It's a bit more interesting and somehow I had a hunch to take it. It was surprising though, to find things taking that course. Possibly no one else wanted the job.

WEDNESDAY 14 MAY

The chief topic is still the Hess mystery and it seems that all the world is discussing it, even Germany where they still cover it by alleging insanity. To make sure we have medically examined him and pronounced him perfectly sane. As a support, it is said he had never flown a Messerschmitt 110 before, had never baled out before, and had a map in his possession showing his intended route. We are a queer nation. In Germany Hess is a gangster; in England we survey him with benevolent interest. The paper says he has been talking freely with Kirkpatrick of the Foreign Office. Let's hope he has been spilling the beans.

At times one gets so tired and full of jobs that little time is left for this excellent diary. For instance, we were blitzed again on Sunday and I only now record it. It was a full moon a day old and a clear sky so Jerry found us alright. At the same time we found him, reports saying he lost two planes around here. He dropped a terrific thing at Bramford just as I was undressing at 1.30, and the blast really hit me at the window. It was followed by another and we got the kids down. Then he tried Ipswich and plastered the tram depot at Felixstowe Road and carried on with various other salvoes. One plane came so low I distinctly saw him all the time. He was the one they say a fighter shot down. We took the kids down the dug-out just as the last bomb fell and eventually went to bed at 3 o'clock.

Was up again at 2.00 last night making the ninth consecutive night I had been up.

WEDNESDAY 21 MAY

The Duke of Aosta has surrendered and the Abyssinian campaign is nearly over. His force at Amba Alagē was the most important of three which he had divided after leaving Addis Ababa in order to prolong resistance. The other two, Gonder and Jimma regions, are presumably not composed of such important troops. He should have surrendered today at midday but no news has so far been received. Hope we haven't been had.

9 p.m. I hear he has now surrendered and the total captured is 18–19,000. Quite a help.

Most important of all, Jerry is now attacking Crete using parachutists, airborne troops and surface naval craft, supported by dive-bombers and Messerschmitts. It started yesterday, about 4.30 (presumably a.m.) when 3,000 men were dropped and these had been cleaned up by 6.30 and 'the situation was in hand by 9 o'clock'. Naturally that was not the finish of it and naturally, it won't all be as easy as that. Jerry is using parachutists who land and signal to pals above when they are safely down and overcoming resistance. Their pals arrive in transports and towed gliders.

The last bit is interesting. We've heard about them but I've wondered just how successful they would be. If designed for high speed they will be noisy and lose their advantage of comparative silence and if slow, should be easy meat. Wonder if the troops bail out and the glider returns or does the glider land? There are few details about anything yet.

It is anticipated that at least one airborne division is taking part, consisting of about 7,000 men, besides the parachutists. Some planes have crashed on landing, which suggests traps and obstacles, and I gathered from the news just now that we are not doing too badly. On the other hand Jerry won't mind losses and will keep pegging away until a bridgehead is maintained if at all possible, so we must be prepared for bad news possibly coming along. He will naturally put all he has into it and we laymen are not permitted to know what forces we have in Crete. Let's hope they are adequate.

FRIDAY 23 MAY

Last night I felt something inside say Crete would be lost to us very soon. Tonight, though still apprehensive, I don't feel quite so doleful. There are three main positions of combat: the capital Heraklion, which we used to know as Candia; Retimo [Rethimnon], where the enemy are being held and the position is in our favour; and Maleme, near the western extremity, where Jerry has captured the aerodrome and has today landed strong reinforcements. If we only had some fighters there he wouldn't have done, but we haven't. With a spotting plane we should be able to bombard the place from the sea; there should be no artillery opposition and no mines.

This battle is very decisive for Hitler. If he loses, he loses much and that's the danger. He will do everything possible and throw everything into it until sheer weight of numbers count. Oh, for that fighter force!

News tonight that our submarines have sunk a troop-ship of 9,000 tons, a 7,000-ton tanker, and two ammunition schooners and torpedoed a destroyer, probably sunk, on their way to Libya.

SATURDAY 24 MAY

Empire Day. I know how I'd like it celebrated. Kicking the invaders from Maleme would do very well indeed. Maleme is still held by Jerry but it's the only place. He has tried again at Heraklion and Retimo, possibly because of the quay facilities there, but has been 'dealt with decisively', to use the official phrase. At Maleme reinforcements have been landed by air with a few small field guns, but the place is under our artillery fire which should be effective. To my lay mind I would have preferred a few of our heavy tanks trotting around the 'drome but perhaps gunfire can deal with it as well and, after all, shell bursts on the flat make subsequent landings hazardous, and perhaps tanks can be used more usefully in rounding up parachutists. They know best.

Our Archie shot down sixteen Junkers 52s, a decent effort, and now I see our Egypt-based bombers and long-distance fighters are in action, which should ease matters. The bombers have destroyed ten troop carriers and four more fighters, modest claims which give one confidence in the news bulletins as a whole.

9 o'clock news. Bad news. *Hood* has been sunk in a naval action off Greenland. Results of the action not yet to hand. A big loss but I suppose we won't get through this war without such losses.

TUESDAY 27 MAY

Have just been listening to a most thrilling story about the locating, chasing and sinking of the *Bismarck*. The compiler of the news item must be human, he made it so interesting. It's hopeless to repeat it all here and, if I ever want to refer to details, I suppose others more gifted than I will have described it.

As a summary though, it all started last Wednesday when we discovered the *Bismarck* and *Prinz Eugen*, an 8 in cruiser, in Bergen. Next day they had left and *Norfolk* and *Suffolk* found them later between Iceland and Greenland and shadowed them south-west. *Hood* and *Prince of Wales* arrived and engaged them, when *Hood* caught a chance one at 23,000 yd range and blew up. *Prince of Wales* engaged, damaged the *Bismarck* so that she caught fire and dribbled oil, received slight damage herself and lost contact. A Catalina found her next day and a huge hunt by sea developed. She was found to be 550 miles off Land's End. *King George V* came off convoy work in the Atlantic, Somerville with *Renown* or *Repulse* and, I believe, *Ramillies* came up from Gibraltar; *Rodney* and another joined in and, fittingly, *Ark Royal*. This besides various cruisers like *Devonshire* and *Sheffield* and three Tribals *Cossack*, *Zulu* and another.

The *Ark Royal* planes found her and made two attacks. One torpedo had hit her off Greenland and now two more did too, one amidships and the other astern, causing her to go round in circles with steering trouble. Then the Tribals went in and hit with two more and she stopped. Just before, an artillery duel took place, results of which are not to hand, and the *coup de grâce* was given by a cruiser with more torpedoes.

I must say a little about Crete. Jerry has gained a success at Canea [Khania]. He has all the while been landing reinforcements, and some reports say small tanks too, and now he has advanced from Maleme towards Canea and penetrated our defences. I don't like the sound of that. True we have landed reinforcements too which include heavy tanks, I hope, so there is still hope.

It has now been released that we have lost *Gloucester*, *Fiji* and 4 destroyers (2 Kellys and Javelins), and 2 battleships and 4 cruisers hit, but not seriously. One boat, presumably a battleship, was attacked continuously for fourteen hours by 100 planes at a time. It said they hadn't time to count the planes they shot down but there were scores. She had 186 near misses in one attack.

SATURDAY 31 MAY
It's a bright spot so let's report it. Rashid Ali has fled from Iraq and Iraq has asked for an armistice, so that little potential trouble spot has been cleared up and Jerry forestalled a bit. News today stresses that our tenacious resistance in Crete has undoubtedly held up Germany's aid to Iraq.

Position in Crete still glum. *The Times* today calmly says we have no tanks there. If true, it's a ruddy calamitous mistake. A gaggle of medium tanks at Maleme would have made all the difference. Or is that just the mouthings of an ignorant layman?

Interesting cargo arrived from America. It is the first food ship under the Lease and Lend Bill. Quite cute to think that the Americans are sending us stuff, including food, free of all charge, but, after all, we are doing the fighting for them. Generous all the same.

SUNDAY 1 JUNE
News tonight said we have landed 15,000 men in Egypt from Crete. So the evacuation has started, or taken place, and the Crete campaign is over. Well I may be daft and I may be foolishly optimistic but I've an idea this is our last defeat. If Jerry attacks Cyprus I've a better-shaped idea that he will be beaten back. If we lose Cyprus the bottom will have dropped out of everything and we are governed by ruddy old women.

An armistice has been signed with Iraq and that's summat in our favour. Hope we don't have to pay for that.

Clothes rationing announced today to come into force at once. We'll be allowed sixty-six units a year. That seems plenty to me.

9 o'clock. Nothing further about the Crete evacuation except to repeat that it may not be complete and to warn us that our losses were severe. So were Jerry's. An RAF officer says Jerry used over 1,000 planes and lost over 200 and that in spite of no aerial opposition. We've come out but we certainly were not hopelessly defeated and I still think that, with a few heavy tanks at each aerodrome, Crete would still be ours.

Things don't seem calm in Germany. An undercurrent shows the disturbances by surface ripples. Admiral Boehm, Commander-in-Chief of Norwegian naval affairs and a friend of Hess, has committed suicide. Some attribute it to a visit Himmler paid him last week.

SUNDAY 8 JUNE
Well, it's happened! Really!! We've actually taken a land offensive. This morning at 2 a.m. we crossed the border and entered Syria. Gen de Gaulle is there and Gen Catroux[2] has sent a message to the Syrians suggesting they should collaborate with us, promising them self-government and an outlet for their trade. Planes also dropped leaflets asking the French to come in with us. Whether they have, or will, I don't know and daren't hope, as the only news available is that we have entered the south-east corner and are making for Homs on the oil pipeline. Fighter escorts have met no opposition so far but that's not to say they won't.

An estimate of the French force is 45,000, 15,000 of which are French, the rest are Syrians etc., with a small air force and some tanks. Now one must wait with patience for news. A lot depends on the next few days. If the French turn up pals it will save much trouble and bloodshed. If they don't it might lead to anything, even France actively entering the war against us, and almost certainly clashes with the French navy. The *Express* today says Weygand has been upsetting Darlan's[3] plans of Vichy–German collaboration and refuses to take any military action against Britain, which is hopeful. The next few days will be fateful, but I don't think we would have advanced on an offensive without well-prepared plans.

Churchill will defend the Crete campaign in Parliament this week. Possibly we shall hear that Crete was all along only intended as a delaying action. I've an idea it was.

Though it's full moon tomorrow Jerry has been very quiet lately. There were few heavy raids anywhere last week. Touch wood.

TUESDAY 10 JUNE

The most recent news from Syria says we are 35 to 40 miles over the border and meeting very little opposition. Some French are coming over to us and the Arab population is friendly, the latter being helped by the fact that we are taking food with us and distributing it. The critical time is approaching and the attitude of the French will affect the issue quite a bit. Rumours say that Weygand and the Vichy French militarists are not in favour of any military action except in protection of the French empire, Syria being only mandated and expired at that. The navy is the crucial point.

I fancy that by the weekend we shall be fighting France. A crisis seems to be developing and I shall be surprised, and overjoyed too, if French public opinion is strong enough to counter the Darlan section. And I used to think he was OK because he was a sailor!!! He's a disgrace to salt water.

The Crete debate has opened in Parliament. The only interesting facts so far are that Jerry lost 5,000 men drowned when we found the convoys, and 12,000 in the land action. Also he lost 180 fighters and bombers and at least 250 transport planes. They are not bad figures considering they were mostly brought down by gunfire. Damn good in fact.

I think it is shameful that I have said nothing in this otherwise excellent diary about our Spotters' Club. I really must. It started last February with a letter in the *Star* from Buxton, who is now our secretary, suggesting forming a club in Ipswich. A dozen of us met and the club was duly launched. After a few weeks we advertised and had a bumper meeting of twenty-five, whereupon we decided to elect a committee and that an attendance officer was necessary and, what's more, I was good enough for that bit. We've invited Chief Inspector Simpson for Vice-President, Gladwish as Competition Officer, so we are on the safe side of the police and, so far, most of us are showing keenness and enthusiasm. It is a little disappointing that the Army has claimed our President and will shortly take others but on the whole we are thriving. Meetings are fortnightly and we should have some good lectures.

WEDNESDAY 18 JUNE

A little of last year's feelings back again. Have seen 2 flights of 6 fighters returning to Martlesham and 12 higher up, going further. Can expect to hear in the morning that the Channel ports have been heavily bombed again. With the belated weather improvement the air war is speeding up. Yet again we visited Cologne and Düsseldorf last night. I hear Stirlings went over this district the other night. Wish I'd seen them. It's now 11 o'clock, just finished gardening, perhaps I may see one before bed.

THURSDAY 19 JUNE

The invasion scare is about again. We have been handed leaflets saying that the authorities may not be able to put in hand the evacuation plans in case of invasion but, in case they can, we must register all school kiddies 'cos they will go first. Registration to be finished by the 28th. If parents and young kiddies want to go with them, they must register too.

That means more mild worrying. To help matters we are hammering the invasion ports and the hospital which was going to operate on Godfrey flatly refuses to take any more patients. What does it mean? Have they more news that an invasion will be attempted? Is it to be the alternative if there is no trouble with Russia? Suppose we must just wait and hope for the best. It is all so unsettling – they tell us to 'Stay put' if invasion comes and then say 'Well, you are special. Please evacuate' and now they speak of compulsion. We have written to Sylvia to see if Dora and the kiddies can go there but I somehow doubt if they can get there as we only intend to go if necessary and if Jerry attacks the first thing we will know is that he is here and railway and road traffic is stopped. Then there is poor old Ma too. Heaven knows what will happen to her unless I can get some nurses or Win to come in and attend to her while I am on duty or at work. Poor old dear! If they move her it will be the end, I'm afraid. All the old distressing feelings which we had last July and August are coming back, the most prominent being 'How awful if I have to run my spade through everything in that lovely garden to stop Jerry having it'. Well, if he comes and I can get the women and kiddies away I'll tack myself on the Home Guard somehow.

SATURDAY 21 JUNE
There's a horrible nagging, back-of-the-mind air about. Everyone is discussing the probability of evacuation. From one person's opinion and another I fancy that when the registration is completed next week they will send the kiddies away, even if invasion is not actually impending. That would just about do for our Margaret if, with Godfrey in the nursing home and Dora with him, she has to go away alone. We have written to Sylvia and she will take Dora and the kiddies anytime, so it seems we must try somehow to anticipate the order and take Margaret to Thelnetham. Poor old Ma. Wonder what will happen to her? I don't want her to go out of my sight. Am afraid these are damnable times.

If invasion comes here, I wonder what will happen? If Ipswich is not attacked naturally things go on as usual but if we are attacked, I wonder what the effects will be? What will wardens do? Where will we feed? I believe I would sooner try starving than go to the communal feeding centres in the town. Priggish, but that's how I feel. Wonder if I could offer to do any spotting for the HG? Wonder what action I shall see? Wonder if I shall come out of it alright? At any rate I anticipate enjoying myself after getting used to seeing mutilations. The big snag will be leaving my treasured garden and allotment.

The longest day today. It is now 10.35. Dora is chatting in the garden, there is still lots of light about and if I were writing this at the other side of the room I wouldn't need the light on. This double summer time is a glorious boon. The other day I finished gardening at 10.45 and then came in to supper. It doesn't seem any different from other years in the morning either.

Well, we know now what the masts are for round the coast, Bawdsey in particular. The news has been released that they are for radio-location on the principle of an ether radio wave hitting an interposed object. Now we know how our subs avoid minefields. The secret was let out in an appeal for maintenance men and operators for a new small wireless set which will locate planes. They have promised us they are pretty effective and will reduce the damage from night bombing but haven't said how the plane will be engaged.

SUNDAY 22 JUNE

I woke with a jump this morning. At about 8 o'clock I dimly heard one newspaper boy say to another 'Was it Germany or Russia who declared war?' but I wasn't certain what he said. Out of bed in a flash I grabbed the paper but there was nothing there so laughed at myself. All the same we were careful not to miss the 9 o'clock news and, sure enough, it was true.

At 5.30 a.m. Goebbels broadcast a message from Hitler to the Reich saying Germany had marched on Russia. Though it is serious news the report read like a Saturday evening music hall. Germany was marching to protect the whole of Europe. She was marching to prevent a stab in the back. She was tired of the obtrusive propaganda and the menace of Bolshevism and, sure enough, a document had been found in Belgrade when Jugo-Slavia had surrendered. Naively enough they can't say yet what was in it. Perhaps they haven't quite finished writing it yet. At the end came the remarkable statement that the Führer's patience is again exhausted.

Well, that's that. I was so relieved that I gave Dora an extra kiss. Invasion seems at least a month further away and now it all depends on how the affair goes as to how likely an invasion will be at all, but we hadn't better think like that just yet.

Grand news tonight. A daylight sweep over France, as usual, this afternoon and the amazing score was twenty-seven Jerries to one of ours. We saw twelve Hurricanes go up from Martlesham about 7.15, probably to take part, so it gave us a personal interest in the business. They were Messerschmitt 109F planes, the new model. Probably all the 110s are on the Russian border.

TUESDAY 24 JUNE

News from the front is rather meagre, perhaps naturally. The Russians say that Jerry has been held in most places, that his drive has met with no success, and claim 300 German tanks destroyed, 128 planes shot down and 5,000 prisoners. They also admit the loss of Brest-Litovsk and two other towns.

Jerry, on the other hand, claims air superiority and land successes but merely satisfies himself with saying operations are going according to plan and successfully, without stating specific gains. Reading between the two I fancy that the Germans are not having it all their own way. I'm glad of that as it may win me a shilling. Green reckons it will all be over in three weeks and I countered by saying the Russians wouldn't be conquered by this time next year, so we compromised on Christmas with a shilling bet on it.

SUNDAY 29 JUNE
Let's talk about grub for a few minutes. Eggs are being rationed from, I believe, this week. It's a bit hazy and there was a little bother about it from which the government, in the guise of Lord Woolton, food controller, had to change its proposals. They said at first that all hen-keepers with more than twelve birds must sell their eggs to the authorities, to which the immediate reply came from the backyard producers that they would sooner kill off all their birds above twelve to save the bother. Wonderfully, the government heeded and changed it to all who own above fifty birds should sell to the authority after deducting a quantity of eggs for their own use, and that's been accepted with better grace.

Prices of foods are being controlled in some fresh cases. Tomatoes for instance. A little while ago they were selling for 4s per pound. Yesterday week they were 3s 6d, 3s and, later in the day, 2s 9d and the next day the controlled price came into effect of 1s 2d per pound. It caused a lot of concern to people like Day who have spent a lot of money on coke for heating the greenhouses in this foully cold spring, but after all 1s 2d isn't bad for a pound of tomatoes I suppose. The immediate result was that tomatoes went off the market, simply because the demand went up like a rocket and because, as a substitute for fruit, they are about the only thing available. Now we have another notice in most fruiterers' windows 'No tomatoes'. Strawberries too. They are now coming in and selling at 1s 10d but I hear that tomorrow they are controlled at 1s 2d as well.

There was no sugar allowance this spring for soft fruit jam, which is a darn shame. Our raspberries are coming on fine. They are, however, allowing double ration for all July for the stone fruit season. That comes to 2 lb extra per person total allowance. Dora should be able to make a little jam which is very laudable.

Meat is going up from 1s worth to 1s 2d per person from this week. They say that there is an extra large supply of Australian meat

in this country which suggests the *Bismarck* and that pocket
battleship we stopped were intended to do a bit of damage and
didn't.

A week's fighting between Germany and Russia has ended with
evidence of stronger Russian resistance than many people cared to
prophesy. Jerry has made advances towards Moscow but only there,
if anywhere, is he on Russian soil. Am now listening to the anthems.
Wonder if they <u>will</u> include the Red Flag? Now Russia is an ally I
suppose something must be done about it and many people are
wondering.

SUNDAY 6 JULY

Heavy raids on Germany again last night. This time we penetrated
to Magdeburg, Osnabrück and other places, one of them only
seventy miles from Berlin. That, considering it was a short night and
almost full moon and a clear sky, is very creditable. Magdeburg,
alone, had a heavy raid, the place being 'a mass of flame' and I guess
about 500 planes were used. We lost 3.

The daylight raids started almost as soon as the night ones
finished and we sank three patrol boats and a few supply ships off
the Dutch coast and then paid another visit to the factories at Lille.
Our losses were 2 bombers and 7 fighters. Jerries were 11 fighters
and a lot of factory and railway damage.

The Russian campaign has been on for a fortnight and we have
the peculiar effect of the newspapers assessing the progress and
comparing it with other campaigns as though a fortnight was a
long time. Suppose it is though, as the French were broken,
whacked and defeated in twelve days.

Jerry has gained the Baltic States and pushed the Russians out of
most of Poland but not Transylvania or Bessarabia although they
have occupied most of them. The panzer drive past Minsk to
Smolensk has been halted and there is not much of Russian
territory proper which is occupied, though there is much fighting.
The battlefield is huge, being 200 miles deep round Minsk. Being
halted there Jerry tried two other thrusts, one north towards
Leningrad, the other lower down towards the Ukraine. Both have
been checked and the Russians have now counter-attacked and
made some successes. One of the counters is 40 miles behind
Jerry's forward troops. In one part of Poland Jerry claims to have
surrounded about 160,000 Russians and annihilated them, while
Russia says they are still fighting. In the lower parts Jerry has been

a fortnight crossing the Dnieper, I believe, and losses have been huge. The Russians estimated Jerry's losses at 700,000 killed and wounded on Friday and say the carnage is such that that figure is being well increased now.

THURSDAY 10 JULY

Last Monday Roosevelt set the world talking. America moved into Iceland, setting free our troops 'for service elsewhere' and forestalling any possible Nazi move to establish bases there. Also they decided to patrol and guard the seaways to Iceland to ensure no interference with maintaining communications – in other words our goods will be convoyed from America to Iceland without the system actually being announced. We have only to see about them from Iceland, 500 miles or so. I begin to see what Roosevelt meant when he promised we should get the goods over.

Confusing news from Syria. Gen Dentz asked for an armistice on Tuesday but we don't know what his answer is to them. They are stubbornly defending Beirut and we sent an ultimatum to Dentz giving him till 5.30 a.m. today to declare Beirut an open city and get out, the idea being to save Syrian lives and property. No answer is known yet. A little while ago when he refused to make it an open city the Syrians said 'Why? You didn't bother to defend Paris!' It seems the campaign will soon be over thank goodness, two prongs are thrusting in from Iraq and making towards Aleppo and the pipeline to Beirut is mostly in our hands.

A lone Jerry paid us a visit at 4.00 yesterday morning. He dropped a bomb in Cecil Road, near the hospital, which didn't explode and one in Surrey Road which did. Quite near Aldy's dad, poor old chap. One man killed, ten injured, several houses uninhabitable.

I fancy he will be over again this evening. He's getting a bit more active, which is a success to us in drawing planes away from Russia.

THURSDAY 17 JULY

I'm almost wishing for an excuse to spend all the evening indoors so I can enter more of this diary. There's so much happening and developing now. Jerry says 9 million men are engaged in the fighting in Russia. Comment is that it's probably correct and that it is the biggest clash in history. In general Jerry is advancing slowly but at huge cost. He reckoned to be in Moscow in two or three weeks and he is a long way off, though reported to be near Smolensk. Russia claims to have knocked out 3,000 Jerry tanks.

The Japanese cabinet resigned yesterday. No reason given. Reports suggest Japan is contemplating forcing Vichy to grant her bases in Indo-China. Wonder what our reaction would be to that? Could we do any effective objecting to it?

THURSDAY 24 JULY
So much happening and so little opportunity recently for recording it.

Japan is reported moving troops north toward Siberia and is certainly extending influence southward. Vichy, the home of the dirtiest, white-livered scum in France, has given Japan permission to establish bases in Indo-China. It's near to the Dutch East Indies and the Philippines and Singapore.

We are still bombing western Germany heavily each night and raiding France most days. In France the fighter defence is strengthened and losses are a bit more even now, though yesterday's were 12 Jerries to 6 of ours. Incidentally it is a good sign that we are using Stirlings for day raids. I saw 2 on Monday evening and Hattersley saw 12 with 52 Spitfires as escort.

SUNDAY 27 JULY
The Russian battles are now five weeks old. The whole campaign is so huge, so vast, that I can't write a consecutive series of notes about them. I can't even absorb the scanty news items intelligently as one knows subconsciously that if Jerry claims an advance and the Russians claim a successful counter, they may both be right. The only thing we can do is to try to get away from the new news and form a perspective a few days after.

Doing that, it appears firstly that Jerry has either overestimated his strength or underestimated the Russians. Instead of being in Moscow in three weeks he has not penetrated far into Russia proper. There seem to be three main sectors, the central one a drive from Minsk to Moscow via Smolensk, the northern one parallel to the Baltic coast towards Leningrad, and the southern to Kiev and the Ukraine, and Stalin has appointed three generals to deal with them.

America is acting again, this time has placed the armed forces of the Philippines under American control, which means it is on a full war footing and is an outpost of America. Wonder if the Japs expected such actions? It seems only a matter of time before shooting starts. The Japs are losing a little face.

WEDNESDAY 6 AUGUST

Am writing this by the faint light of a bedroom lamp, keeping Ma company, poor old dear. At least, I hope it's faint as seen from outside. I haven't any blackout up, must have some air, and I hope the drawn curtains will be enough.

We made particularly heavy raids last night on Hamburg, Hanover and Karlsruhe, besides other smaller affairs. Jerry contents himself, touch wood, with sending very few planes over here. Since 10 May we've only had three sharp raids, two on Southampton and one on London as a reprisal for a Berlin raid. It suits us, of course, and means short alerts at night, when we do get them. Ipswich being near the east coast I suppose we get as many as any district. Altogether there have been about 500 alerts during the whole war, mostly in the last 12 months. Our outlook on alerts is far different from what it was 12 months ago. When the raids started we didn't know what was coming and there was a tendency, I fancy, for most districts to think themselves Most Important Districts. I well remember feeling a little thrilled (blast, there goes the damn siren, I thought there were a lot of planes about), a little dismayed and a little apprehensive last summer when we were told at a wardens' meeting that raids were expected to start in the near future and would probably be coming every night. That was about May, before France collapsed.

We certainly thrilled in those days to the sirens. Last night it went and I only vaguely heard it. Previously, at 10.45, I fancied it was a Jerry going over and got into bed and was asleep in very few minutes. Blasé and I hope we keep so. There are certainly plenty of fighters going up from Martlesham. Twin-engined most of them.

Rumour says *Warspite* has been sighted out Malaya way. Probably true.

SATURDAY 9 AUGUST

My vigil lasted till 5.20 when I crept out and went to bed. Poor thing, she just faded away at 1.45 p.m. the same day, Thursday the 7th, while I was home to dinner thank goodness. Incidentally it was just about the turn of the tide if that's worth anything. Don't know what made me think of it but I fancy it was something which put Henry V into my mind. If this were not a war diary I could spread myself on poor Ma and how I miss feeding her and how the poor dear suffered before she had morphia enough to dull everything. Thank goodness for morphia and thank goodness, much more, for friends. They pop up from everywhere it seems.

On the same day Mussolini lost his son, Bruno, in a flying accident. Tough on the poor old devil I suppose but he is, I believe, the cove who took an active part in the Abyssinian campaign and wrote a book on his experiences in which he described the 'sport' of bombing natives and seeing them blown to pieces 'opening up like a rose'. On that account I can't see Haile Selassie[4] sending a wreath.

They published the silhouettes of the Stirling in the *Spotter* this week and also give the Beaufighter top speed of 330 mph with 1,500 mile range at 200 mph.

Gen Dentz, the Syrian Vichy bloke, has been arrested with thirty-five cronies. The dirty tykes have dishonoured the armistice by holding back seventy-five of our officers taken prisoner during the campaign. The French are not cultivating an honourable name over this business.

TUESDAY 12 AUGUST
We buried Mother yesterday at 10 a.m. at the church. There are several things I shall never forget connected with it – the most impressive was the reception at the church on Sunday evening and the beautiful little service. Am afraid I was touched once or twice, the coffin looked so beautiful with the flowers smothering it and so many people were so obviously genuinely sorry and there was the dimmed light, the organ, Handel's 'Largo' and the dear old canon. Yesterday I didn't feel so bad until they played the 'Dead March' as we followed down the aisle. It was quite easy to imagine Mother inside the coffin as we followed. It rained heavily all the time and while we were at the cemetery. She's at peace and at rest now, thank goodness.

Tension is growing out East. Australia is saying the situation is critical and war is very near her shores. Japan is outwardly cool and unruffled and Thailand, which is threatened by Japan massing on her border, says she will fight if attacked and will not hesitate to use gas if necessary. America and Britain have warned Japan, who will naturally take no notice, so the stage is set for a very interesting and sanguinary flare-up. Those weak, contemptible Nazi-ridden Vichy French!

Jerry is making a huge thrust with a million men in the Ukraine and is making headway towards Odessa. A bit late though, as most of the harvest is in.

We put the clock back one of the hours Saturday night and now we blackout about 9 o'clock. It's horrible after those wonderful light nights. Never mind, we had 100 days of it so marvellously light. Let's hope it comes next year too.

TUESDAY 19 AUGUST
I don't like the way in which the news is preparing us for bad news from southern Russia. Jerry has captured Nikolayev, a naval base east of Odessa. Odessa is still being held but Jerry says he is heavily bombing naval attempts to evacuate the troops. Actually the main position is that Marshal Budenny has withdrawn his men, 400,000 of them, across the Dneiper.

If I had the foresight and the money I might have started a barbed wire factory before this war. They must be using hundreds of miles of it round or through Ipswich. It's a bit alarming to find the defence line runs along the railway cutting, well into the town, up our end. Lots of it is that coiled concertina stuff. It looks as though they think we shall see something of him, if Jerry comes at all.

SATURDAY 23 AUGUST
Most exciting. Saw two Beaufighters yesterday – my first.

For some time the government has been getting disturbed about the number of German 'tourists' which have gone to Iran. Several thousands went there and last week Russia made a protest to the Iran government about it. Sort of suggests we are much stronger to feel able to do that. It wasn't an ultimatum but near it and gave no time limit for an answer. The answer has now been received and, like the verbal predecessor of a few days ago, it is not very satisfactory. The text is not yet public but it does contain references to 'determination to resist aggression from any quarter', the phrase which is getting a bit worn by now. America considers war is inevitable out there and I shouldn't be surprised either. We have big interests out there and also, if Jerry gets southern Russia and occupies Iran, he has robbed us of an oil supply, has enveloped Turkey, Iraq and Syria, and is too near to India.

There is a tendency, taking the long view, for the Russian battle to appear improved. Germany has been publishing huge claims of Russian losses which are today refuted by Russia. She says that after two months of war her army is 'increasing' in strength and resistance. Suppose she should know.

A week ago Bader, the British pilot with false legs, had to force-land his Spitfire in France. He was written up a lot, being a wonderful bloke and squadron leader of a crack fighter squadron and had twenty confirmed victories. He damaged a leg on landing and I'm pleased to read that Jerry was sport enough to tell us and to offer uninterrupted passage to a plane carrying a new pair for him. This has been done. There are still some humane Jerries about.

TUESDAY 26 AUGUST

Another decisive step taken yesterday. I'm very glad to say we have been strong-purposed enough to invade Iran yesterday morning. Russia moved in over the Caucasus and we landed a party by sea, capturing seven Axis supply ships in the process, and crossed from Iraq as well. News is sparse but we are occupying oil refinery towns and are taking wheat from India for the population's use. Good propaganda.

A crisis has sprung up in Australia. Mr Menzies suggested coming to London for staff talks but wanted the Labour Party behind him, but they were not agreeable. He countered by suggesting a coalition but the LP suggested he should resign and make way for a Labour government. This they are considering.

Am thrilled. Saw a Tomahawk and a Mohawk this evening.

THURSDAY 28 AUGUST

Good news tonight. The Iranian government resigned yesterday, a new government was formed which has now ordered all resistance to us to cease to avoid bloodshed. Germans in Iran are reported to be in panic.

Yesterday came news that Laval and the chief of French Fascists were shot by an assassin or should I say 'a hero'. Today, news is he has a bullet in the liver, in the arm and under the heart. Seems serious.

SUNDAY 7 SEPTEMBER

A National Day of Prayer today. The Civil Defence Services have paraded at St Margaret's and the Home Guard is in the park. I went at 8 a.m. and Dora has just gone at 6.30.

Well, well! The spark was almost put to the powder magazine last Thursday, possibly it may even have ignited a slow fuse. News came that a Jerry submarine had attacked an American destroyer, the *Greer* about 450 miles south-west of Iceland. More than one attack was made and the destroyer retaliated with depth charges, with some measure of success they think 'cos the sub was logged as immediately below when they attacked. Roosevelt stated he had personally given orders to ships in the vicinity to hunt the sub and 'eliminate' it. Now Germany admits a U-boat made an attack on an unnamed destroyer, firing two torpedoes, but claimed the destroyer attacked first. On top of all that, the world was set agog at an announcement that Roosevelt will broadcast on an important, but unstated, subject tomorrow night.

These last few days have brought a succession of Admiralty reports of our submarine activities in the Mediterranean, where they have been playing about with Musso's shipping. Altogether two cruisers have been hit, two transport liners sunk, a tanker and several supply ships sunk and others damaged and sunk by aircraft. General opinion expects an offensive by us in the near future on the Jerries in Libya and Cyrenaica and these naval activities are a preamble. Hope we do mean business.

Saw a Whirlwind this afternoon and a high-wing plane which might have been a Botha but don't think it was. This summer has been a bit disappointing regarding the number of types of aircraft I've seen. It's probably because of the Russian battle and in that case I'm glad it is so but I certainly expected to see Typhoons and Tornados and Manchesters, etc. My total bag so far is a 3 and a 2 of Stirlings, a 10 and a 1 Whirlwinds, 2 and 1 Beaufighters, a Tomahawk, a Mohawk, a Martlet, a possible 2 110s, a Junkers 88 and what I thought was a Lockheed Lightning but turned out to be a Focke Wulf 189. Still, the autumn isn't over yet and something may be in store, though I hope it isn't.

SATURDAY 13 SEPTEMBER
Roosevelt made his promised statement on Thursday night, which was Friday morning here. Briefly he stated that, since the American destroyer *Greer* had been attacked and three cargo boats sunk and a battleship had been stalked by a submarine, he had given orders that the American navy is now to shoot first if any Axis subs or surface raiders were found in any waters where American ships have a right to trade and commerce, or indeed, where any other nations' ships were bringing American trade. He said too many neutral countries had hesitated to look the Axis menace in the eyes until it was too late and they had them by the throat, and America was not making that mistake.

Well, that puts America as near in the war as it's possible to be without actually declaring it. Her navy will now be fighting Jerry's, her aeroplanes are being used against him and, indeed, all her supplies too. By the end of the year she will be making one supply ship every two days.

Things are delicate in Russia. Jerry is attacking Leningrad and it is reported orders have been given to take it at any cost and they are attacking in that style. The city is almost besieged and surrounded but Voroshilov is countering with some success. The carnage is very heavy, the worst of any district the Russians say. Soon the winter will break out there so if Jerry doesn't force a capture, the troops will be in a state. At tea in the canteen the other day Rolfe was in his rather pessimistic strain about it, taking it as settled that Leningrad would fall so, without thinking, I had to reply with as much confidence as I could assume, that it would not fall. Hope I'm right.

In the centre Timoshenko's offensive is still on but slowing up while, a little lower down, Jerry has captured another town and is thrusting south-east towards Kiev, threatening the east bank of the Dnieper. On the other hand the Russians have crossed the Dnieper at four places and also Odessa is still holding out.

MONDAY 15 SEPTEMBER

Jerry appears ominously successful in the lower part of the Russian front. He is continuing his south-eastern thrust from Gomel and is threatening to encircle Kiev. He has also managed to establish a bridgehead on the east bank of the Dnieper so the usual pincer movement is developing. We have sent a complete air wing to Russia complete with personnel. Probably it's a fighter wing.

A few days ago Jerry claimed to have attacked an Atlantic convoy and sunk twenty-two ships. He usually exaggerates but I wondered what the truth was and it has been released. Attacks were made by U-boats and aircraft over 3 days and the subs sunk 3 and the aircraft 4 ships and one more floundered due to a gale. They also just missed a surface raider. I suppose we can't always have cruisers about but it was disappointing that only destroyers (only one mentioned) and a sloop were in protection.

On the other hand, Jerry and Musso find it necessary to provide as many escort ships as supply ships. Their convoys usually consist of six supply and six escort vessels. We have been attacking them again in the Mediterranean and off Norway, with suitable results.

Went to the hospital and donated a pint of blood to help win this war yesterday. No after effects and felt as fit as a fiddle today. One or two blokes passed out up there though I didn't see any. Too much imagination I fancy.

We are to be allowed to join the Home Guard but to be called on in that capacity only in the event of enemy action in this vicinity. Warden's work comes first. I'm joining. Dora doesn't mind, bless her heart. I'm in for a darn busy time this winter with senior warden's duties, the HG and one lecture each week and one each alternate Sundays, and then the control of the Fire Guard. Morrison mentioned the new Fire Guard in a weekend speech. I know I ought to feel interested and astonished at the wonderful organisation but somehow I'm not.

SATURDAY 27 SEPTEMBER

Was on the allotment this afternoon and saw the Hurricanes go out, followed by two Hurricane IIs with the prominent cannon. Later, eleven came back. Sort of brings war home to one. We heard on the news that we have made a daylight attack over France at Amiens and shot down 21 Jerries for 14 of ours with 3 pilots saved. The Mark IIs have been at Jerry's flak ships and minesweepers again, setting two on fire and damaging others. They must have a devastating effect on planes, the MG-type fires 14,400 bullets a minute. Coo!

This has been 'Tanks for Russia' week and the whole tank output has been allocated to Russian use. M Maisky, the Soviet ambassador, has just told us the week's output has been 10 per cent up on last week which was a record itself.

Have today been gathering in my main crop from the allotment. Have had about 4 or 4½ cwt of potatoes and not far off a cwt of main-crop carrots altogether. We sent some carrots, beans and tomatoes to the harvest festival at St John's. Somehow I felt awfully bucked at doing it. I've never done, never been able to do, that sort of thing before. Dora's idea; I hadn't even given it a thought.

SUNDAY 28 SEPTEMBER

Somehow I've a premonition we are going to hear some big news. Wonder if it's merely indigestion. Went out to tea to Win's this afternoon. (That in itself is big news.) We did not take our respirators, in fact they are not seen so much nowadays. At the beginning of the war everyone dutifully obeyed the government instructions to carry respirators. They didn't need the wardens' pleadings, their own imaginations and sense told them to, and we all took little cardboard boxes suspended from string and strung over our shoulders. Then various cases appeared and the cardboard was hidden, but in those first days Hitler had levelled us all to a common footing. By degrees they were left at home until, by now, only 20 per cent take them, excepting school kiddies who all take them. Naturally common sense says no gas will be used over here while Jerry has his hands full in Russia, so there is some reason.

We have three types: the civilian type which is light with the container hanging from the respirator itself; a civilian duty style which is similar but much heavier rubber; and the service type which has a face-piece connected by a tube to the container in a haversack. The common civilian has the first type, wardens the second and police, special police, Home Guard and soldiers the third. Wonder where gas will first be used?

FRIDAY 3 OCTOBER

Let's say something about the ladies in this war. On the whole I fancy their effort is a little more than last time. They are in the tram and bus services as conductors and making a good job of it; either the right type has been chosen for the job or they have adapted themselves well, but there is no fumbling or slowness and I must say that a girl with curls showing under her hat looks more of an asset to the tram than some of the men conductors.

Their biggest effort is, naturally, in the factories and Bevin has made such calls on the female population that they are all registered up to, I believe, twenty-five years of age and are called up for war work as men are for the Army. If eligible they are compelled to do a job either in the factories or the Services. Naturally some are unpatriotic enough to dodge it and get married for that purpose as it is reckoned that if a woman has a husband and home to look after, she can be exempt.

There are several branches of the Services, with various illustrative names, the NAAFI, the ATS, the WAAFs and others. They are doing work in photography in the Air Force, and predictors with the AA and, I fancy, with the radio-locators.

In the factories the different age has made a difference from the last war. This time they wear green overalls and there are lots of them in our Works, and it's pretty they look, except for one thing. The overalls are boiler-suit type with legs and they show off, or accentuate a little, the ladies' extra width across the hips. In other words their bottoms are more prominent and made even more so by high-heeled shoes. It seems ever so peculiar to see a large stern taper down to two one-inch heels.

On top of all this there is the multitudinous mixture of part-time jobs. Sewing for the Forces, canteen work, knitting work, and Miss Robinson was saying today she goes periodically to the YMCA, mending soldiers' socks and doing odd sewing jobs to their uniforms.

Yes, the women are doing quite a bit and, with the continual call-up of the men and raising the reservation ages, I can see women coming even more into the fore.

FRIDAY 10 OCTOBER
It's now been released officially that we are catapulting fighters from merchant ships in convoy to deal with planes like Kuriers. If the action takes place within 500 miles of land the fighter pilot makes for it, if further away he pancakes on the sea near his boat and hopes for the best. A darned good answer to air attacks. America says they are Hurricanes but there is no confirmation in England.

Last week the total of war savings reached £1,000 million. We have been holding an intensified savings campaign at work, aiming at £750 in twelve weeks to buy two ambulances. Actually we reached £1,141.

Excellent news this week from the Mediterranean. Our subs torpedoed eleven ships, four being certainly sunk, others almost certainly sunk and others damaged. Then the Air Force got jealous and attacked a convoy, torpedoing three more and probably sinking them. The drawback is that neither sub nor plane can hang about long to see results.

Have sent an article on height estimating to *Aeroplane* today. Wonder what luck? Shall be tickled if it sells.

Dora went and gave a pint of the best last Sunday.

TUESDAY 21 OCTOBER
Am a bit pleased. Went to the explanatory meeting last night at California Schools, where the Home Guard chiefs explained to us wardens the scheme whereby we could join. Am afraid I joined, am now looking forward to training in rifle, BLA, hand grenades, Northover projector and machine-guns. Quite candidly I think the whole thing is a bit of a plant but I am swallowing the bait quite willingly. The Home Guard is getting smaller and smaller; men are being called up and there are lots of slackers and I am pretty sure the authorities are trying it on with us, flogging the willing horse sort of style. Never mind, I always did think every man should be able to use a gun nowadays and here is the opportunity. All the

same I would like to gloat a little over some of the things achieved
and taken up during this war. I have done, am doing rather,
warden's work and have taken on the maid-of-all-work senior's job,
have taken up first aid, have become fairly efficient at plane
spotting, am digging for victory and, after all, am working on war
work, also have given blood at the hospital. Suppose I am doing a
bit now. Swank.

THURSDAY 23 OCTOBER
Jerry's drive on Moscow, though sustained, is slackening a little.
The Russians have been countering and Jerry has now switched to
the southern wing. He is attacking the Crimea through the
Perekop Isthmus and has pushed right along the north of the Sea
of Azov. Odessa was evacuated about a week or fortnight ago, the
men being used elsewhere. Timoshenko has been relieved of his
command of the Moscow front to take over some other area.
Rather interesting. The Moscow Conference is just over and
Wavell is back out East. Is there some mutual action being
prepared? Rumour says Jerry is massing ready for a thrust through
Turkey so it's quite likely Timoshenko and Wavell are hatching up
some counter between them. Good old boys.

Oranges are about now. They are distributing them by allowing
1 lb for a child's ration book (under five) for last week. This week
they surprised us by allowing 2 lb. It's a good sign to have oranges
about again even in those small quantities.

Generally speaking, though some foods are short, the whole
situation is good. Meat, sugar, butter and margarine, cooking fats,
eggs, bacon are all rationed, but we have not found any real
shortage yet. Naturally schemes are advertised for saving foods and
we are economising but the allotment, so far, has provided lots of
vegetables and we don't feel the lack of meat which still stands at
1s 2d worth per week. In fact I sometimes think the dishes we get
now are more delicious than before the war.

Some time ago we were asked to stock food for a fortnight's
supply. The condenser effect has enabled us to get over shortages,
for instance breakfast cereals are a bit scarce. Eggs vary from one
per month to about two. Now kiddies under five can have four this
month, but eggs never did worry me. We have been out gathering
hips from the hedges and Dora has made a syrup '15 to 20 times
as rich in vitamin C as orange juice' for the kiddies. Dora cuts fat
off the meat, boils it down, and makes cooking fat. Wheatmeal

flour is common now and she makes the bread half that and half stone-milled flour, the result being the most delicious bread ever. The only thing wrong with it is it won't keep.

We recently changed our suppliers from the Co-op to a small personal shop. The service is better and supplies more regular and ample, reason being a large concern is just too large to obtain supplies adequately in these times.

SUNDAY 2 NOVEMBER
An interesting experiment in food rationing announced today. On 17 November we will be rationed for canned meat, fish and beans. We are to be issued with coupons which we collect ourselves (the government decided, wisely, to economise on clerical staff and postal services) and we can spend 16 coupons per month per head. One pound of meat will take 16 coupons, such fish as herrings 12 coupons, home produced meat 8 and beans 4. The big thing is that we may shop anywhere, the idea being to bring back competition to shops and as a shopkeeper will be able to restock according to coupons he holds, it will pay him to attract custom. The idea may spread to other foods later if workable. America has been sending us all the stuff and we are distributing to the shops by 17 November 35 million lb of meat, 35 million of fish and 12 million of beans, all in addition to present ration of meat and other foods.

Germany has suddenly reopened the attacks by submarine on the American destroyers, saying the destroyers attacked first. It is suggested in the *Express* that they are trying to invoke the Tripartite Treaty with Japan and Italy under which any attack on any of the three will bring the others to their assistance, thereby inviting Japan to try conclusions with America.

TUESDAY 4 NOVEMBER
Haven't said much about Russia lately. The position now is that there is an effort to get Finland out of the war. Roosevelt has asked her to do so; if she doesn't she will incur the displeasure of America. This is immediately after Russia asked that we should declare war on Finland, Roumania and Bulgaria.

Leningrad is still holding and countering the German attacks. Moscow holds out too and 200,000 men have just arrived from special winter training. Jerry keeps making vicious thrusts to encircle the place but so far his thrusts have been stopped. Germany, however, shows signs of renewing attacks heavily soon.

In the south, Jerry has forced an entry into Crimea and is now overrunning the place, Sevastopol looks like being a loss. It is in this direction he is making most progress, after oil probably. He has traversed the north shore of the Sea of Azov but is held at Rostov, so far, that place being the terminus of one pipeline from the Caucasus.

Things are serious down there. If he gets down the east coast of the Black Sea the oil will be in sight and our supply line from Iran will be severed. However, Timoshenko has made a new defence line running north-east from Rostov and it will be seen how effective that is.

A sidelight on the situation is that the biggest convoy the Navy has ever guarded has arrived at Archangel, some of the contents being aircraft and airmen. Also I heard a pointer at work on the spring tank programme and it appears to be fairly reasonable.

Bevin is still driving for manpower. His latest is that women between twenty and thirty who are in full-time voluntary work, except Civil Defence, must leave to take up war work, probably in factories.

Jerry has torpedoed another American ship, a tanker this time, off Iceland. She made port however.

Later. News that our submarines in the Mediterranean have sunk 6 more supply ships and torpedoed 4 others, 2 of which were armed merchant cruisers. Poor old Musso. Some were troop transports.

THURSDAY 13 NOVEMBER

Signed up with the Home Guard today. The paper, I noticed, definitely said we, as Civil Defence men, were only to be called on in the event of enemy activity in the immediate locality. Well, I'm in it now. First parade tomorrow night and equipment probably next week.

Churchill opened Parliament yesterday with a speech containing a few facts. He said our shipping losses for March, April, May and June averaged 500,000 tons. For July, August, September and October they averaged 180,000 tons a month, a respectable reduction just when one would have expected an increase. Estimates say Jerry keeps 100 or 200 subs at sea.

Rather tense events in America tonight. They are taking the final vote, or something, on the repeal of the Neutrality Act. It's illustrative of the way in which things may swing completely round in wartime. A few days ago it seemed certain that the repeal would go through. Jerry has been playing about with Uncle Sam's shipping,

even the Isolationists have been favourable and calling for real help
to us and Russia. Now there are big strikes threatening in the coal
mines, in steel works and in aircraft factories and the opinion is that
unless Roosevelt takes, or promises to take, a strong hand with these
labour troubles, the senators will feel that this repeal will bring them
nearer to war without the very necessary labour support to provide
munitions. We should hear the result tomorrow morning, so I guess
I shan't miss the 8 o'clock news bulletin.

FRIDAY 14 NOVEMBER
The Neutrality Act was repealed by 212 votes to 194. A close shave
but good enough. All that's wanted now is the President's signature
which should be given on Monday. So now all the shipyards are
ready, and have possibly started to arm the merchant ships.

This is not so good. *Ark Royal* is at last sunk. Am very sorry to
hear it but it is the fortune of war. She has led the Jerries a dance
and must hold the record for number of times 'sunk'. Early in the
war she suffered a near miss from a bomb and Jerry claimed she was
sunk and even decorated the pilot responsible. After that she was
claimed again about every six months and at last some Wop has
torpedoed her from a submarine. Curiously we gave the news before
Jerry claimed it, which suggests the sub responsible was duly sunk.
She sank while in tow, having the opportunity to save most of the
crew. A fine ship gone. May she be speedily replaced.

SATURDAY 15 NOVEMBER
Went to first HG lecture last night. Thought it was a little
elementary at first but changed my mind later. We went over the
names of all the parts of the rifle and then discussed cleaning.
Tomorrow we go on parade. Major Barnard said we were to learn
how to form threes and march in case the war was over before we
finished our course, and we had to go in the peace parade. Some
hopes, I'm afraid.

Good news tonight that only one was lost off the *Ark Royal*. The
poor old lady went down eventually only 25 miles from Gibraltar
which was really bad luck.

SUNDAY 16 NOVEMBER
Went for my first day's parade in the HG today. We did 1½ hours'
marching and absorbing parade ground information and I
thoroughly enjoyed myself. I wanted to giggle at first but that soon

passed and I found myself taking it as seriously as the others, swinging the arms, pushing out the chest and holding the head up as though we were eighteen year olds. There were thirty of us and although we could have kept better time and finished up with straighter lines, Major Barnard said he was very pleased with us. I must say we did manage a certain amount of snap in the movements. Am looking forward to Sunday week.

We have had a windy and wet day since midday, a really miserable looking day. We also had an alert for nearly two hours – Jerry reconnoitring I suppose. I expected heavy raids before now but, touching wood, they haven't materialised yet. The casualties for October were 262 dead and 300-odd injured, compared with over 6,000 killed last October. Have been on 10 to 2 this week but the weather has been bad and have not had to turn out at all.

THURSDAY 20 NOVEMBER
A ripping piece of news this morning. On Tuesday at daybreak we again advanced into Cyrenaica. Not a raid this time, it's grim earnest and fight like hell. I'll bet those chaps are putting their backs into it too, the first time we have met Jerry on an equal footing in this war and I guess they will do their very best, whatever the outcome is.

There is very little definite news beyond the fact that it has all started. Control says the action is very like a sea war with wireless silence, but I shouldn't be surprised at a thrust straight to relieve Tobruk and cut off Jerry in Bardia and Hellfire Pass. Should have news by tomorrow though. Interesting that we have Beaufighters there; it indicates we have plenty.

Like old times on Tuesday evening. Jerry came from Harwich way where they plastered him, then again from Nacton where we saw the old familiar rows of red tracer going up and he suddenly roared over here, low down, about 1,000 ft or less. I thought the docks would get it but he oozed off without dropping anything.

SUNDAY 23 NOVEMBER
There's been a sort of quiet excitement these last few days. The Army is fighting in Cyrenaica and we all want to know how it is getting on. Every news-time we tune in to see what's for us, we dash home just a minute early to get there before the 1 o'clock, but only now and then do the bulletins come through. Through it all is a realisation, I think, that this is a testing ground and a decisive

part of the course of the war. If we lose this action we shall never win any but if we win we are well on the way to Jerry's downfall.

So far our confidence seems well placed. On Friday night came news that the tank action has been joined, the Wops losing 57 and Jerry a total of 130. Then we were 10 miles from Tobruk and Rommel was cut off. Our avowed aim was not to gain territory but to destroy every German tank in North Africa and to cause as much loss as possible to their personnel, and by Jove! we seem to be keeping to it. We haven't even bothered to relieve Tobruk but on the other hand tanks have been landed there and the garrison are rallying to help the main army.

The position now is that Rommel's force has been treated to our version of the German blitz tactics. We penetrated to behind his lines, aiming at Tobruk, and cut him off around Sollum, Bardia, etc. and now have penetrated his lines at several points and cut his force into four areas which are still being attacked. An estimate states he has lost a third to a half of the Axis tanks in North Africa. Our losses are about one-third of his and today we hear we have captured Bardia.

In spite of the cold Jerry has launched a heavy thrust on Moscow and the Russians have been compelled to give a little ground. Jerry now claims to have captured Rostov in the thrust in the south. Wonder what his losses are? Must be getting on to the 5 million mark.

Dennis came round today. He is LAC now which isn't bad considering he joined up at the end of July. Now he is going to Stranraer for flying training in Bothas.

SATURDAY 29 NOVEMBER
Tanks and troops massing for further battles in Libya, and rumours that gliders and boats are assembling in Crete and Greece, presumably for reinforcing Rommel.

We are to have exciting times next weekend. The district is being 'invaded' and all services are to take part in the exercises – HG, Army, wardens, police, first-aid services, etc. Even the public has been asked to cooperate by acting as casualties. It is to last from 1400 hr on Saturday till dusk Sunday, a total of 28 hours, and things will be happening all the while.

Should have recorded that Gonder surrendered on Thursday. There were still 10,000 of them left. So closes the Abyssinian affair and so ends Musso's central African empire. Let's hope the North African empire will soon follow suit.

SUNDAY 30 NOVEMBER

Tigris and *Trident* have been covering themselves with glory. News has just been published that they sank, between them, 8 ships carrying troops or supplies and damaged 6 others (4 probably sunk) off the north of Norway, round Murmansk way. My dehumidifiers weren't used there for dehumidifying, I'll bet. Good gals.

There's more behind the Far Eastern question than we are allowed to know. The talks still go on in Washington but this weekend Manila was blacked out as a precautionary measure, leave and shore leave were cancelled at Singapore last night, reinforcements have again been landed there. Lord Halifax cancelled a tour of ordnance factories to return to Washington to talk about Japan, Japan has started bombing the Burma Road and the Jap prime minister speaks of purging hostile nations from Eastern Asia. It is all set for a helluva scrap.

Went Christmas shopping yesterday with Dora and the kiddies. The use of wrapping paper has recently been forbidden so we returned home with all sorts of things unwrapped in baskets. Luckily we were able to hide two stockings in a big paper bag without the kiddies seeing them. Toys were very difficult. There seems a fair supply of books and cut-out toys and box games but poor little Godfrey seems sentenced to go without the motor car he wants. Metal toys are practically non-existent. Footmans had two motor cars with clockwork such as they used to put on penny toys, priced 4s 6d. We didn't buy. Prices are high generally, but chiefly on paper goods. I wanted a calendar for Ven and the one I wanted, not too splash, was 6s 3d, pre-war would have been about 2s 6d. Purchase tax accounts for some of it I know, but it seemed excessive. On the other hand electric torches were little above old prices, so were things like ball-sets, but I wish I could have bought a railway train for my boy.

WEDNESDAY 3 DECEMBER

People are getting a little dissatisfied over the Libyan campaign. On Friday Rommel bunched his tanks together and drove at the corridor we had established from Tobruk to the forces south of it and at the same time his troops to the west drove in the same place. The result was they pierced our corridor and took Sidi Rezegh which we had captured. Suppose we can't expect everything to go all our way but after our high hopes of whacking Jerry now we have equal equipment it's a bit disturbing. Actually the wireless news is a very mixed blessing. If we had to wait a few days before getting news we wouldn't be so impatient. Anyhow we simply <u>must</u> win this little scrap or the results, and the inferences, will be tremendously ominous.

Went to headquarters and collected my equipment last night and came home with rifle, bayonet, haversack and odds and ends, respirator, trousers, blouse, greatcoat, forage cap, badge, boots and anklets, all on my bike. It was foggy too, to make matters more pleasant, but perhaps it helped to conceal me. It's all second-hand, I fancy, but can't expect anything else. The rifle seems a decent one and that's the chief item.

Churchill spoke in Parliament yesterday and introduced new conscription measures. The upper age limit will be 50 instead of 41, the older men going to Civil Defence, and the lower limit will be 18½ with all youths of 16 being registered. Reservations will be on the individual and the job he is doing and not on class of occupation, and the existing scheme of age reservation will be advanced one year per month in the new year. Also all single women of 20 to 30 are to register. They want a certain amount of labour and mean to have it.

Prince of Wales and another, possibly *Malaya*, with escort have arrived at Singapore.

SUNDAY 7 DECEMBER

A wealth of news items. Wonder if I shall report them all or fall asleep?

At 1 a.m. we were in a state of war with Finland, Roumania and Hungary. It was so expected that the occurrence has passed almost unnoticed in the papers. It is possible too that a feeling of regret at becoming official enemies with a people with whom we were willing to take up arms only a short while ago makes us unwilling to notice it too much publicly. All the same we are now free from an embarrassing situation regarding the restoration of the territory Russia took in early 1940.

Situation out East is rather more tense. I fancy the talks have broken down and today it is announced that Roosevelt is appealing personally to the Mikado, which suggests a last appeal to reason. If so, am afraid I can't see it coming off and then what? Hope we haven't underestimated out there too.

Well, our looked-forward to exercise has ended. The invader eventually captured the town, I fancy, but not until the Home Guard let them through, having decided to go home for a rest. My only informant is Reg Thrower, who is very tired but supremely happy and pleased with himself and his comrades, so I must reserve final summary.

The official title of the Exercise was 'Scorch' and Ipswich was attacked by the enemy distinguished by a yellow St George's cross on hats and vehicles. The town was only defended by Home Guard in our district anyway and all we saw were yellow crosses, and no white ones which were British troops.

We manned our post at 1400 hr and saw a party of HG man the air raid shelter at the side of it. Lysanders started to drone over. They were to drop parachute containers each representing thirty parachutists but I saw none dropped. Six Tomahawks then went south-west. They were to be dive-bombers but they disappeared without doing any.

Maun had given us an inkling of where our incidents were to be and at 1640 they started. So did the actual invasion. Bren carriers and lorries came into view and went by, preceded by motor cyclists, and the reports came in from the incidents. I was the mutt at the telephone and missed a little fun. I got the first report through the report centre and had to wait 32 minutes before finding the six available lines disengaged and had express reports waiting too. While hanging on I heard the police had nobbled a fifth-columnist officer and had arrested him. He yelled to two passing carriers who rescued him firing blank rifle shots. The police tried to truncheon one stopped carrier and I could stand the other chaps' comments no longer. I dropped the damn phone, and my sense of duty, and had a glimpse in time to see the police attack repelled by rifle and revolver fire. One poor devil had a blank charge in the eye at about 1 ft range, and came to our post half-blinded.

The carrier passed, reports came in and eventually I got through to report centre. That seems a weakness which has been shown up very well. They must have more than six lines to deal with a blitz. I think there were 800 incidents over the whole weekend.

I came home to tea at 1715 hr and returned at 1800 hr to find the post surrounded, the enemy in charge and established at the Royal George, sentries along Sidegate Lane and Colchester Road with Brens in gateways and a soup kitchen in Bertie Beechener's driveway. Our phone was officially out of order so we were instructed to man the post with two wardens till further instructions and discharge the others.

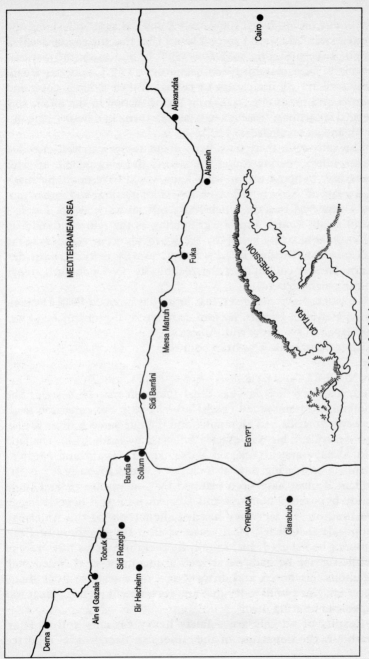

North Africa

Was due on again at 1400 hr but found the post locked and the exercise over, and wasn't sorry. I heard later that the enemy actually captured the post after we left at 0800 hr and made the wardens prisoners, even marching one over from along Colchester Road. They couldn't get out except by taking off their denims, coats and helmets and promising to take no further action in the affair, so I escaped something. Wasn't sorry, having spent 11½ hours there out of 20, and was real glad of a bath.

This afternoon there have been about twelve carriers, crowded with soldiers, tearing round the streets shooting people up with blank fire. Suppose that is what Jerry would have done. So that's all we saw of 'Scorch' exercises. It was interesting, and rather fun, but I expected to have much more official work to do. I didn't patrol at all, though I'm not grumbling as the rain continued till about 0600 hr. Have heard the breakthrough occurred because the HG out Woodbridge Road way was mostly working Saturday afternoon and couldn't get the roadblocks up. Upon such things do campaigns depend.

9 o'clock. News just given that Japan has bombed Pearl Harbour in the Hawaiian Islands. By tomorrow we shall probably be at war with Japan in sympathy with America.

Later. Manila has also been bombed.

MONDAY 8 DECEMBER
Well, it's started. Japan has done things in true Nazi style. She bombed and bombarded Pearl Harbour, sank two American ships between America and Honolulu, and then declared war on Britain and America. This was quickly followed by landings in Thailand and Malaya and attacks on Wake Island, Guam and Midway Island. Considering this all took place simultaneously it's pretty evident it must have been planned days or weeks ago and those ruddy hypocrites Nomura and Kurusu were still negotiating in Washington. In fact they handed their reply to the American proposals to Cordell Hull an hour after the bombing of Pearl Harbour had started. Incidentally he told them in his fifty years of public service he had 'never seen a document so crowded with infamous falsehoods and distortions – on a scale so huge that I never imagined until today that any government on this planet was capable of uttering them'.

Results of all this are a fairly heavy casualty roll at Pearl Harbour, the departure of the American fleet to sea, reported sinking of one of the Jap carriers which did the bombing and four of their subs, but it's only reported. Tonight comes the news that they must have had some success in Thailand as the fighting has ceased and negotiations will be commenced.

Wonder what the result will be and when? Some opinions in the papers are that Japan may be committing suicide. At first sight that seems the most likely result and I hope it is the correct one. Japan is the most dependent nation on outside supplies and a blockade should produce results. Her navy is smaller in size than the American and British Pacific Fleet, but one mustn't forget that the Americans have Atlantic commitments and that Japan will be fighting at home. I can't see clearly what I think the course of events will be. I have an idea that *Prince of Wales* has *Duke of York* as her companion and I rather incline to back them against Japan's new 45,000-tonners. It will be a naval war, naturally, so America's seventeen new battleships will grow very rapidly I guess. I believe it is eleven of them which will be 45,000 tons and some have whispered that some will even be 58,000 tons. Yes, it will be a naval war alright.

Tonight we heard Roosevelt's declaration relayed, marvellously clearly, from Washington. It was simple, direct and short but the drama and dignity of it was rather spoiled by some Congressmen showing their approval by whistling like cockneys at the theatre. Tonight Churchill will broadcast.

9 o'clock. Have just heard Churchill, who covered the events until the reply declaration by America and us. He spoke confidently but warned us against over-optimism.

Casualties at Pearl Harbour are higher than previously reported. They amount to 3,000, nearly half being killed. An old battleship, *Oklahoma*, and a destroyer were sunk and others damaged. They certainly attacked heavily.

WEDNESDAY 10 DECEMBER

Bad news. *Prince of Wales* and *Repulse* have been sunk off the Malayan coast. Details are not yet to hand but the Japs claim they were sunk by air action. If that is so it is certainly an achievement and they deserve all credit for it, but one must wait for further information before making or passing an opinion. It seems, however, that my query of whether we have underrated them had a certain amount of foundation.

THURSDAY 11 DECEMBER
News today just a little better. There are 2,000 survivors from *Prince of Wales* and *Repulse*. Americans claim to have bombed a Jap battleship and set it afire, though probably not seriously. We seem to have pretty well cleaned up the Tobruk area of Libya and the Russians are still advancing in the north and south ends of their Leningrad-Rostov line. To round things off Germany and Italy have declared war on America. I suppose the American reply will come soon.

The loss of those two ships has caused a big stir and lots of concern in the country. Undoubtedly it is a heavy blow and now everyone is waiting, with some underlying apprehension for our revenge to be announced. *Prince of Wales* was the pride of our Fleet and for her to be sunk by a nation like Japan in the opening days of the war, and by air attack too, makes one wonder just what we are up against and hope that it doesn't occur again. In the extreme, if Japan is using suicide squads, one can almost imagine the control of the Pacific passing completely into her hands. Heaven forbid. Well, we've taken knocks before so I suppose we can take this one. If it has the effect of instilling even more grit and determination into us and the Americans it will have done something.

I wonder what the Isolationists in America are thinking to it all. What ostriches they have been! Thank goodness Roosevelt was able to see the light and act as he has done. He has had 18 months high-class experience in armaments production by helping us and that in itself should be sufficient recompense for the goods they have sent under the Lease and Lend Act. Let's hope they make good use of that experience.

9 o'clock. The survivors from *Prince of Wales* and *Repulse* now number 2,300. The attack was apparently made while engaged with Jap transports. Three high-level attacks were followed by three torpedo low-level attacks, each of nine planes. A Jap battleship is sunk, so is a cruiser and a destroyer, so we are a bit repaid.

America has duly declared war on Germany and Italy. At last their Congress is united, the votes being absolutely unanimous. Once more Hitler has found documents, this time saying that Roosevelt has been ceaselessly working for war since 1939. What fools they must think we are.

SUNDAY 21 DECEMBER
A week without an entry! As excuse am working till 11.30 each night on Margaret's dolls' house. Such a lot to enter.

Went on a Home Guard route march this morning. As Civil Defence section we had an invite to turn out with the others but am afraid I was the only one. It was a frosty morning and I thoroughly enjoyed myself. We went about six miles round Tuddenham way and on the way took cover a few times from attacking aircraft, which had to be imagined as there were none of ours about, fired from cover at the enemy in Rushmere Wood and then exterminated an MG post in Wright's Farm. It was rather fun trespassing over the railway line and climbing embankments while encircling the farm. I learnt quite a lot and there was a different atmosphere from lectures, while out with the 'regulars'. It was a case of doing something because it was ordered rather than trying something out as an exercise and I fancy I didn't do too badly.

There is a certain amount to attend to in spare time. Buttons must be cleaned, rifle kept clean, and it's amazing how dirt gets into the barrel even though tucked up in the corner of the room. Haven't yet had a chance to clean my respirator haversack, indeed only bought the cleaner yesterday. I expected to find the regulation Army boots rather heavy but it is not so. They are second-hand: being reserves, naturally, all our stuff is second-hand, but there is virtue in that as they are already broken in. I had no trouble this morning with them.

MONDAY 29 DECEMBER
For the third time the Christmas period has been free from air raids on either side. One Jerry did some machine-gunning on the east coast on Christmas Day but otherwise we all kept at home. I don't think it was because of bad weather, though one can't judge all Europe's weather from one's own, but Saturday evening was wonderfully clear and sure enough I heard the Wellingtons droning over going Ruhr-wards.

Yesterday morning was cold, darned cold, but fine after the first fall of snow this season. Turned up to parade for HG and they ordered 'greatcoats off', gave us 20-min drill on the field then a route march through Tuddenham and back, about seven miles. Having been the week before as well I felt an old-stager to the other fellows and was quite superior to the two who were moaning about their heels. One vowed he would take off his boots when he got home, even before his respirator. This week we started BLA instruction and, last Monday, had our test on musketry. Lt Cotton took us and, like the Bliss bloke the week before, kept plugging

away at the inefficient ones with the result, I'm afraid, we made a
rather poor show. One chap didn't even remember using hot water
to clean a rifle after firing. With the honour of the class at stake
when they asked for a volunteer to demonstrate 'lying load' I
sacrificed myself and got through with the comment 'Quite good,
except he moved about enough to be seen at 1,000 yards'. I did, to
keep my eye on him, but I did not move when firing. I know there
were at least half of us who could have answered 95 per cent of his
questions, but we were just not asked. However there's always the
future, perhaps we can shine better at the BLA.

We seem a keen crowd, quite enthusiastic and nearly as smart as
the regulars. We were, naturally, the rear platoon on the route
march yesterday, and Nos 9 and 10 were on the parade ground
when we arrived back, and I think most of us were conscious of
critical eyes as we marched to our place and did our best to appear
smart, in spite of tired thighs from keeping legs continually tensed
against slipping on the everlasting ice on the roads.

Those Japs seem to be having things mostly all their own way.
They have now landed on Sumatra and Sarawak and reinforced
their troops on the Philippines, using eighty transports in one
concentration. Sometime the Americans may perhaps do
something about it. Manila was declared an open town to prevent
unnecessary civilian injuries last week. The Japs replied by
bombing it heavily, and at leisure, there being no defences.

WEDNESDAY 31 DECEMBER
The Russians have given us good news today. They have recrossed
into Crimea and recaptured Kerch and Theodosia about fifty miles
along the coast, the object being to relieve Sevastopol and possibly
to make Jerry retire along the north of the Sea of Azov by
threatening his rear.

Jerry is excusing himself for retreating by blaming the weather
and is conducting a big campaign at home, asking the people to
give up all the winter clothing they can to send to the front. No
doubt the Russians have the better of them regarding winter
clothing; they always have to dress for extreme cold. Captured
Germans have been found wearing even women's silk undies and
fur coats. That fact itself shows how badly Jerry estimated the
Russian strength and how he reckoned he would have conquered
all he wanted before winter.

NOTES

1   Amy Mollison Johnson, famous pre-war flier, and holder of many records.
2   General Georges Catroux, senior Free French officer in North Africa.
3   Admiral Jean Darlan, pro-Vichy French Minister of Marine. He was later held responsible for the destruction of most of the French fleet.
4   Haile Selassie, Emperor of Abyssinia (later Ethiopia), forced into exile when his country was conquered by the Italians in 1936 in spite of inept attempts by the League of Nations to prevent it. He spent his exile in Britain, returning to Abyssinia in triumph five years later.

1942

*Probably the worst Christmas of the war for bad news was followed by
an equally calamitous New Year. The Japanese swept all before
them and were soon to capture the supposedly impregnable Singapore
with horrendous consequences for the 60,000 Allied troops and
thousands of civilians caught in the trap. Japanese forces soon
established themselves in Java, Burma, the Philippines, New Guinea
and most of the islands between before their advance to Australia was
halted by the mighty naval engagements of the Coral Sea and Midway
in early summer.*

*Meanwhile, the see-saw battle in the western desert continued and
Commonwealth forces were flung back into Egypt to El Alamein only
forty miles from Alexandria. The depression cast across the British Isles
by this news was further deepened by the disclosure that a reconnaissance
raid on Dieppe by mainly Canadian troops had gone badly wrong and
resulted in many casualties.*

Earlier, in February, the German cruisers Scharnhorst, Gneisenau
and Prinz Eugen *stole out of Brest, where they had been effectively
trapped for a year, and headed for home.*

*In the air, however, Bomber Command – lately joined by the USAAF
– was doing much better and in May it launched the first 1,000-bomber
raid, the attack on Cologne. This provoked retaliatory missions by the
Luftwaffe who attacked in strength one English city at a time as selected
from the famous Baedeker travel guides.*

*Invasion was still a possibility in the early months of 1942, the news
from the fronts was not good and Richard Brown was stretched to the
limit, juggling the various demands of ARP and the Home Guard with a
full-time job. Constantly disturbed nights compounded the mounting
tension as did family worries. Richard Brown echoed the words of most of
Britain's population when he admitted to being very tired and sometimes
'jumpy'. In August after weeks of waiting for some kind of definite sign
about the way the war was going he wrote, 'I have an idea that when we*

look back some time hence, this period will be regarded as a sort of transition or waiting period'.

But the wait was nearly over. General Bernard Montgomery chose 23 October to launch his counter-attack from a spot in the desert which was to become one of the great turning points of the Second World War – El Alamein. This time there was no repeat of June's setbacks. This time it was Field Marshal Erwin Rommel who was forced to retreat. The church bells rang out and Churchill announced it to be 'the end of the beginning'. The news of Operation Torch, the Allied landings on the coasts of Algeria and Morocco, was the icing on the cake.

SUNDAY 4 JANUARY

Wonder what 1942 has in store for us? I can make no prophecy at all, the tendencies and indications are all so vague and big developments may take place so suddenly and alter the whole course of the war that it would be foolish for a misinformed bloke like me to attempt it. If I knew each nation's possession of arms it would be different. I do, however, feel the year will bring no large-scale offensive because Churchill has billed it for 1943. The chief point one wonders over is the ever-threatening invasion attempt. They keep telling us that Jerry has sufficient forces for it and that he will probably make it in the spring; they quote the huge fleet of gliders and transports he is building, and say it can only be for one purpose.

If it does come I must confess I have a preference to keep the wife and kiddies here in Ipswich. With Jerry invading, nowhere is safe and I might be able to keep an eye on them. That's a selfish outlook I know but the thought of them pushed about over this inhospitable country is not pleasant either. People don't take in evacuees from love and pity but only for what they can make out of it. There are exceptions but not many where kiddies of Godfrey's age are concerned. Well, well, let's hope it doesn't come, though if it does thank goodness I am taking an active part. Even if I don't come through it I shall have done all I could and I would rather do something than come through this war with the thought that all those in the HG had volunteered and fought for me and I'd done nothing to help. Fortunately it seems now that I may be of use. We have started BLA instruction now. About four more weeks and we go on to the tommy-gun. We are getting on, slowly.

SUNDAY 11 JANUARY

Saw a Spitfire yesterday and that's rare enough lately to deserve comment. Sinclair has told us that the weather recently has been the worst for fifteen years as regards flying and certainly we've seen very few planes round here. Today we've had our first heavy snowfall. It's still at it and from a south-easterly wind too, so I guess flying is still off the menu.

Talking raids, last week we paid five successive night visits to Brest and sometimes Cherbourg to let *Scharnhorst*, *Gneisenau* and *Prinz Eugen* know we haven't forgotten them. Hope they were hit well and proper.

In Russia the Russians are still chasing Jerry who has now abandoned his previously stated intention to establish a winter line and says the war has reverted to one of movement. Jerry is in force in Mozhaysk, in front of Moscow, and the Russians are playing the Jerry game by making a huge pincer movement round it. Looks like succeeding too while the general offensive is taking place all along the front. Did I report that in this offensive ever since 8 December when it started, the Russians make very little mention of prisoners. If reports of what they have found in places like Rostov where Jerry has executed civilians and left them hanging as warning, are true I guess there won't be any prisoners either.

Have been to Chatham on *Taku* to investigate a dehumidifier modification. They certainly know how to pack machinery on those subs, but I suppose that when analysed each main or pipe can be found to be just what was necessary and installed in a perfectly orderly manner. There were only two destroyers in the docks, an American and a Tribal, and I saw little of interest. It was again a little difficult to get past the bobby on the station and the guard at the dock gates which I think was gratifying.

Saw quite a bit of damage in London going from Liverpool Street to London Bridge by road. The bombs used were no lightweight, judging from the huge buildings completely blown out leaving only a shell of walls half standing. Coming from Liverpool Street to Ipswich, too, there were whole blocks of houses in the slum district completely empty and damaged, but not razed flat, and several factories, smallish ones, just empty shells with hardly any walls left.

Spent an hour last night sewing on flashes to my tunic and greatcoat, while Dora was knitting me some khaki socks, so today I went on parade resplendent in HOME GUARD in brilliant yellow flashes on my greatcoat. We did two hours' squad drill and field drill on a frozen playing field. I didn't know my rifle was so heavy.

WEDNESDAY 21 JANUARY

There is an alert on just now; it went while I was at Win's. Saw one or two white flashes, presumably bombs, out Felixstowe way and heard some 'wunks' presumably gunfire. I must own to a certain feeling of apprehension just lately when the alert goes, due, I fancy, to a consciousness of the reduced activity of recent months, the probability that the lull will end some time and the possibility that that time has now arrived each time it goes. Jerry drops in on some unlucky town now and then, plasters it from a few planes and clears off with all the immunity enjoyed by the lone hit-and-run raider. Sometimes he is brought down but not often. Last Saturday Lowestoft caught it. It was a dull afternoon and rumour says the shop windows were alight, it being before blackout, making a good target. Happily a crash warning had sent many assistants to shelter but there were fifty-five deaths besides a café containing about sixty naval men which had a direct hit. Some say Woolworths, others Boots, also Hills and Steels and Marks & Spencer were flattened.

This light business should be ruled out completely. Here in Ipswich they do the same thing. Coming home about 5.45 one sees many shop windows blazing in the twilight as though the advertisement value were enormous.

Last night, I hear, Felixstowe copped a packet. If it is there again tonight they'll be getting a bit fed-up.

Mozhaysk is fallen, am glad to report. The paper says the Russians pushed Jerry out in 55 degrees of frost.

SATURDAY 31 JANUARY

Again lots to report and not much of it is favourable. For some time now we have had a stock sort of newspaper headline reading 'Japanese . . . miles from Singapore'. It started at 300 miles or so, then fell by steps to 200, 180, 100 then 75, then down to 18 in a jump and now we won't see the headlines again because we have retired to Singapore Island and blown up the causeway connecting it to the mainland. The GOC says he will hold the island till he receives the reinforcements which will surely come. Let's hope they do and that they will be strong.

Then in Libya – it would be laughable if it were not so damn serious. We attacked on 18 November, only escaped being kicked back a few days later by a hair's breadth, as we now know. Instead we kicked Rommel well and truly across Cyrenaica until he decided to stop running. To our surprise here at home we suddenly heard he had retaken Ajdābiyāh and now the blighter has made us run and he has retaken Benghazi. Is it that 6-pounder gun tank against our 2-pounder again? We have had to admit, after saying how his tanks were being slaughtered, that he has somehow been reinforced. A pity, that.

The debate in Parliament ended on Thursday with a vote of confidence being carried by 464 votes to 1. Jimmy Maxton was the one, his two pals couldn't vote, being tellers, so it seems that though many criticised the government as a whole no one wants to lose Churchill. However, they had a minor victory. When Churchill came back he proposed that his big speeches in Parliament, such as last Tuesday's, should be recorded and broadcast to save him repeating stuff, with the result that the expression should not suffer and to save him valuable time. This was defeated because the puny opposition would not be granted the same facilities.

News about *Barham*'s loss is now published. She was hit by four torpedoes in the Mediterranean off Sollum while in the company of *Valiant* and a destroyer screen and sunk in 4½ minutes with the loss of 700 men.

WEDNESDAY 4 FEBRUARY

Not much news. The chief thing of interest is this ruddy winter. We get nothing but snow, signs of thaw, a little thaw, shift in the wind, more frost then the cycle over again. The temperature varies from 33° to 30° I fancy. The roads today are bad for cycling, half slush, half irregular lumps of bound-on hard snow, with a sprinkling of cyclists like me probably intent on saving a bob a day in tram fares, even if there is space on the trams for them. One can't take dinner to work with the present rationing system though Dora manages one well when I have to stay.

Talking of food, I haven't yet mentioned, I believe, our points scheme of rationing. Books are issued like ration books with coupons marked A, B and C. At the moment A is worth one point, B two and C three; there are four of each available for each fortnight. One uses them by going to any shop one chooses and buying what goods they cover. At present they are for tinned goods, meat, salmon, etc. and dried fruits and cereals like rice. One gets a choice that way and, if preferred, can spend all on sultanas, within limits.

TUESDAY 10 FEBRUARY
The situation is looking bad. The official description in the news today was 'grave'. The Japs have crossed the Johore Straits and have landed almost at will on the island, and today they claim to have mended the breach in the causeway which we blew up and that their troops are pouring across. Where are those reinforcements? One is tempted to say rather bitterly that they are probably now being sent out. The stark damnable tragedy of the whole situation, too, is our lamentable weakness in the air. It seems from the usual report that 'the Japs raided Singapore. One plane was brought down and another damaged' that we have no more than one squadron of fighters there. Someone ought to be disembowelled for that. Even in peacetime it ought to be better defended. Well, there's the position. We have 'been withdrawing', the Japs are only ten miles from Singapore town, the naval base is evacuated, and it seems highly probable that those wonderful reinforcements are too late. This is one of the hard knocks that Churchill warned us to expect, I guess.

Soap is rationed from yesterday. It is on the points basis, each person having four points per four-week period and each point will allow for 4 oz hard soap or 3 oz toilet soap and other fancy flakes pro rata. Quite a liberal allowance.

We had an exam on the BLA last Friday. Am a little conceited at scoring eighty-five out of a possible eighty-five marks. Only two of us did it, though it was really rather elementary. Still, much more satisfactory method than the aural method Lt Cotton tried over musketry.

FRIDAY 13 FEBRUARY
Friday the 13th! A fitting date for the news we were served up. Yesterday *Scharnhorst*, *Gneisenau* and *Prinz Eugen* slipped out of Brest and went home. Almost like that. They chose a day with lousy weather, and hugging the French coast probably, with an escort of destroyers and a huge umbrella of fighters, were only sighted at Le Touquet. Naturally we attacked with Swordfishes, Beauforts, bombers, MTBs and destroyers. Our losses were 6 Swordfish, 20 bombers and 16 fighters, 1 of which crashed in Ipswich – Jerry lost

Richard Brown, photographed in the mid-1950s. (Brown family collection)

Reavell & Co. drawing office, 1923: Richard Brown is fourth from the right, Dora fifth. (Brown family collection)

The Ranelagh Works, Reavell & Co., 1948. (Brown family collection)

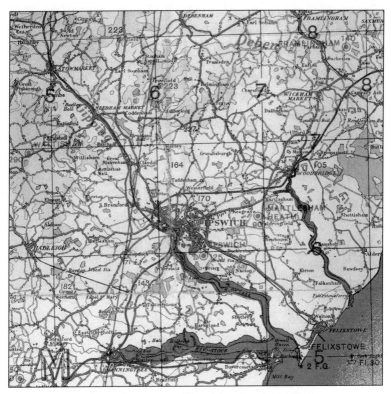

Ordnance Survey map of Ipswich and environs, 1943.

Leopold Road, Ipswich, still much as it looked in 1939. (L.W. Millgate)

N.R. 50.

NATIONAL REGISTER.

NATIONAL REGISTRATION DAY IS FRIDAY, 29th SEPTEMBER, 1939.

SEE INSTRUCTIONS IN SCHEDULE AS TO "PERSONS TO BE INCLUDED."

RATIONING.—The return on the schedule herewith will be used not only for National Registration but also for Food Rationing purposes. It is to your interest, therefore, as well as your public duty, to fill up the return carefully, fully and accurately.

Help the Enumerator to collect the schedule promptly by arranging for him to receive it when he calls. Do not make it necessary for him to call a number of times before he can obtain it.

When the Enumerator collects the schedule, he must write and deliver an Identity Card for every person included in the return. Help him to write them properly for you by letting him write at a table.

If the whole household moves before the schedule is collected, take it with you and hand it to the Enumerator calling at your new residence or to the National Registration Office for your new address. The address of this office can be ascertained at a local police station.

Wt 28033—171 12 50

National Registration Day official instructions.

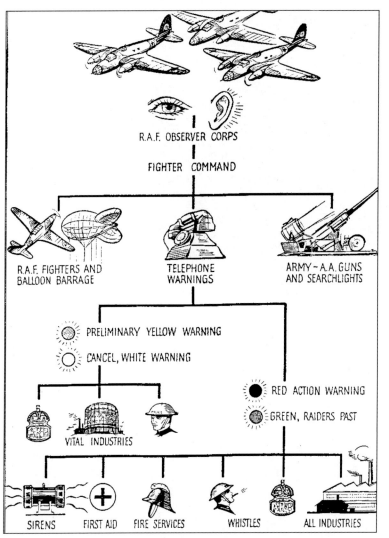

R.A.F. OBSERVER CORPS

FIGHTER COMMAND

R.A.F. FIGHTERS AND
BALLOON BARRAGE

TELEPHONE
WARNINGS

ARMY ~ A.A. GUNS
AND SEARCHLIGHTS

PRELIMINARY YELLOW WARNING

CANCEL, WHITE WARNING

RED ACTION WARNING

GREEN, RAIDERS PAST

VITAL INDUSTRIES

SIRENS   FIRST AID   FIRE SERVICES   WHISTLES   ALL INDUSTRIES

The Siren System, reproduced from the Ipswich ARP magazine, The Warble.

The Altmark *aground in Josing Fjord, February 1940. (Imperial War Museum)*

MTBs in port. (Imperial War Museum)

Concrete road blocks, July 1940. Similar road blocks were erected in Ipswich and around the country. (Imperial War Museum)

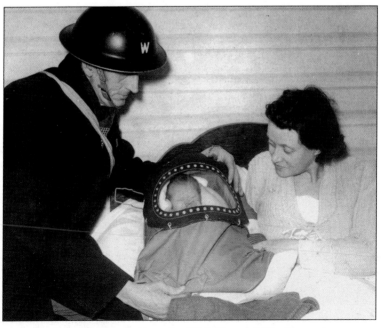

Baby in gas mask, November 1939. (Imperial War Museum)

Crashed Dornier 17 'Flying Pencil', Gippeswyk Park, Ipswich, 21 August 1940.
(David Kindred)

Italian prisoners of war watching a football match 'somewhere in Cambridgeshire'.
(Cambridge Collection)

Evacuated schoolboys smiling for the camera in Cambridge.
(Cambridge Collection)

Road signs removed with the intention of confusing the enemy.
(Cambridge Collection)

British prisoners of war, Benghazi, captured in Rommel's counter-offensive of April 1941. (Imperial War Museum)

HMS Prince of Wales, *Singapore, 8 December 1941. Two days later she was sunk by Japanese aircraft. (Imperial War Museum)*

Myrtle Road, Ipswich, after the raid of 2 June 1943. (David Kindred)

Fruit stall during the Blitz, London. Note the sign 'Our oranges came through Musso's Lake'. (Imperial War Museum)

ARP wardens at post. Richard Brown is on the right. (Brown family collection)

The Royal George, Ipswich. Former ARP post and social centre. (L.W. Millgate)

Home Guard in action with Molotov cocktails. (Imperial War Museum)

Filling the pig bin. Everyone helped with the war effort. (Imperial War Museum)

*V1 crashing near Drury Lane, London. Some passers-by do not appear to react.
(Imperial War Museum)*

2-5-45 1172 al"t" = Spaid (Goagsityn)

Plane Production in U.K. New Plans.

	1939 Sep-Dec	1940	1941	1942	1943	1944 JAN-JUNE	TOTAL. SEPT'39-JUNE'44
Heavy bombers	—	41	498	1976	4614	2889	10,018
Medium + light bombers	1072	3679	4170	4277	3113	1391	17,702
Fighters	447	4283	7063	9850	10727	5655	38,025
Naval	165	476	1232	1082	1720	1533	6,208
Trainers	772	5125	6614	5940	4825	2070	25,346
Recce, transport etc	468	1445	516	566	1264	1071	5,310
	2924	15,049	20,093	23,671	26,263	14,609	102,609

RAF losses, up to 28-4-45.

Bomber Command ~~7,997~~   7,997
Fighter Command (in defensive + offensive ops)   2,998
Coastal Command   454
                                                11,449

Statistics on British plane production, Mr Brown's diary, 2 May 1945.

Gliders at Woodbridge with their Halifax tugs, March 1945.
(Imperial War Museum)

GIs on the march somewhere in England. (Imperial War Museum)

VE party complete with bonfire and effigy of Hitler which Richard Brown helped to build, Leopold Road, Ipswich, May 1945. (Brown family collection)

18 fighters – and a lot of prestige. We have bombed Brest 112 times
since they have been there and, though they were immobilised for
almost a year, we didn't do any vital damage.

SUNDAY 15 FEBRUARY
Well, it seems it's happened. The 6 o'clock news stated that
Churchill will speak tonight at 9 o'clock and that the Japs have
announced the unconditional surrender of Singapore. Only this
morning the news announced the situation was unchanged out there
and that tanks were in action. This being the first announcement of
us having them, we assumed that reinforcements had arrived and the
situation had improved, and now this blow has fallen, and in such a
vague way, it's all very disturbing. One even wonders if our
reinforcements have been intercepted and sunk, together with the
attendant fleet. We have ordered Singapore to surrender to save
unnecessary loss of life. We must wait with what patience we can till
9 o'clock. Certainly we've had the bad sign which usually precedes a
surrender – the Singaporians are going to fight to the last man and
last round. That always means the same thing.

9.30. Yes, it's true. Churchill has just spoken and put the plain
facts before us to show our genius for quiet fortitude and grim
determination in the face of threat. At the same time he reviewed
the situation and the changes since he last spoke six months ago
and, without whining, reminded us that America is now with us
and that the Russians are keeping Jerry on the run in a way we had
not dreamt of then.

On the whole the situation though bad, is indeed better than it
has been, e.g. in June 1940. I would still rather be English, as I am,
with the Englishman's chance of survival than a Jerry with his
chance. The recent flight of *Scharnhorst* and *Gneisenau* and *Prinz
Eugen* under our very noses, Singapore, the Libyan position, all
make us lose face abroad. Australia is getting a bit shirty and with
cause, I'm afraid. Still, the tide must turn. Wonder when and how?

WEDNESDAY 18 FEBRUARY
Saw a powerful sight yesterday. Had to go to Chatham again on
Taku for heated dehumidifier air trials and, coming out, we passed
into the torpedo room. It was more spacious than I expected, for
handling purposes I suppose. Everywhere was neat in a new coat
of white paint, a little brass work here and there, but chiefly and
dominantly were four torpedoes in racks, painted a lightish royal

blue. They looked so smooth, and shapely, and I suppose coming on them suddenly made a difference but I thought it was mechanically one of the most beautiful sights I have seen.

The whole boat looked neat and trim. She was painted dark blue-grey outside, in fact was almost ready for sailing. Brave chaps who sailed in her. Hope they come back safely and, if possible, covered in glory.

Japan has been joyfully celebrating the capture of Singapore and taking a national holiday over it. Wonder what they will do if we can manage to get it back?

SUNDAY 22 FEBRUARY
Have another unfortunate personal loss to record. Poor Win died very suddenly on Thursday, the 20th, about 11.15 a.m. It was such a shock to see Den when I arrived home at lunchtime and heard the news. Poor thing. I don't think I shall ever forget her poor face as she lay there. It was bronchial pneumonia with influenza, the immediate cause being heart failure. This damnable, completely pitiless, winter was no doubt the cause. She was at tea here on Sunday, though, and did her cycle round as usual on Monday. With this piercing weather I suppose it was only a natural outcome. Plucky kid. She worked like the very devil and said how she dreaded this winter as though she guessed it would be the worst for about a century. We've now had an unbroken frost and snow for seven weeks, with intervals of only a few hours' thaw at a time. The remains of the snow I grumbled about last are still in the side-streets.

All we can do now is to do our best for Den and to keep the grave tidy. At any rate she is at last at rest and hasn't got to work at that excessive, though plucky, pitch.

The Japs are now concentrating on Java and Sumatra. Part of the strategy embraces Bali Island and there has been a bit of an action out there between naval forces, and our planes. Full results are not to hand but we claim to have sunk a Jap cruiser and two destroyers, damaged badly or just damaged six more cruisers and a few destroyers and sunk one transport. Japan can't build so quickly as America and us.

SUNDAY 8 MARCH
No news at all from Java today which is significant.

Had a strenuous morning at Home Guard parade today. For the first hour we had drill movements with rifles at the slope. Not being used to it and having overcoat on, my poor arm ached and then for the second hour we had bayonet fighting. Thank goodness I'm not writing with my left hand.

Bayonet fighting is a gruesome business but, if it ever comes to that, I believe I could do it. The thought that that bloke over there is an invader, a cove who wants to upset our little home, who has the damn cheek to set foot on this little island and who wants my blood into the bargain, would make it quite easy to give, say, Nos 3 and 4 butt or to boost his lungs up to his throat as Welham advises.

We have tommy-gun exam tomorrow evening. If I do as well as in the BLA exam I shan't complain. It's a wonderful gun, so simple in use and design. All the same I would rather have a BLA I fancy. It is so accurate and it appeals to me to be able to place twenty shots accurately without any bolt movement.

Am just a little thrilled. I heard a thunderous drone this afternoon from up above the haze suggesting a squadron of bombers going southwards and have just heard on the news that we have attacked a factory near Paris. I thought they sounded like business.

MONDAY 9 MARCH
It seems that Java has gone. The Dutch have been swearing to fight to the last man and now the Japs report that 93,000 and 5,000 Australians, British and Americans have surrendered unconditionally. The two statements fit in. It seems to be the style of this war to swear to fight to the death, then just give in tamely five minutes later. What is the mystery? It happened in Singapore as well. It makes one shudder to think what may happen if Jerry attacks here. We boast and shout of how he would be beaten and then things like Libya and Singapore and Pearl Harbour and *Prince of Wales* and *Repulse* happen. We prate about lessons to be learnt from those defeats but we seem to be bad learners. It is all so disturbing.

For some weeks now they have been making a roadblock at the station bridge on the town side. They've certainly made a job of it, digging down trenches about 5 ft deep or more and 3 ft wide, and filling up with solid concrete with recesses for steel barriers. They must have some special cement as they were making it in most of the cold weather and the frost hasn't seemed to make much difference. Now they are also doing the Woodbridge Road railway bridge.

FRIDAY 13 MARCH
Rangoon was evacuated last Monday. The Japs are pushing on but
there is some doubt whether they will reach the borders of India
before the rainy period sets in.

Let's talk about home news. Last Monday the local grocers
stopped delivering groceries and the Monday before that the
butchers stopped deliveries. It releases both more labour for the
factories and more petrol for other purposes. Dora fetched her
groceries last time in her basket, a bag and the boy's pram. I
suppose sugar, jam and suchlike soon weigh a lot and last time was
the day for the month's jam ration.

Talking of petrol, pleasure motoring will be stopped altogether
on 1 July and until then the petrol ration will be halved. That
means that a 10 hp car gets 2 gal for April, May and June each.
Not a lot but, after all, to hear the planes about all day makes one
realise the petrol must come from somewhere. I refer of course to
the days when flying is possible.

SUNDAY 15 MARCH
Three weeks ago the Americans landed 'thousands' of troops in
Australia. They suffered no losses but hinted that some Jap subs were
sunk on the way.

There's to be another 10 per cent cut in paper for newspapers
tomorrow. Some people who take the papers on chance sale will be
disappointed as papers like the *Express* will be cutting down supply.
The *Telegraph* did that some time ago rather than reduce the size
but tomorrow, I fancy, they will commence cutting the size from six
to four pages for Monday, Tuesday and Saturday, leaving six for the
other days. It's all because of the effect of Japan's entry on the
shipping position. That will also mean reduced rations of meat,
butter, cheese and clothes soon.

There has been an outcry against the Japs last week. Eden stated
publicly in Parliament that he had conclusive proof of Japanese
atrocities on our troops and citizens in Hong Kong. They bound
fifty officers and men and then bayoneted them to death; rape,
naturally, was committed and one section of the Chinese quarter
was just set on one side as a brothel irrespective of occupants.
Feeling is pretty sore about it, as the general opinion is that for Eden
to make it public it must be genuine. For my part I can't get worked
up about it as one always expects atrocity stories in war and there is
always that lingering doubt as to how much exaggeration is present,

but I must say I would still cheerfully deliver No. 4 butt on any Japanese, so it doesn't need the incentive of atrocities in my case. Perhaps I may, some day. Who knows? This war has taken so many twists and turns that anything may happen.

WEDNESDAY 25 MARCH
That damned invasion bogey is lifting its detestable head again. The local special police have been allotted certain sectors and have been instructed to contact each household and inform that, in the event of evacuation, notice will be given of from ten hours to four days. In that event the sector forms somewhere and is marched to the station. Harry is given Leopold Road and Sidegate Avenue and we go to Derby Road station. That may be only merely to get the thing organised, just in case, but warnings of possible invasion, and instructions to stay put unless otherwise ordered, have been officially given out so one, naturally, wonders what is coming.

Thank goodness I'm in the HG this time and shan't have to leave, though there's not much chance of survival, but it will be an awful wrench for the wife and kiddies to have to go and face the foul business of travelling just somewhere, but all the same a place where they will not be wanted. What a business! This time though Harry will be going too and I think I can be assured that Dora and the nippers will be looked after the best possible. Let's hope it never comes.

Milk ration will be increased on Sunday. It was 2 pints per week for an adult (more for kiddies) and rose to 2½ pints about three weeks ago. Now it will be 3 pints per week.

EASTER SUNDAY 5 APRIL
A whole week since the last entry but that doesn't mean I've had time to spare. With the lighter evenings and the fact that those pestiferously unimaginative coves at Argyle Street have decided that the spring and summer are the correct periods for ARP lectures, one doesn't get a lot of free time to oneself and on top of that I am now busy renovating that wardrobe for Den's room. Last week we had three evening lectures, the week before five and a Sunday morning parade.

The sirens were kind last week. I was on duty 7 to 1 a.m. All the week I expected a call-out at each of those three lectures but actually only on one, Friday evening, did it go and then just as we were ending and clearing away chairs. Nowadays I'm supposed to go on duty with a white tin hat, a khaki greatcoat on the sleeves of which are slipped two dark blue Civil Defence armlets and, on those armlets are corporal's stripes, two of them. I don't mean one stripe on each sleeve like a common lance-corporal, but two on each, a full-blown corporal. That's what they think we seniors will fall for, just to get a little discipline into the CD service. Barmy, I call it. I don't want any distinction. My white helmet is enough for me.

Out in Burma there is the same old story of retreat with the Japs now seriously threatening the oil wells out there. I suppose they will go with the rest and then the Japs will halt till the rains are over; they are due in about a week. Did I report we had evacuated the Andamans? It succumbed about a fortnight ago. Possibly operating from that base the ruddy Japs have today bombed Colombo with damage unreported as yet but we have shot down twenty-seven planes with thirty heavily damaged or probables, our losses being slight.

Double summer time starts today. Cheers. Breakfast cereals and tinned milk go on points scheme tomorrow.

THURSDAY 9 APRIL

Another chapter is closing in the history of this war. The Bataan peninsula which has been such a thorn in the Japanese flesh is at last overwhelmed and the defence which has lasted about three months has ended. One phrase says 'the Japanese attacked the 3rd Corps and the 3rd Corps was ordered to counter-attack but the move failed owing to the exhaustion of the men'. It appears some have reached Corregidor Island in the fairway of Manila harbour and they may carry on from there. Plucky men. They have been completely cut off all that time without hope of relief and yet fought on against terrific odds. If there is one prisoner missing after this affair the Japs deserve to have Tokyo completely flattened.

Another chunk of bad news comes today with the loss of *Dorsetshire* and *Cornwall* which were attacked by Jap planes in the Indian Ocean. No details are given but I guess they were sent to deal with the carriers which bombed Ceylon and the carriers found them first. Hard luck.

THURSDAY 16 APRIL

Tuesday was Budget Day and, of course, it brought new taxes. Income was not affected, remaining at 10s in the £1, but tobacco, beer and purchase tax were soaked. Cigarettes, decent ones, at 9d for ten are now 1*s* for ten, and tobacco has gone up by 6½*d* or 7*d* per ounce. Stuff like St Julien is now about 2*s* per ounce. Coo!! Naturally chaps at work are trying to cut down, some to cut off altogether. We are chipping them and they seem a bit lugubrious over it, though sticking to it.

Beer is up 2*d* per pint and whisky is up 4*s* 6*d* per bottle to 22*s* 6*d*. Entertainment tax is up 2*d* on 1*s* 2*d* and 10*s* 6*d* on 2-guinea seats for example. Purchase tax is doubled on a big list of articles, now standing at 33⅓ per cent, the increase making it 66⅔ per cent. There is a little relief for lower paid income tax payers, otherwise that's all.

THURSDAY 30 APRIL

Norwich caught it again last night, the raid being short and sharp. Casualties are unknown but I hear there were 80 dead and 200 injured Monday night. They went to York Tuesday night.

It seems an incredible thing to report, and I should not do so if it were not that I had heard it referred to on the wireless, but Jerry has definitely said he is to concentrate on towns and buildings of historical and architectural interest as reprisal for the civilian damage we did at Rostock which included churches at places. He referred to 'three star towns in Baedeker' as objectives so, naturally, they are being referred to as 'Baedeker raids'. What an incredible intellect. He seems to have forgotten the boasts he made to neutrals, as a warning probably, after his Warsaw and Rotterdam raids, showing pictures of the 'cultural objects' he had damaged. He is squealing now, good and proper if the newspaper reports are to be believed, and doesn't like the tastes we have given him of his own medicine, although he started the business.

TUESDAY 5 MAY

Great news today. We have occupied Madagascar and tonight we await Laval's comments. This morning's news merely stated we had arrived off the coast at dawn and this evening we hear we are occupying and meeting with little opposition. Vichy is calling on the French forces there to fight to maintain the honour of France. As though France has any honour left after letting us down in 1940, handing over Indo-China to the Japs, the Syrian business and working in with Germany.

I think it is excellent news that we have strength enough to do it at all and now we have got in before the ruddy Japs it should make all the difference to our supply lines up the African coast. There are no details of any importance except that the landings were made under naval and air protection which indicates the presence of a carrier and a fair naval escort. About a fortnight ago we were told that three French cruisers had arrived there from Dakar. Wonder what's happened to them? How fine if they came over or we took them. Was surprised to find Madagascar is nearly 1,000 miles long and is three times the size of England, Scotland and Wales. She has an excellent harbour too. America has warmly praised the act and bluntly warned Vichy France that any armed resistance would be an act against the Free Nations which includes America, so she must look out.

Mandalay has fallen and the Japs are pushing ever on and on. Things are serious indeed out there for our Army. The rainy season is due soon and it may save them. The British Army waiting for rain to save them! Soon the boot will be on the other foot and then Japan will be glad of anything to save them.

Saw a Halifax this lunchtime and three Mosquitoes during the weekend. Was quite thrilled.

Jerry reports a naval action on one of our convoys in the Arctic. He claims a cruiser and admits a destroyer heavily damaged and also claims some merchant ships. Shall be interested to hear the real facts.

THURSDAY 7 MAY
Unfortunately Jerry told the truth for once. We did lose a cruiser, the *Edinburgh* though we had to sink it finally ourselves, and some merchant ships by torpedoes from planes. He lost one destroyer and another damaged.

News from Madagascar is that all resistance is now practically finished at the naval base end of the island. The base, Diego-Suarez, has surrendered as has the adjacent town and we expect our Fleet to enter the harbour this afternoon. The French lost some ships but I'm not certain of the total number. Quite a good effort and it seems that the Japs were forestalled for once.

Corregidor surrendered yesterday. Brave lads. Wish Singapore had such a record of guts. The Japs can now release a huge load of troops for other purposes, possibly invasion of Australia.

This ruddy pestilential weather! Was there ever such a year? We get the coldest winter for many a year, then weeks and months of east wind culminating in an east gale, and such a gale, which lasted six days. I just couldn't do any top gear work anywhere coming home during that time. Then it changed, having dried all the land

and the seeds in it, and we had a few days south-west wind but still no rain, and the skies were still glorious and cloudless until this afternoon and the wind is now again a half gale from north-east. There I suppose it will stop for another six weeks, and all the crops will just die or not come through at all.

SUNDAY 10 MAY
Chief news, rivalling in importance even this ruddy continual east wind, comes from the Far East like a breath of hope. Though details are meagre, piecing together all the reports, it appears that Japan was massing ships for the invasion of Australia, in spite of my contrary beliefs, and was watched by American reconnaissance planes. When they moved the Yank fleet was there and for about six days various actions were fought, supported by Fortress land-based planes. For once the Japs were apparently the weaker side and the results so far are Jap losses 2 carriers, 1 heavy cruiser, 1 light cruiser, 2 destroyers and others totalling (I believe) 10 warships sunk, others badly damaged including a heavy cruiser and an aircraft tender of 9,000 tons. Our losses are 'comparatively light' but unable to be stated because Japan would like to know them.

Malta had 6,000 tons of bombs during April. Coo!! The Madagascar incident closed with the surrender of the French, our losses being under 1,000.

Had a form from the Central Register last week asking for more particulars of my employment and what proportion of my time is actually spent on war work. Shall see K¹ in the morning and get his opinion as to how much I must tell them and if he wants to hang on to my valuable services. I don't particularly want a job out of the town, especially as after the war fresh jobs will go to ex-servicemen in preference to others, only right too, the alternative being the Forces. With luck I could get a commission in either the RAOC or RAF, preferably the latter, but leaving the wife and kiddies would be a strain on them. Leaving them in an invasion area isn't too comforting. Quite frankly I'm a bit apprehensive. I don't want to leave home, Ipswich, the HG, the warden service and Reavell's but I know I could get a better job and I think I should be happy in the RAF, at least doing something.

9.45. Have just listened to a wonderful speech by Churchill. Bless his dear old heart this is the second anniversary of his taking over office as Prime Minister and he was in excellent form and good humour. I think that if ever I can and want to refer to the good speeches of this war, this one must surely be well worth the reference.

WEDNESDAY 27 MAY

News tonight: Rommel has started what looks like an offensive in Libya. Report just states that his armoured forces have advanced 'in some strength' at a point below Gazala and that we have engaged him. He is using dive-bombers which suggests it is a real offensive, though it is too early to say what is afoot or if it is only a mere raid.

In Russia things are critical and, I'm afraid, interesting seeing that they will possibly decide the course of the war. The papers call it the Battle of the Bulge and von Bock is still attacking the southern part of it, Timoshenko's left flank. Jerry claims to have surrounded three Russian armies and Russians say they have broken the counter-offensive of Jerry's. The struggle grows fiercer every day, each side reinforcing, but it is encouraging that the Russians have countered von Bock's thrust and cut off the spearhead. The next few days will be critical.

In Czechoslovakia someone has taken a pot at Heydrich, the thin-lipped Nazi butcher. Unfortunately he is only wounded and rewards are out for the one responsible. They only value him at £60,000 though. Naturally he will not be found and, naturally, there will follow an orgy of butchering of innocent hostages as is going on every day, almost, in France and Holland.

SUNDAY 31 MAY

Thrilling news. About three weeks ago the papers said we were considering the possibility of operating 1,000 bombers a night. Last night we did. 'Well over 1,000 bombers' raided the Ruhr and Rhineland, chiefly Cologne, and in addition night fighters and Coastal Command planes were out too. Even at the 6 o'clock news no details were available except that the fires could be seen from the coast of Holland 150 miles away and this morning reconnaissance planes found a pall of smoke 15,000 ft high over the city. Losses were forty-four in the whole night's operations.

It is obviously the heaviest raid of history though the majority of planes were twin-engined, Wellingtons and Hampdens I suppose. Even so well over 1,000 tons of bombs must have been dropped. What a raid! All in 1½ hours too, so the rate of dropping was over

10 tons per minute. At his heaviest Jerry never operated more than 500 planes per night.

Last night I had a troubled sort of sleep, sleeping yet all the while conscious of continual droning of aircraft. No wonder!

This afternoon twenty-two Spitfires went out south-east flying very low. Possibly some naval affair in the North Sea. Churchill has sent a message to the RAF congratulating them on the big raid. Significantly he referred to it as the first of a series of similar raids which will be aimed at each city in turn.

TUESDAY 2 JUNE
The queerest birthday so far I believe. Jerry must have heard of it for he illuminated the town with flares in honour of it at 2 a.m. With Cologne in mind we arose hurriedly and I opened up the dug-out. The fires seemed out Martlesham way but when planes came round this district I packed Dora and the kiddies down to the shelter. Then the fun started. There seemed the usual sequence, first chandelier flares, then incendiaries, then HE. This happened three times altogether. It's now 0615 hr so I don't know any details. It lasted about one and a half hours and I guessed about ten or twelve planes took part.

They made their runs from over us and the whistling of the bombs was a little questionable at first. We couldn't just make out where they were likely to land as the note was a falling one, so I lay in the gutter once or twice till I was used to it. Twice I diagnosed parachute mines at 3 and 2½ miles away. There was low cloud about, lit up by the fire glares, so I saw planes on four occasions clearly enough for identification. Two were Dorniers of some type or other, 215 or 17 or 172 or 217, etc., two others Junkers 88. From what we could see the fires were soon dealt with. I guess the NFS round here is pretty good.

I was a little apprehensive about our Magna shortcomings. We've nearly finished the cadge so there are no first-aid kits about just yet. The best I could do was to contact two of the three ladies who were to tackle the tea and ask them to put the kettles on. Suppose I ought to explain that Dora and I have, or are, canvassing the sector locating hot water bottles and blankets, and cadging old sheeting for bandages. We are also raffling off a cake, at 2*d* a time, so far have made £2 on it, and scrounging spoonfuls of sugar here and there for the tea ladies, in addition to a pound of tea, already subscribed. It's quite fun and I like the job, though I wasn't a bit keen at first.

Dora has gone off at 6 o'clock to see her mother, poor thing, so it's going to be an unusual birthday. There's a lot of trouble in the world and the worst of it is that damnable cancer. Poor old dear, like mother, she doesn't deserve that lousy complaint. Hope Dora gets home tonight, shouldn't like her to get in a blitz on the London scale.

Tuesday evening. Naturally raid news. Broadly the scheme seems to have been that Kesgrave got it with incendiaries and Harry has met a local bloke who claims to have beaten out 'hundreds' with the flat of his shovel. Here in Ipswich they dropped a line of eighteen, Rushmere Road direction then some more on Bixley Heath. The fire service let them blaze so Jerry bombed the blaze. Unfortunately Bixley Road got the bad shots and some people were killed and quite a lot of damage done.

Round Aldy's way IBs were showered down and he enjoyed himself putting them out, attending to five himself. His opinion of Jerry's IB is very low. Nacton Road school is damaged and a house burnt out killing one girl.

Last night Jerry claims to have visited Canterbury. Does that mean we may expect him again tonight round here? How tired I do feel. Hope he gives me a night's rest and keeps away. Two-and-a-half hours' rest after a strenuous night's scrounging wasn't really enough. Tried to get the first-aid dressings and so on today but did not call at a convenient time.

MONDAY 15 JUNE

Libya looks critical for us. Why the hell can't we learn how to fight? Rommel is out-generaling us altogether. He thrust with all his strength at Bir Hacheim and we withdrew. 'It makes our forces more concentrated,' we said, the old signs creeping in again. Within an hour Rommel, having safe-guarded his southern flank by that move, thrust madly north for Tobruk and district and the best we could say was that 'he is fourteen miles away from Tobruk at nearest and we are holding him'. Why the blazes couldn't we hit him? This evening, news is that the fighting has suddenly turned fluid, whatever that may mean, probably it's to Jerry's advantage. If we lose Tobruk it will be serious for us, perhaps for that very reason we will hold it, but I don't like the way in which we seem to neglect chances. Our Air Force is doing wonderful work on his supply columns but I'll bet he has an ample reserve of supplies and can stand it. If only Wavell were there.

For our part we are now officially committed to a Second Front
in Europe. Eden promised it in a public speech last week and now
it is fashionable to refer to it in speeches. As a pointer another big
contingent of American troops escorted by [the] American fleet
arrived in Northern Ireland on Saturday. Significantly their chief
weapon is the tommy-gun.

Had a personal thrill on Saturday. *Torbay* is in the news having sunk
70,000 tons of shipping. On one occasion she went into an Axis
harbour and torpedoed two merchantmen lying there and got away
again. Having been aboard I feel a personal interest in her and bet
Chatham is proud of her.

THURSDAY 18 JUNE
Very bad news from Libya. We have retired from Sidi Rezegh and
El Adem and there are indications that we are scooting for the
Sollum line leaving a garrison at Tobruk. What a defeat! And what
a lot it portends! It means, as I see it, that we haven't a general to
match against Rommel and, likely enough, all Jerry's generals are of
equal training so it augurs badly for any chance of opening a
Second Front in France. One may say that there is a terrific
difference in our lines of supply, comparing Jerry's few miles across
the Mediterranean to our 18,000 round the Cape but against that is
the fact that we have been told that we started with equal forces and
equal tanks. The men are better than Jerry's but one quakes when
thinking of our leaders. Green always declares that the ne'er-do-well
of the family always goes in the Army. I'm wondering if he's right.
We even jib at air raids on nights of poor visibility but I seem to
recollect the dozens of times I've been on duty in pouring rain
when Jerry has droned over uninterruptedly. He didn't find bad
weather a hindrance.

Seem to be feeling doleful lately.

SUNDAY 21 JUNE
Dolefulness justified. We skedaddled back to the Sollum line and,
this dinner time, we heard that Jerry had penetrated the outer
defences of Tobruk and occupied a considerable area inside.
Teatime came the news that Jerry has claimed the occupation and
surrender of Tobruk itself. Pity. Now what will the Excuse
Department produce?

We had a surprise announcement on Friday morning that
Churchill is again in America. The giddy old buffer flew there,

which suggests either urgency or can't spare the shipping, which I think is more likely.

It is officially released that American troops are in this country and an open secret that some are around this district near Woodbridge. A whole area has been evacuated so they can move in and train and there has been a little to-do about it.

TUESDAY 30 JUNE

If only I could record good news from Egypt! Yes, it's Egypt now, not Libya. It's just as well perhaps as I was never too sure how to spell Libya and where the 'y' went.

Back and back we go, though the speed is slower now. They are giving the positions as being so many miles from Alexandria. It wouldn't be so bad if only they wouldn't lead us up the garden so much. Last week, for instance, Attlee told us in Parliament that

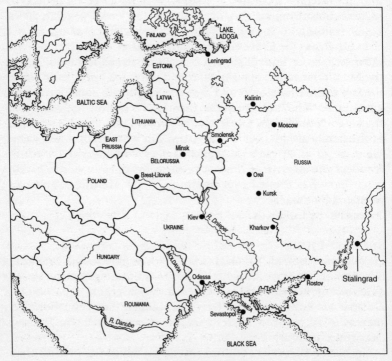

The Russian Front

Ritchie[2] was receiving, and would receive, reinforcements and now they tell us today that Auchinleck is playing for time till he gets reinforcements. Rommel's supplies seem inexhaustible, the *Express* the other day said he had 600 tanks and 10,000 lorries.

Today's news is that the 'Auk' [Auchinleck] took over command last Thursday and also that the position is grave. Fighting is fierce and I know that to be so regarding the individual men but I'm afraid, candidly afraid, for the way they are handled.

I know I sound dolorous but our stock is not very high just now and we have surely lost face. To think that we had the Libyan campaign in our hands soon after it started and failed for lack of guts! Well, stock being so low, it's time it started to rise so perhaps we can expect something soon. We may expect, shall we receive?

To get to brighter matters, a fortnight ago I treated myself to a pair of second-hand field glasses. They are fine and have given me a heap of enjoyment so far. It's amazing how they show up colours of camouflage and lettering when the unaided eye cannot see anything at all.

TUESDAY 14 JULY

Situation in Russia very grave. Jerry is attacking on a 650-mile front from Kalinin to the Sea of Azov. He has managed to pass many divisions over the Don and is heavily besieging Voronež. Besides all that the Russians have lost a big grain producing area, in addition to coal, iron and industrial districts. The key town or rather the chief one at which the fiercest fighting is progressing is Voronež. Jerry claimed its capture over a week ago but though he looks like taking it, it hasn't gone yet.

WEDNESDAY 15 JULY

I mentioned a push on our part in Egypt a little while ago. It just occurred and then we sat down and consolidated the new positions. Since then Rommel has made three attempts to dislodge us but unsuccessfully, though the last attempt was last night and results are not yet to hand. He made it last night because our fighter-bombers are proving rather effective.

Don't know if I'm getting a bit run-down or what but I'm getting a bit jumpy at night-time. Jerry has been in the district a bit, sometimes with and sometimes without an alert, but I usually hear him in my sleep and wake up, sometimes before the crash warning goes from Ransome's. The other night planes were low

and I heard one go into a shallow dive. I was out of bed like a flash
but nothing occurred. Later I saw flickering white lights shining on
the opposite side of the street and took them to be flares quite
near. Out of bed again saying 'Flares!!!' and dressing quickly. Dora
went to the kiddies and called back 'only searchlights' and they
were, practising some patterns and apparently guiding planes
either out or in. Once you experience a mild blitz you seem to be
on the *qui vive* afterwards. There's something so ominous, so
continuous, even so efficient-sounding, in the buzz of the planes
shallow-diving in their runs then wheeling back for another, mixed
with whines and the crashes of the bombs. The big urge at night is
to get dressed and as prepared as possible. With kiddies there is so
much to do in such a short time. If we could only rely on the alert
giving us a reasonable warning it wouldn't be so bad but we can't.
Incidentally, on the evening I just described there were no enemy
planes over the country at all.

BANK HOLIDAY MONDAY 3 AUGUST
Certainly am on holiday. Awoke at 8.50 convinced that I shouldn't
have been any earlier had I been at work. Dennis is home, being
transferred to a bomber station on Halifaxes when he goes back
and he minded the kids while Dora and I went to the pictures this
afternoon. Quite a treat and an unlooked-for one.

Woke again, at 3 o'clock, to the sound of gunfire last night. Had a
confused idea we were being blitzed through hearing the planes so
got up quickly and dressed. Went downstairs and while I was opening
up the dug-out in case of need, Dora thought she saw a plane
brought down. The sound of engines ceased suddenly and there was
a glare on the ground, so probably she was correct. We then found
there had been an alert and both of us slept through it. Dear me!

That makes six nights out of seven I've got up for something,
either alerts or gunfire. One night Arthur Mayhew, Reg and I
passed the time cursing those who do nothing for the war. Am
ashamed to say there are still some, lots in fact, who don't do
much. They find themselves eligible for HG or ARP work so,
instead, they make themselves fire-watchers. At our place for
instance they spend a night at the Works now and then, have a
good night's sleep and get paid 5s for it. Some even go to a shop,
buy a badge with FW on it and wear it in their buttonhole, as
though they are virtuously doing their bit. As though FW can ever
hope to compare with ARP or HG.

SATURDAY 8 AUGUST
First week's holiday over. Weather has not been too good; there's been no real sunshine; Tuesday we were glad of the fire Dora lit for airing; and today has been rather wet. Now Godfrey is a little more fit perhaps it will improve for next week.

News in general is very disturbing. I have an idea that when we look back some time hence, this period will be regarded as a sort of transition or waiting period. I suppose I ought to take a long view but there is a tendency to see only that which is before one's nose and candidly I feel a bit depressed. And so we just wait. We are doing just nothing beyond attending a conference in Moscow which is reckoned to have some bearing on a Second Front.

In Egypt conditions make me nearly sick. The papers tell us, as though something to be proud of, that Rommel is reinforcing and our fighters are carefully keeping watch on the streams of supplies. Ye Gods! 'Keeping watch'!!! Then they say he is getting supplies by sea and by air from Crete – and we thought we had a Navy out there which might be considered strong enough to stop a convoy right on its doorstep. Apparently it isn't. It might even be evacuated from the Mediterranean altogether for all we know or hear of it.

Jerry is using new incendiary bombs. His original 1 kg is now fitted with a respectable nose of HE which goes off after five minutes. Bigger ones are now using phosphorous and we are warned that if touched by it to keep it wet. Our officials have a peculiar sense of issuing instructions. They tell us to deal with the first type preferably from behind a brick wall. I suppose we utilise the five minutes in building one.

Went to a concert this afternoon by a Polish army male voice choir and a pianist. I was chiefly attracted by the probability that he would play the Polonaise in A and he sure did. It was grand, played with terrific vim. The singing was really excellent. The bass soloist, a huge chap, was better than others I have heard. All were officers, about thirty-six of them, and I guess they are excellent ambassadors especially by reason of going to the trouble to learn some of our English songs.

Had a short alert last night. One of our chaps, who shall be nameless, is I fancy a little windy. Must bear that in mind.

THURSDAY 20 AUGUST
Yesterday we made our first daylight raid on occupied France. It was a big affair, although how big we don't know yet. Rather

disappointing to us impatient blokes but the official bulletin is not yet issued. The raid was on Dieppe district involving three landings, the flanks being commando raids designed to overcome the defences and the centre one being the tank landing forces.

I've just been listening to an eye-witness account by a BBC observer, quite thrilling. He described how one commando force landed and destroyed the six 6-in gun battery commanding the beaches and blew up an ammo dump. The other flank had the misfortune to run into a small Jerry convoy offshore and suffered some casualties. However, they landed but were not strong enough to capture their battery so they took up sniping positions and prevented it working at all during all operations. What the tanks did we are not told but it is certain we had an excellent umbrella of fighters all the while.

Preliminary reports say we lost 98 fighters with 30 pilots safe and Jerry lost 92 with 100 more probable. The latter figures will probably go up. Jerry claims 1,500 prisoners and 3 destroyers, 4 transports and 3 MTBs sunk, probably exaggerated.

A new term has been used – TLC – which stands for Tank Landing Craft, the square-ended barges for transporting tanks. The whole affair lasted nine hours and we broadcast to the French emphasising that it was only a raid and asking them not to interfere and expose themselves to Nazi revenge. We promised to tell them when invasion does start and that we will keep our promise. Naturally Jerry describes it as an invasion and is preening himself no end at being able to repel it.

WEDNESDAY 26 AUGUST
The Duke of Kent died yesterday. He was on his way to Iceland when his plane, a Sunderland, crashed in the north of Scotland. The only survivor was the rear gunner who is seriously injured. Poor thing. A lousy way to go out for a chap in his position.

Actually the fact was hardly mentioned at work today. Poor Ray Nursey was killed last night and it has cast a gloom over the place. Jerry came over soon after 10 o'clock and dropped three bombs. One is unexploded in Harmony Square, one dropped on the Recreation Ground smashing Porter's house and killing Nursey and the third hit an Anderson in Lindbergh Road killing a woman and her eight children and seriously injuring her husband. Aldy was only 100 yd from the second one and he declares he didn't hear the thing drop.

A second Jerry arrived and we gave him the biggest reception I've yet seen. It was huge, including Bofors from the dock and also the new rocket gun. He came over our post, where I was, and I watched with my glasses. He dashed into a cloud and then down came the shrapnel. It was just like the beginning of a storm with heavy drops pinging on the road. Three shell cases from the rocket guns came down in Colchester Road so I guess I'm taking more shelter next time. After all I suppose it was a bit foolish to keep popping out and enjoying it like I did. Poor Ray has given many of us that opinion.

Godfrey can't make out why I didn't shoot Jerry with my gun. I believe he thinks what's the sense of me having a real gun like that if I don't use it?

We had an RAF morning this morning. I suppose Jerry came over to see. This dinner time Haw-Haw said many incendiaries and HE were dropped on barracks (!!) and docks and outlying aerodromes of Ipswich, much damage being done. Let's hope they believe it.

The biggest American convoy yet arrived here some time ago. I guess some are in this district which is one of the signs I considered essential for a Second Front.

Another naval clash is in operation in the Solomons. Again news is scarce and again we don't know many details.

Good news from Russia, at last they have launched a big offensive north-west of Moscow, advanced thirty to forty-five miles on a big front and captured 250 tanks alone. Is this a damp squib or is it at last the counter which will tie Jerry up in the Caucasus. On the other hand the position at Stalingrad is grave. He has made a breakthrough and seems likely soon to take the place. Come on Russia! Get to it.

THURSDAY 3 SEPTEMBER
Today has been celebrated by services all over the country, the King having appointed it a day of prayer. The factories have ceased work for a quarter of an hour at 1100 hr for a broadcast service. We went in the packing shop, the first event of its kind.

Well, the fourth year opens with some auspicious events. Jerry is using a million men against Stalingrad and things are grave again. He is also moving against Novorossijsk, the last naval base the Russians have in the Black Sea, and, I'm afraid, with some effect. Further north the Russian offensive is proceeding but slowly.

In Egypt Rommel started an offensive a few days ago. He wheeled round our left flank, at the Qattara Depression and advanced north. For the last two days fighting has ceased which suggests we had something ready.

At home we are centred on the coming Second Front, at least I am. I can see signs of it coming – there have been Spitfire squadrons, some Spit sixes, freshly arrived at Nacton and Martlesham and the town now boasts about twenty or so Americans in twos or threes every time I go to work. They must be Yanks. I saw an officer sitting on the pavement in Princes Street today.

THURSDAY 17 SEPTEMBER
I didn't bother to wake; I was too darned tired. The alert went at 2345 hr and so did the Grove Farm guns. Jerry had arrived and by the time the kids were in the shelter and I was at the post he had gone home. It was a short, very short, raid with plenty of gunfire and he dropped an oil bomb at Gippeswyk Park and about eight 50 kg HE which didn't explode. One landed near Reavell's water pump house and another went into the pattern stores. I looked at the latter, my first UXB, and I don't want to have to investigate another though I would prefer UX to X. The storekeeper showed me where it was without going near so I went to investigate. It was a neat hole in the roof and some patterns were smashed but otherwise no damage. Some ass reckoned it had exploded. Don't know what he reckoned 50 kg could do when it went up. Actually it has gone down and they dug 6 ft and couldn't find it so they have left it. Probably it has gone down to the bottom of the marsh.

Last night he came again and I'm afraid I thoroughly enjoyed it after the hectic start. I was coming home from HG lecture at 9.30 and ran when I could see what was coming but the firing had already started. It came all so suddenly. I found Dora a bit disturbed, to my surprise, but when they were safely in the shelter I could look round. The gunfire was terrific at times, we certainly have some guns round here now. We had no bombs here in Ipswich, touch wood, but Colchester caught it a bit. Will know more tomorrow, but there were no casualties anywhere. It's interesting to see the balloons soar into the sky when the alert goes but am not at all impressed with their usefulness beyond preventing accurate dive-bombing.

Stalingrad is being savagely attacked, and still we do nothing. Those poor devils are surrounded now except on the Volga side and they are fighting house to house. What spirit! Jerry is taking a terrific hammering but still pushes on, inexorably, it seems. His resources must be immense. Immense, yes, but not endless. He must be living on his capital.

We made a landing at Tobruk last Saturday night. Results are not published except we lost *Zulu* and *Sikh* due to the embarkation being in daylight. There was a heavy air raid at the same time.

Last night we made our ninth raid on Germany this month, and each raid used a heavier weight of bombs than Jerry ever dropped here in one night on the whole country. Heartening – a little. Losses varied from 2 when we went to Wilhelmshaven to 39 last night on the Ruhr with a 'very strong force'. Total losses for the nine raids were 120.

Have heard from Dennis this week. He says German flak is worse than ours, so he has apparently made his first trip. Thank goodness he returned safely. May he always do so.

SUNDAY 20 SEPTEMBER
Let's talk about salvage and economies in general. Chief articles of salvage are paper and cardboard. It is an offence to burn or throw away clean paper but we are allowed to dispose of private papers by burning and there are many economies practised. My *Spotter* and several periodicals are now published only fortnightly; the *Telegraph* has four pages Monday and Saturday, six other days; envelopes are used again and again by business firms using stick-on labels for resealing; tinned goods have only a small label; and customers have to collect their meat, fish and bread, etc. with their own paper bags. We are encouraged to save all bones for grinding into glues or fertilisers and of course all metals are wanted. Since Japan collared all our rubber sources naturally rubber is valuable and all rubber articles are to be salvaged by law. It is even an offence to wear a tyre beyond the stage at which it can be remoulded. Rags and woollens too are required. This last week specially labelled dustbins have been distributed in the streets for people to put scraps in for pig food.

Yes, salvage is certainly well organised now and very little goes into the dustbin in the garden. It is only emptied fortnightly and on the alternate week the dustman collects salvage. It's quite a game being super careful with materials which might be useful and big quantities are saved.

Well, the moon will be full next Thursday and still we have done very little aggressive action in this here war. When will they open the Second Front? The Russians must be feeling despondent and left alone. If it doesn't come along with this moon I shall give up a lot of hope.

SATURDAY 26 SEPTEMBER
Let's talk about coal. Lots of others do, so why shouldn't I? Actually the situation has been decided as serious. There have been many miners called to the Forces, which is strange seeing that the government seems to have tried to avoid such situations, but perhaps they volunteered early on. Anyway the coal output is less than we want and coal rationing was promised for last winter, but was eventually deferred. The view was adopted that it would be better to economise in fuel usage than to break up sections of the Army by withdrawing fully trained men and sending them mining again. This year . . .

SUNDAY 27 SEPTEMBER
. . . Dennis came home on a surprise visit, 48 hours' leave before being transferred to a fully operational bombing squadron.

To continue, this year with the increase of munitions factories and the alarming statement that the output per miner has gone down, they have spent the late summer (summer!!) warning us that we must be economical or rigorous rationing will be introduced. To encourage us we have been allowed to buy up to a ton of coal in June, ½ ton in July and now ½ per month providing a house of our size has not more than 1½ tons in store. In addition we have been presented with a fuel target.

This target varies with each house and is made up like this. Each house is allowed a certain number of fuel units which varies according to the number of habitable rooms up to a max. of seven rooms, and which varies according to the district, being rather higher in the north, lower in the Midlands and lower still in southern counties. Suffolk is reckoned Midlands and we, with a five-room house, are allowed 110 units. In addition there is a personal allowance of 15 units per person, us four therefore having 60, making a total of 170 units. This we can distribute over what fuels we choose in the ratio that 1 fuel unit will equal ½ cwt of coal or coke, 500 cu ft of gas or 50 units of electricity. On those terms we will be well under our target figure as, unless it is another exceptionally severe winter, I guess we will not use more than 2 tons of coal.

There are few private cars about now and those chiefly on business. Our trams too are restricting their services, the last one leaving Cornhill or Electric House about 9.30 p.m. That, incidentally, will make it better for the lady conductresses for getting home with the earlyish raids we get nowadays. In most places are slogans and reminders to help us economise in light and coal and all things using fuel, even water. I suppose we shall get down our consumption and save that 10 million tons they want to save somehow.

Stalingrad still holds and, though I hardly dare write it, the Russians are reported as slowly driving Jerry out. The fighting, chiefly in the streets, is still intense and must be terrible. The winter draws on and we are all holding our breath and saying 'Will it hold?' It means such a lot if it does hold that we just hope, with a kind of faith in the Russians but fears for Jerry strength.

Yesterday was the first official mention of the Mosquito. Four of them went to Oslo on Friday in daylight and raided the Gestapo headquarters when Quisling was billed for a speech on some festive occasion. It was cancelled. We lost one plane which is a pity as it was an audacious affair.

SUNDAY 11 OCTOBER

On Sunday we made a ten-man commando raid on Sark in the Channel Islands, with the object of finding out what has happened to British residents who remained there. During the event they captured five Jerries and tied their hands for security reasons while they were being taken to our boats. Four of them ran for it and were shot but one was taken off.

Now Jerry has had the confounded cheek to object to soldiers' hands being tied and says it is against the Geneva Convention. What a sauce! The scum who introduced poison gas, who invented the flame-thrower, who was the first to bomb open towns, who gloried in 'Coventrating' towns one after the other, who cheerfully machine-guns people in the streets, has the audacity to object to tied hands. I won't mention things like concentration camp horrors nor the way in which he shoots literally hundreds of innocent hostages for one Jerry soldier killed nor his atrocities in Russia. As a reprisal, and incidentally reprisals are against the Geneva Convention, he threatened to put in chains all the 2,500 prisoners he took at Dieppe and in fact chained 1,367 of them on Thursday. We replied by doing the same to an equal number of Jerry prisoners in Canada. He said if we did he would do it to three times the number of our men, banking on the fact that he has more of our chaps than we have of his. At the same time Musso is darkly threatening reprisals on us for crimes of some sort in the Egyptian fighting and now the Japs are joining in with similar threats.

THURSDAY 22 OCTOBER

Quite a lot to report. Jerry came over East Anglia on Monday morning. It was a cloudy day. The alert went at 8.45 a.m. until 1.15. All that time single cloud-dodgers were thoroughly (presumably) enjoying themselves swooping on dozens of towns and villages in the district from Brentwood to Norwich. We had five RAF warnings during the morning and he visited Ipswich during the fourth. Our famous balloon barrage was up but was no deterrent as he just went through it and dropped a bomb on Cranfields and another in Belstead Road at the top of Willoughby Road. From the shelter I saw him go by at about 150/200 ft, a seemingly brand new Dornier 217 in new bluish paint, then felt the blast from the delayed-action bombs. I hear thirty-seven people were injured but none fatally. Even inoffensive little Needham Market collected two bombs and G— says he gave first aid to about twenty people there, mostly kiddies. Hoffmans caught a packet and so did Colchester bypass road. Hatherley had his house damaged. In all about twenty people were killed and many injured in the whole area while two Jerries were knocked down, with others probables.

This morning was again cloudy and he smashed up Orford. There were eleven killed and many injured and lots of damage. All this has made us take Jerry a little more seriously. Dora has declared she won't let the kiddies out of doors during an alert, seeing that he did machine-gunning on Monday. I'm all for extra caution of course, as I have an idea we shall get a nasty packet before the winter is over, but I don't agree with her suggestion that the kiddies should keep down the shelter if it were dry enough. All the same they certainly would be safer there.

Saw a Liberator on Tuesday, my first. The wing looks ridiculously small and the rudders huge but all the same they work.

SATURDAY 24 OCTOBER

Out in Egypt we started the offensive last night with a full moon and heavy air support against feeble air opposition but a strongly made defence line. Let us pray it goes well for us and is the last offensive out there and that it results in clearing North Africa completely of Jerry and the Wops.

The 9 o'clock news has just stated that it is not clear yet if the Egyptian action is the big offensive or not. It would seem so, however, as the Navy has been bombarding Mersa Matruh.

Out in the Far East the Japs and the Americans are still jockeying for position. The Yanks are using principally the air arm and keep nibbling at the Jap fleet. They have just made a big raid on Rabaul and sunk or damaged 10 ships, a cruiser and a destroyer and 2 transports being sunk and 6 transports damaged. Tonight's news reports a naval bombardment of the Gilberts by the Yanks which is something else for the Japs to worry about.

SATURDAY 31 OCTOBER
Had an afternoon out today. Dora and I went to hear Solomon and as Dennis came home unexpectedly yesterday, we were able to give him a treat and take him also. I enjoyed it very much but am afraid the Chopin group, coming last, completely overshadowed Brahms and Schumann and the 'Waldstein' so that it was with just a little impatience and only a little curiosity that I waited till it was played. After each playing I am once again almost resolved that I can never again find enough personal enthusiasm to try playing again myself.

To wind up we went to the Ritz to tea and a very excellent tea it was considering wartime conditions. I felt very much more at home than I did last time when Harry and I took Mother there to tea when Dora was away in Northampton. This time there was no feeling of being out of it while sitting with the Army and Air Force representatives. I'm doing a bit more myself now and can rub shoulders with the Forces without any shamefacedness, even if it was only inwardly.

Still the battle is raging in and around Stalingrad. Jerry makes a gain of a few yards, or part of a factory, then is forced out after a day or two and news always comes of the Russian relief armies getting closer. They were in sight of Stalingrad about two weeks ago so the pace is rather slow.

News tonight says there was a raid on Canterbury this afternoon, large enough for nine Jerries to be brought down. So they've started day raiding on a biggish scale again.

FRIDAY 6 NOVEMBER
Wonderful news yesterday, the kind of news we have been hoping for, when we dared hope at all. The *Telegraph* headlines met me with 'Axis Forces in Full Retreat' with the reassuring word 'official'

behind it. After over two weeks of restrained news bulletins and warnings not to expect too much it was one of the most thrilling things I could have read. Then came the news bulletin at 8 o'clock confirming it all and the details in the paper – 260 tanks, 9,000 prisoners, 270 guns, 300 planes, 300 more destroyed on the ground, 50,000 tons of shipping sunk, 50,000 more damaged. All that was unloaded on us and behind it one could detect the official news censor saying, 'Well it's safe to give those details anyway even if we are pushed back again.'

Today the bulletins are again full of it. Jerry is being actually routed and we are following hard. The Wops have asked for an armistice to bury their dead; we have now destroyed 350 tanks, estimated to be four-fifths of his tank force, two Jerry generals are killed, our planes are hammering and Jerry himself is scorching his own stores – an excellent sign. Rumour says he is rushing four divisions from the Caucasian front and flying some over, while we have sunk six more supply ships, some of them small ones.

Well, it's good news and Montgomery deserves all the praise he is going to get. Somehow I haven't feared the outcome ever since it started but didn't expect a collapse like that. Let's hope it continues though one mustn't expect miracles. After all there is that old problem of supply lines and it's a long way to Tripoli. We haven't even kicked him out of Egypt yet.

An interesting sidelight on the Egyptian affair – there has been no Axis tanker able to get through to Rommel for six weeks. That's a good pointer to the activities of the Air Force.

SUNDAY 8 NOVEMBER

Wonderful news again today. If we go on at this rate the Ministry of Information will be charging us entertainment tax.

At 0200 hr today the Yanks landed at several points on the Mediterranean and Atlantic coasts of French North Africa. Excellent and tonicky news. No details of operations are given but Vichy says the landings are near Algiers, Oran and Casablanca. So that's what the fleet of 125 ships, which included 25 supply ships and transports, was doing at Gibraltar.

We've saturated the radio with messages to the French. Roosevelt has explained that he is getting there first before Jerry, that our only object is to prevent Jerry taking the bases and to free France from the invader and has promised to leave immediately Jerry is kicked out of North Africa and is no longer a menace. We have radioed that it is not yet the beginning of operations in France itself and that we will keep our promise to tell them when it is. Gen Eisenhower, the Yank GOC, has radioed to the places concerned not to resist, that he will not fire first and that, if they wish to cooperate they should display either a French and an American flag or two French tricolours. By night the signal is a vertical searchlight beam. A French general, Giraud, who recently caused a stir by escaping from Germany, has broadcast on the Algiers radio appealing to the French there to cooperate.

So that's that. The stage is set, the curtain has gone up and the play is started. What will be the developments?

My opinion is that the French will fight. They may even issue an ultimatum and follow it by declaring war but I don't think that will happen. All the same Darlan toured Dakar, Casablanca and all the rest a little while ago and undoubtedly stiffened their ruddy jelly backs a little.

I should have said it is not altogether an American affair. It is supported by our Navy and our landing forces and several divisions from home are on their way out there.

Oh for news! Amazing statements are made about Egypt. Figures issued this evening say Jerry has now lost 500 tanks, about 1,000 guns and between 30,000 and 40,000 prisoners. Many of the latter were taken because there just wasn't any transport for them and forward tanks are radioing 'what are we to do with all these prisoners', while the old stories of December 1940 are being repeated, of masses of Wops coming in under very small escort, perhaps two British privates, and of tanks overtaking 50 or 100 enemy and just advising them to walk eastwards instead of west.

Montgomery last Friday said to a band of reporters that it is a complete victory. Incidentally the Jerry general, Thoma, was captured and Montgomery had the satisfaction of entertaining him and discussing the battle with him, together with how he intended to develop it. Unprecedented goings-on I should say.

Last news was of fighting around Mersa Matruh and of New Zealand tanks racing ahead to cut off the retreat and to pin Jerry against the sea. Let's hope they do it and let's hope the Wop fleet is not able to make a Dunkirk of it. With our Air Force and our Fleet I don't think it will.

Today is held as Armistice Sunday. We, the Home Guard, went to St John's church this morning together with B Company and enough civilians to completely fill the place. I think the turnout was quite good and indeed Cobb complimented us on our marching. The markers made a bit of a hash of pacing out after the service but apart from that we were pretty military.

9 o'clock. Jerry has crossed the frontier into Libya and we are after him. The French fleet has put to sea from Toulon and I guess they will fight. Vichy says 'the situation at Algiers is serious'; the Americans are each side of Oran and have captured the aerodrome at Casablanca. A rising was also attempted in French Morocco.

WEDNESDAY 11 NOVEMBER
Have been to HG tonight so can't report the latest news except by hearsay and the tail end of Churchill's speech to Parliament which I heard, but, oh boy! what news there is today! Event after event has tumbled over its predecessor and the air of jubilation is still evident.

This morning Hitler ordered an entry into previously unoccupied France and Corsica. I had expected that on Sunday, so wasn't surprised, but I did jump at the reason. He actually told Pétain it was done to anticipate a British attack on France and Corsica which would take place in 24 hours!!! Gee whiz, I just don't believe it.

At midday came news that Casablanca had surrendered and tonight it is followed by the information that all fighting in French North Africa has now ceased. Now, what about Dakar? Will it be attacked or will discretion tell them to surrender and come over right away? One report says some of the French fleet has come over to us, which may or may not be true. A still more exciting report says that Pétain and Weygand are missing. If they have the ruddy impertinence to come over and call themselves 'Fighting French' I hope we pension them off somewhere where they can't spread their natural defeatist minds. This morning Pétain protested against Hitler's occupation of unoccupied France saying that the action has nullified the armistice. Treacherous old dodderer, he wants to steal any glory that's going round at the settling up after it's all over, I guess, if he has come over.

Churchill has made another of his wonderful illuminating explanatory speeches to Parliament on the Egyptian battle and I'd love to report it but don't know all about it yet. Two points, however, I must mention.

In the artillery barrage with which we opened the offensive in Egypt we had a 25-pounder, or bigger, gun every 23 yd!!!! To make a bit of a celebration of the victory the bells will be rung next

Sunday all over the country. I'm glad we are a little proud of
ourselves for once. He also said that the next few days would see
events of great importance.

FRIDAY 13 NOVEMBER
Bardia was occupied yesterday and Tobruk today, that much
fought for port, and the chase still goes on. Churchill reckoned
Jerry had lost 34,000 men in killed, wounded and prisoners and
the Wops 25,000, while we had lost 13,600. That's chiefly owing to
our air supremacy.

Darlan, the old sinner, has surprised us by broadcasting to the
French fleet at Toulon advising them, not ordering them, to sail for
Gibraltar or alternatively to scuttle themselves. So far no result has
appeared but I fancy Jerry will now occupy Toulon on that pretext.
Green, today, called him the 'Vicar of Bray' and that about
describes the old turncoat.

One interesting item of news is that six Italian troop carriers
were shot down into the sea loaded with Jerries and they, they were
the complete convoy, were going north. Wonder why? Should have
said it was north from Tunisia. Most peculiar.

SUNDAY 22 NOVEMBER
The tempo of the African campaign is slowing a little which is only
natural. In Tunisia we have contacted advanced Jerry.

First, though, I should report another personal matter. On Tuesday
the 17th Dora's mother died, another victim to that damnable cancer.
Poor old soul, the thought of twelve months' suffering such as she had
makes me savage and wonder when we <u>are</u> going to do something
about it. We buried her yesterday at Barkingside. Naturally Pa and
the girls were upset, indeed I think most of us were affected. And
so ended a life which, for the last twelve or fifteen years, had been a
time of struggle and disappointment with not much compensating
pleasure but certainly with no grumbles. She deserved a more kindly
end than that, poor old dear.

SATURDAY 28 NOVEMBER
Again must plead lack of time as an explanation of six days without
an entry. Big things have been happening too.

Yesterday, for instance, came one of those events which thrill
and, all in a day or less, vitally affect the course of the war. Hitler had
apparently found some more documents – an achievement in a

special line in which he is becoming very adept – in which it appeared that Darlan had given an order to the French fleet not to fire if the British landed in France. As a result he marched on Toulon and the French fleet promptly scuttled itself. I think it an amazing thing that Hitler ever did refrain from occupying Toulon and we must probably wait till all this warfare is over before knowing why he did so but whatever it was it ceased to have any significance and now there are more bumps on the ocean bed, sixty of them.

What a blow to the French! There were, as far as we know, 3 battleships there, *Provence*, *Dunkerque* and *Strasbourg*, 4 heavy cruisers, 4 light cruisers, an aircraft transport, 18 contre-torpilleurs, really light cruisers, 10 destroyers and 20 submarines. Rumour says 2 subs escaped and the news today says we are patrolling to help out any others who may have escaped. What a catastrophe! They were all blown up and not merely scuttled by opening the seacocks.

Well, that's that. It's settled once and for all the question of who is having the French fleet and may release one or two heavy ships of our Mediterranean fleet though I don't think so as we must keep a big one there nowadays. Wonder what the units in Alexandria and Martinique will elect to do now?

The Russians are attacking again and in huge force. They are performing a pincer movement some distance west of Stalingrad and claim to have cut off 250,000 Jerries. If that is so Hitler, in his capacity as supreme commander, will have a few sleepless nights I guess. Wonder why the Russians gain so much spirit from their hard winters? It's just as cold for them as it is for Jerry and to perform a feat like that needs overwhelming superiority. It's possible that they may cut off the whole Jerry force in the Caucasus.

WEDNESDAY 2 DECEMBER
Dennis turned up again on 48 hours' leave. He seems much more settled this time; I wondered if he was a wee bit apprehensive on his last leave. He was full of the wonderful sight of Stuttgart in flames and was keen to get to his new appointment, day raiding in Lancasters. A new pilot, a seasoned Norwegian, has made him much more settled and he says he could go anywhere with him. When he does I hope he comes back again and safely.

SUNDAY 6 DECEMBER
Today we have had a Home Guard exercise in which the defences of the town were tried out. Naturally I can't say what conclusions were

arrived at, no one ever is allowed to know, but I enjoyed myself and have come away with the opinion that, providing Jerry has no heavy armour, we can deal with most of what he can put over.

We were in position by 0800 hr and it was worth getting up early to see the wonderful rose and light blue horizon with the oldest moon I've ever seen holding a khaki-coloured disc in her arms. We on the reservoir were mobile reserves and I, poor mutt, was a ruddy runner. I suppose it's something to be picked for a singled-out job, even though it is only a runner, but I'm still kid enough to have preferred being with the section on standing patrol at Westerfield.

Waiting there all morning, except when taking a message to Coy HQ, I had the absurd feeling that I could be sorry for a gear wheel in a motor car gearbox. It doesn't know what all the fuss is about and is only there to fulfill a small part in the scheme of things, like us.

By 10.30 'Jerry' had made a few appearances and we were sent to stop infiltration at Park Road–Westerfield Road. We arrived at the same time as four Bren carriers and had a delightful scrimmage though, being behind with Richardson, I didn't see all of it. Those Brens were actually turned back three times by our thunderflashes and clods and rifle fire. One shed a track and the crew took to gardens and bombed us with clods but not very effectively. I had the joy of dashing to the gates and bombing with a chalk bag when they were fumbling to undo it but they emerged brandishing Brens, so did we, waving rifles, and the umpire gave us 2 Brens and 1 crew disposed of for 6 casualties. Actually I feel all four were destroyed, possibly being a little biased at the sight of such things as our fellows preparing to draw a flank with four Hawkins (represented by clods) tied thereon across the road under their tracks. After that we manned the garden wall at the crossroads and waited till the end at 1600 hr, but nothing more took place. It was a good day.

Atmosphere was provided during the morning by Mustangs diving over the town and rather loud explosions provided by the RE who took a joy in exploding 2-lb charges of HE for bombs, one of which 'blew up' our reservoir and destroyed the town's water supply. I guess the CD services had a busy time in some districts. So did the HG in other parts of the town from the continuous rattle of explosives and cracks down Norwich Road direction, but we had only a little up our way. I can see, however, that if only we had improved communications, such as wireless, it would make heaps of difference.

TUESDAY 15 DECEMBER

The chief event is that the El Agheila line was broken on Sunday and Rommel is in retreat once again. Now, will the next stop be Tripoli I wonder? It looks like it this time. Our Air Force is again very helpfully active and our bombers have been in support too. Up in Tunisia things haven't been quite so successful for us. We forged ahead, it seems, with a rather unwise spearhead and Jerry attacked our right exposed flank forcing us to withdraw. We moaned in excuse that we lacked fighter support and airfields but that the former were being supplied and Eisenhower came to the rescue with the statement that we were a month in advance of schedule anyway. So now we are again fencing, probing for weak points, and Jerry's forces there are now estimated at 23,000 men. This sounds discouraging, am afraid, but is not meant so. After all we are fighting on new, mountainous country and Jerry has such a little way to go for reinforcements. On the other hand, in the six months preceding the last fortnight, he lost sixty-two ships in that district with a similar number damaged. He packed quite a lot of supplies and equipment in sixty-two ships, I guess.

In Russia Jerry is still on the defensive round Stalingrad from which he has been driven over the Don and in the central sector round Velikie Luki. The Russians are not having it all their own way however. We've heard nothing more of the 300,000 Jerries who were surrounded and facing annihilation outside Stalingrad, presumably they have learned the art of extrication as well as the Russians. That's not meant spitefully but there is a tendency for people to think that now the Russians are on the offensive they will have cleared Jerry right out of Russia by next spring. I think that opinion very unwise. Jerry will fight like blazes in retreat and I shall be pleasantly surprised to find him driven much further back than Rostov, Kharkov and Smolensk.

I haven't said anything about an affair out East. Briefly it's this. Some time ago the Japs, who had established bases in the north of New Guinea, struck over the Owen Stanley Mountains through heavy jungle towards Port Moresby, the capture of which, being opposite Darwin in Australia, would have been a threat to Australia. They beat the Aussies back to within 30 miles of Moresby and then the tide turned. Slowly they had to retreat, beaten at their own game of jungle fighting, back over the mountains, down the slopes towards their bases at Gona and Buna. All the while the Yank air force was hammering the Jap bases and their fleet's attempts at landing reinforcements, incidentally sinking several Jap destroyers and cruisers in the process.

Eventually the Japs were cornered in a triangle of Gona, Buna and a village inland, then each was taken, the last, Buna, yesterday. Now only a few pockets of Jap resistance are left; when they are gone one more threat will be removed and one more lesson will have been given to the Japs on overreaching.

The secret session in parliament took place the other day in which they considered Darlan and his position. I would love to know what was said.

SATURDAY 19 DECEMBER
Things are certainly moving. Today we have moved into Burma. Let's hope Wavell has been reinforced heavily and that he will retrieve fortunes at least so far as to reopen the Burma Road.

We have been chasing Rommel all this week and are now past Nofilia, some distance west of Agheila. We pulled a fast one over Rommel the other day by sending a force over the desert and then north to cut his retreating column. They cut off quite a force, though how big no one knows, and the papers went mad over the rearguard which was surrounded and facing annihilation. Now, however, news of the action is scanty and we are pursuing the rearguard. No one knows if the first action was successful or if this is a new rearguard.

In spite of the recent moves and Allied victories I stick to my first forecast of 1945 for the end of this affair. If it is taking us all this time to conduct a campaign in Tunisia it will be much longer in a heavily defended place like France and we may even be kicked out again. One never knows. Certainly the reason for the slowness in Tunisia is evident, the country is mountainous and our troops have advanced beyond cover from airfields so our fighters are not as numerous as one would wish and in France we should be able to give better support than that.

SATURDAY 26 DECEMBER
Startling news for a Christmas Day on the radio yesterday. It was that Darlan was assassinated on Christmas Eve at 1530 hr. The assassin was a Frenchman and he was executed today.

Well, that's that. Sounds awfully bad but one way of settling an awkward situation. Wonder what was the truth of the matter? Was he merely a turncoat who took advantage of the situation in which he found himself and did he intend that he should be in Algiers when we landed there and, if so, did he know we would do so, and why was he debated in secret in Parliament? And why did he slate the British so when he was in Vichy? Those are questions to which we may never know the answers but, at the moment, the position is that an awkward situation is solved and the Fighting French, though possibly tending to be more suspicious in the future, will be able to work more harmoniously with their Darlanish comrades.

To my surprise the alert went this afternoon. I had expected a Christmas truce but apparently Jerry spotted a convoy perhaps. I had such confidence in the truce that I didn't put my stirrup-pump out last night when going to bed. Had better do it tonight.

Haven't heard from Dennis since he went back three weeks ago. Hope he is OK. Anyway he might have wished us Happy Christmas but perhaps the post has gone wrong somewhere.

NOTES

1   Lt Col Kingsley Reavell, son of Sir William, and later Managing Director.
2   Gen Sir N.M. Ritchie, then in command of the 8th Army.

1943

January 1943 was a marvellous month for the Allies; the German 6th Army was surrounded at Stalingrad and the siege of Leningrad lifted. Enthusiasm for all things Russian overwhelmed the British Isles and the population was swept along on a cascade of measures which began with aid to Russia, Stalingrad festivals, Red Army Day and culminated in the presentation to Stalin of the Sword of Honour, a gift from King George VI on behalf of the nation.

The tide was truly turning against the enemy. In North Africa the 8th Army advancing from the east linked up with the predominantly American forces in the west, trapping three German divisions, and organised resistance in that theatre of war was effectively at an end. The way was clear then for the attack on what Churchill described to the nation as the 'soft underbelly' of Europe.

On 10 July Sicily was invaded and proved to be the signal for Mussolini's overthrow by his very own Grand Fascist Council. Imprisoned in a village high in the Arbruzzi mountains he was dramatically rescued by a crack German airborne unit after the Italian surrender in September. Marshal Pietro Badoglio's government then declared war on Germany and the Allied advance through Italy was bitterly resisted by German troops rushed down from the north.

Throughout 1943 a series of huge naval clashes significantly diminished the size and power of the Japanese navy and the Americans gradually began to take the offensive. In Burma the Chindits[1] were playing the Japanese at their own game and giving no ground.

Meanwhile, the Battle of the Atlantic was finally swinging in the Allies' favour and the gravest threat to the Arctic convoys was removed when the battle cruiser Scharnhorst *was sunk in Norwegian waters on 26 December – a grand Christmas present.*

The war news may have been better but things at home were no easier. The entire population was now subject to regulations of one kind or another and from April 1943 women up to the age of fifty-one could be sent to work in factory or field adding to the population already on the move. Many of the uprooted were living in uncomfortable and dreary accommodation and rarely able to travel home because of restrictions on transport. Rationing was tightened and everybody who could, including Mr Brown, grew their own food and kept chickens. A bright spot for some in the pervading gloom was the presence of increasing numbers of American servicemen, the GIs. They brought with them chewing gum, nylon stockings and riches in abundance.

For the Browns the year started off badly: Dora's father fell out of a train and died as a result of his injuries. Uncertainty about the future followed for the family. A qualified engineer in a reserved occupation, Mr Brown passed an interview board for a commission in the Services and, in common with many men in the same position, spent many months waiting and wondering whether the call-up would come. In the meantime, Home Guard training fully absorbed him and when the German bombers returned in force and with devastating results, all his Civil Defence skills, nerve and patience were tested.

FRIDAY 1 JANUARY
Don't know what I've done, or how I've done it, but I've an evening off with nowt much to do, except that it's my night on duty if the alert goes.

New Year's Day. Everywhere one hears the wish hopefully expressed that this year will see the end of the war and almost everyone hopes and believes this was the last blacked-out Christmas but without being pessimistic I just can't see it coming off, nor will it end in 1944 either. Hope I'm wrong but we must wait and see. I've just paid a bob to Aldy as a penalty for wrong judgement in August. I said we would land in France and he said 'not this year', backing it with a bob.

Well, we face the New Year certainly with a more hopeful outlook than in 1942. The Russians are forging ahead, there is a sporting chance Jerry will be kicked out of Africa in the near future and we are keyed for a landing in Europe in the spring. Things look rosy but we mustn't, mustn't, get complacent. When we first pushed the Wops out of Cyrenaica in 1940/1 the war was almost over in some estimations, and now we know the real position at that time.

New Year. I ordered my seeds today and we have the prospect of longer days to look forward to. Now we are using summer time it's a bit queer to go to work with lights on. It's noticeably lighter in the evenings though and after a week will begin to be brighter in the mornings. We had a fall of snow two days ago and it was strange to sweep it away before breakfast in moonlight. Fortunately it thawed almost at once and is nearly gone now. Cycling through the town in blackout at busy times is not as hair-raising as I expected. Wet weather makes it a bit exciting when one gets one's glasses splashed and vision is then pretty bad and restricted, but the chief trouble is the pedestrians in dark clothing who walk in all directions across Cornhill completely ignoring traffic like cycles.

America has built 750 ships [weighing a total] of 8 million tons this year, all supply ships.

SUNDAY 3 JANUARY
Let's talk about Home Guard. Our OCs are talking about us so why shouldn't I? Last Wednesday our platoon officer told us we have gone and done it; we've made ourselves so efficient in the eyes of the OC that we were required to parade every Sunday in future, that we were confirmed in our appointment as mobile reserves and he wanted us to train in the new battle drill.

We are getting bouquets from them lately and I'm not too sure that I like it. If they are to be taken seriously we distinguished ourselves at Exercise Orwell, though I can't see what we did so well as all that. We've done well at our lectures, our platoon got the best results at Bromswell range and our PO says the colonel said we were the best platoon in the battalion 'not the company, the battalion' as he emphasised. This morning too we had a snap rifle inspection while we were busy on the field, the result being more bouquets on how well the rifles had been cared for. It's getting all too overpowering, even tame, in its repetition. Incidentally I find I was fourth or fifth in the Bromswell results out of 160-odd who fired, our Sgt was first and our platoon collared the first five places at least.

We started the new battle drill this morning and did the 'Down, crawl, observe, sights' stunt. Sounded childish at first but I'm all for it. It should certainly train us into automatically doing the right thing when in attack. Captain Mee took us for it and also gave us initial tactics for street fighting. That should be interesting as well as exciting, especially if Jerry comes. Capt Mee said it had been decided to toughen us, presumably for street fighting. Working under him we shall need to be tough but he certainly impresses one as being an excellent leader and one that I would follow just anywhere with great confidence.

Have just been out for a walk to try to get tough. Up to the shops, to the school and home by Sidegate Lane in 18 minutes. Not too bad.

We have now been given an additional air-raid alarm signal. If Jerry is within easy flight of the town, presumably the Colchester warning system of 18-mile radius, the siren gives a 'cuckoo' warning, called the 'Alarm', which will have its own all-clear note of a series of 'dashes' for 30 sec. This system will not be operated at night between 2300 and 0600 hr, wisely I think. We had an inaugural test the day before Christmas Eve.

SUNDAY 10 JANUARY
Am writing this at the Schools, while fire-watching at the group centre. Hadn't better say any more; the thought of this impertinent imposition makes me wild.

Chief news lately is about the Russians and their offensives. For several weeks, about six or seven, they have been forging ahead. In Stalingrad district they struck from the north and across the Don, at the position where it runs north-west from below Stalingrad. These thrusts, coinciding with the advent of winter, forced Jerry to withdraw leaving an army of about 150–200,000 men before and in Stalingrad. That army has been encircled and the front is now about eighty miles away and halfway to Rostov. I fancy they are doomed. Jerry has been doing his best to relieve but all counters have been smashed and he has been forced to use Junkers 52 planes; hundreds of them have been shot down.

Talking of that I am taking a morbid sort of pleasure in disagreeing with lots of people who are all seeing the end of the war by this summer. Seems all foolish to me, though I like optimism. I stick to the estimate I made early on that it won't be over till 1945, probably summertime, so say August, and for want of a better date let's say the 11th, so that makes it 11 August 1945 as a day to look forward to. Let's hope we can.

Out in the Far East Japan has been trying to repair her fortunes in New Guinea. The total force of 15,000 men in Papua has almost been annihilated, all the strong points having gone, and she assembled a huge armada in Raboul harbour of transports and escorts. The Yanks attacked by air naturally, time after time, one day sinking nine ships there and shooting planes down sent up as a protection. Then Japan sent some out in an effort to land troops at Lae in New Guinea. Again the planes were attacked and three out

of four were sunk. The Jap won't be discouraged though and I
guess he will carry out the project whatever it was.

SUNDAY 17 JANUARY
Once more, unfortunately, I have bad domestic news to report.
This morning Dora's dad died after three weeks in hospital. He fell
out of a train at Shenfield, hurt his head and has been unconscious
most of the time since. What a run of illness and death poor old
Dora has had. Mother, Win, her aunt Katherine, her mother and
now dad, all in seventeen months. Poor old dad, I fancy he had
little heart to live after last November, though with a fractured
skull he didn't stand much chance. Poor Muriel. There's a lot of
trouble in this world.

Dennis has been home for twelve days, went back yesterday. He
was a little sore about the ops he was missing, all those 'easy' ones
and him not being in them with a chance to raise his ops figure
made him annoyed. He had some twelve when he came home and
it might have been twenty by last night.

Those ruddy French! Even those on our side can't agree in
North Africa. There is some political squabble going on, but I
don't know much about it partly because news is naturally scarce
and partly because I'm not too interested in the jelly-backed lot.

SATURDAY 23 JANUARY
Dora went up to bury Pa today. Even that has been affected by this
war. There was that raid up there on Sunday and again in daylight
on Wednesday and we were all wondering about Sylvia sleeping up
there when she could have come here *en passant*. Apparently even
John was worried over the houseful.

Yes, he came again on Wednesday. About 25 or 30 fighters used
the low cloud cover but 11 were downed. One bomb hit a school full
of kiddies – the death roll is 47 with 60 injuries. To be fair, the
building was one of the high type, unlike our ideas of a school, but
the effects are just as damnable.

We entered Tripoli today and that's the entire Italian empire. The
8th Army has thus travelled 1,400 miles in 80 days, equivalent from
Leningrad to Paris and back, and put like that it seems a helluva
way. That puts the whole of Tunisia and its approaches within
range of our fighters.

SUNDAY 14 FEBRUARY

Tonight we have had another mild thrill of about twenty heavy
bombers going out on a raid; mild because although we haven't
heard them recently they have often passed over our district on their
way to the coast. I was lucky enough to see the first, a Stirling, but
the remainder were above the low cloud. Wonder where they were
off to and wonder whereabouts Dennis is now? Probably over
Holland or western Germany at the moment. This total war is a
damnable business but I think we play fairer than Jerry does and,
after all, with his swank and boasting about 'Coventrating' British
towns, he started it. I read that over 450,000 tons of rubble were
excavated from Cologne after our 1,000-bomber raid last May.

Starting next June we are starting a new publicity stunt. There
are War Saving Weeks for the Air Force coming off and people will
be able to buy savings stamps, cancel them by writing their own
initials and have them stuck on bombs for delivery to Germany.
The money will be a gift but it should catch on. Somehow I think
it will be a bit bloodthirsty but perhaps I haven't learned to hate
enough yet.

9 o'clock. News just in that Rostov is recaptured. Those
Russians are doing fine and deserve more notice than I give them
here but the whole offensive is so vast that the reports become
almost monotonously similar and it is only by studying the maps
that one realises the size of the affair and can appreciate the
continual encircling moves.

We raided Lorient yet again last night in two waves dropping
1,000 tons of bombs. Good, but it is a pity it wasn't on German
soil in view of fresh news of the Jewish persecution. A new
development is that Czech Jews have had their ration books taken
away and are forbidden to buy unrationed food. Sounds incredible
but the facts are verified by secret information. For instance in
Poland 6,000 Jews are still being executed each day and the
complete ghetto established in Warsaw of 43,000 Jews has now
been wiped out. In addition there are to be no Jews left in Berlin
and Bohemia by the end of the month. Perhaps those bombs will
not be misplaced after all.

10.15. Have been listening and trying to see the bombers
returning for the last fifteen minutes. Saw one, a Stirling, very
clearly. The first time I've seen them go out and back before
bedtime. There seemed a note of satisfaction in the engine noise.

SATURDAY 27 FEBRUARY

Tonight am feeling like the 'leisured' class – it's the first free
evening this week. Should be out doing census but am jibbing, just
for once. Was round at the group centre last night, fire-watching
the school which naturally results in a poor, very poor sometimes,
night's sleep. Had an interesting, though a rather illegal, night. I
arrived on time at 8 o'clock and immediately came back to do
some census. After all I was still on the sector. At about 8.30 off
went the alert while I was in Mr Buckle's so I scrammed to the
post and signed on, then went to the school after my tin hat,
arriving at the same time as a red flash to the south. Incidentally
the 'cuckoo' went then and we watched the searchlights groping,
ineffectually of course, for Jerry and passing him on to the next
ones as he came northward. Just like old times.

The all-clear went soon after, at 9 o'clock and then – I actually
went and had one!!! Although it was only a lemonade and lasted
till ten to 10, following which I dashed home to bid the wife
goodnight, and arrived for my fire-watch at 10.15.

Churchill is progressing, having had an attack of pneumonia.

THURSDAY 4 MARCH

Jerry retaliated for the Berlin raid last night. About 34–40 planes
were used and some reached London but only three were brought
down and one of those was over Holland. A bit disappointing but
there was lowish cloud about which probably accounts for it. We
were at HG classes at the alert so those on duty left. We had just
resumed when the 'cuckoo' went, so more went and classes were
postponed.

It was like old times watching a few searchlights shepherding a
plane, or planes, up the Stour towards London. Then a glare on
the coast above Bawdsey seemed like incendiaries or a flare,
followed by flares Hadleigh way. There was a little firing too but
not much round here, only about a dozen rounds from Grove
Farm. It was interesting to hear the shells rumbling through the
air. Couldn't see results owing to cloud but Felixstowe shooting
was very consistent and much better than we have seen.

Can't see any results except one small fire at Kirton and a crater
on the line near Shenfield or Ingatestone or both, and the 8.45
from London ran into one killing the driver and fireman and
possibly others. For once it probably paid to run at 20 or 25 mph
during an alert. Incidentally our 'cuckoo' is a good help.

A tragic accident occurred in London last night during the raid. A woman with a baby slipped down some steps at an underground shelter and went to the bottom. For some reason others behind followed and others from the street, freshly arrived. In all 178 were suffocated and 60 others needed hospital treatment. Terrible. I'd like to know just how people falling can bring others with them, unless the real cause was a missing or broken step.

SUNDAY 14 MARCH
For the past few days there have been items of news showing that there are a few Frenchmen who have courage enough to do something about themselves. There has been shooting in Paris, riots in Paris and Brest and what seems like organised sabotage over the country in general. There are bands of organised 'franc tireurs',[2] as they call themselves, which sabotage the railway and wreck loads of food and burn others. Reports even say the engine-drivers have been known to stop their trains in mid-country when it was known that there were gangs of forced labour aboard so those workmen could escape to the hills. It appears that this Nazi scouring of the country for labour for German factories is the cause of quite a lot of the trouble. The campaign to get the men to volunteer was a complete flop so Jerry is just taking the men, sometimes just driving up to a factory and impressing them.

Anyway the bands of patriots are armed and again reports from Switzerland say the arms are dropped by Allied planes. They must get them from somewhere and, if from us, I guess we are backing them up. Soon? Well, the full moon is next weekend and our bombing is getting into its stride now.

TUESDAY 16 MARCH
Am afraid Kharkov has fallen to the Jerries again and am also afraid that the Russians have now reached approx. the limit of their advance. Gains are still being announced but they are not as large as before and it is possible that I was not so far out in my original estimate that they would do well to reach the Kharkov–Rostov line by spring. There must be some reason why Hitler is not heard of nowadays and if he has relinquished supreme command it should benefit the Jerry army, blow it.

The French partisan movement in Haute Savoie seems to have reached a definite size, as it were. Jerry thinks it is important enough to bomb and many French are joining.

'Atrocities' are things I have been very wary of in this diary but now and again come reports one cannot disregard. It is in *The Times*, surely testimonial enough, that when Rzhev was recaptured only 246 people were found in the whole city of originally 65,000. All the rest were killed or transported for labour in German cities. There are even reports in other papers that Hitler has ordered the wiping-out of all Russians where possible.

TUESDAY 30 MARCH

We went to Berlin again last night and also to Bochum in the Ruhr, losing twenty-one over Berlin and twelve over Bochum. Conditions were very bad, icing and storms, so possibly that helped towards the big losses. A crippled plane might get home but probably won't if half covered with ice.

We now possess chickens. Three of them. In a chicken house in the garden. What's more they have laid four eggs in two days. Most people have backyard chickens nowadays as eggs are rather difficult to obtain. The government has control of all the eggs from holders of more than fifty chickens and private owners like us can have up to one bird per person in the house, on condition we give up our right to purchase eggs from the shop. We, then, having four persons can buy enough grain to feed four hens but we may keep as many hens as we please with the stipulation that if more than four are kept the authorities have the right to consider we must be feeding them on our own rations or illegally obtained food and are therefore wasting food. Dora thinks it will pay because, after illnesses, the kids need feeding up and the allocations are not enough although children under two, or sometimes five years, get four eggs. Since last August we have had seven allocations of one egg per person over five (or two) with sometimes two eggs per person as a treat. In addition we have been able to buy tins of dried eggs but they have only been purchasable on the points system.

A word about these points. We are allowed twenty points per four-week period per head and lots of things are on points. These are cereals, about two per packet, oatmeal about one per pound, dried fruit like sultanas, currants and prunes at about four to eight per pound, rice and suchlike about three, tinned milk, Nestlés, is eight per tin and cheap brands down to two, tinned eggs, tinned fish like salmon which was once thirty-two points per tin, golden syrup and treacle about eight per tin of 1 lb.

Biscuits are eight per pound, chocolate, and four for plain. The system works quite well; they can regulate the consumption by varying the no. of points, reducing where the article doesn't sell and increasing on a too-popular brand.

SUNDAY 11 APRIL
Twelve days since my last entry. What a pity! Can't do everything but I don't want to leave this. Double summer time started last Sunday so perhaps that accounts for a bit.

Chief news is of Tunisia. Out there Montgomery was halted for a few days before new defences Rommel put up at the Wadi Akarit just beyond the Gabès Gap, but he attacked, forced it and is now twenty-seven miles beyond Sfax. He fanned out westward and met the Americans coming eastward north of the Shatt el Jind, the historic (we hope) meeting which we have been anticipating since 8 November taking place with little fuss and no formality.

Rommel is on the run again and as he goes northward the 1st Army is lunging forward in the north towards Bizerte and Tunis to cut off his retreat. The whole object now is to prevent a Dunkirk. Naturally it won't be so easy (!) as we found that, owing to the greater distances involved, the shortest crossing being about eighty miles or so with longer journeys between ports but Rommel is a wily, slippery customer and he will get some away. The general opinion is that preference will be given to his Afrika Korps leaving the Wops behind, while at the same time recognising that anything may happen and that he isn't completely beaten yet.

Our subs are there, comparatively in strength, and ships are continually being sunk. I was surprised to read that since 8 November the Wops have lost five liners taking reinforcements out there.

About three weeks ago I registered as an engineer.[3] All the staff did between certain ages. The idea is that if and when we invade the continent it may be more advantageous to keep the staff we have got going than make new, at the same time realising that they will be taking away from industry men who are engaged in vital work. If accepted, or rather conscripted, it will mean a commission I think and I rather think my chances of being taken are fairly high. I'm about the only AMI Mech E in the DO and it may count. Candidly I'm not keen on going but can, I think, find enough resignation to meet the call. Fortunately Dora is sensible about it and views it very well indeed. All the same, hope I don't go.

SUNDAY 18 APRIL

Another week's gap and such a lot to report that I doubt if it all will be. Still, we'll try.

I've had another visit for the Works, this time to Vickers at Barrow, on the usual sub work. I went on the *Tantalus*, in a half-finished state (the sub, not me) but didn't see anything startlingly new except for tubes. I hadn't better record everything just in case this scribble is scrutinised at any possible time but I did see a finished sub with an interesting name and crew on submergence trials. I also saw two ships, at a guess of 10 or 20,000 tons, surprisingly with only one screw, and intended for a special purpose. I went on a Dido[4] too, again half-finished but with engines aboard and four guns installed. Was rather surprised to find she was just as packed with machinery and pumps and motors and wiring and bottles and mains as the subs. 'Swarming with men like ants' became a phrase with a meaning – they were everywhere. The night I arrived I saw about thirty smoke-generators, portable ones dragged behind lorries, on their way to base for the night. Their function apparently is to make a smokescreen in the event of a visit from Jerry, which may account for the rather astonishing fact that there was no damage to the works or yard evident but lots of damage in the town itself (touching wood on it).

TUESDAY 20 APRIL

Such a thrill this morning. We had an alert, quickly followed by a 'cuckoo', so I proceeded to don my steel hat and clear the top floor as usual. One young lady was eating lunch so I had to go back for her and, even then, had to persuade her to go to the shelter. I mention all that to explain that it was rather late by the time I reached the yard and so proceedings had developed. It was a perfect cloudless sky and a silver vapour trail in a gradual curve showed the reason for the alarm. Then, to our joy, came two smaller and more silvery streaks and Jerry completed his curve into a 180° turn while the fighters cut across to cut him off. Eventually they were a little above him and dived to the attack, at which Jerry dived too and they dropped out of the cloud-forming belt. We couldn't see much then but some said they saw black smoke and, at lunchtime, we heard officially over the wireless that he had been brought down, actually it was off Clacton.

EASTER MONDAY 26 APRIL

Well, that's another holiday over, or nearly so. We've had the four days off but the Works had to go in last Saturday afternoon and Sunday to make up for it. We've had peculiar weather, a little or a lot of rain each day and a helluva gale every day too. I'm certain we had 60-mph gusts today and the wife and I were digging in it on the allotment. Dora is doing more in the vegetable garden this year, more than she usually does I mean, and she usually does help. After all, if I am called up she will probably keep the allotment going and might as well learn how to do it. I can't say I feel remote from the war but if I go the war will certainly be brought nearer to us both.

We haven't heard from Dennis since he returned from leave about three weeks ago. He doesn't like writing but he might consider us just a little bit.

The Tunisia fighting is still fierce and continuous. It is now known that Rommel left Africa on 19 March probably to organise the defence of Italy, so it seems that Jerry knows his time in Africa is limited.

SUNDAY 3 MAY

Sunday again and a cold one. I've just been up to the allotment, for the first time on a Sunday evening, to hoe my potatoes, anticipating a frost. I feel a bit more like writing this evening so perhaps I will.

We are deep in preparation for 16 May now in Home Guard. 14 May will be the third anniversary of its formation so on the following Sunday there will be celebrations. I suppose we Civil Defence section, or rather platoon, are honoured. We are the youngest section of the town, omitting the conscripts, and have been chosen to do a street fighting, house clearing episode on the Cox Lane demolition area and this morning we were rehearsing. Green's platoon will be doing a mock battle in the park also. I'd like to see him make a success of it.

Capt Mee wanted a plan of the Cox Lane area so I've been going to work and home that way, a little self-consciously in case people might suspect some fifth-column activity. We take all this street fighting as something interesting and a little bit of fun perhaps but if it comes to a showdown it will be anything but funny. Wonder if it ever will come? My chief concern at the moment is rather that I hope my knee won't let me down on the 16th.

Tunisian news is unsatisfactory in volume but very satisfying in context. Naturally progress in such highly defended hilly country is very slow and it's only by mentally comparing the line with what it was weeks ago that progress is appreciated. Jerry keeps countering but not often with success. His supplies are being hit too and I guess von Arnim is a bit puzzled how to do it. His shipping was hit so he tried aerial supply with Junkers 52s and we smacked them hard. Then, on one occasion anyway, he tried the Messerschmitt 323 and we downed the complete thirty-one of the convoy. Now comes news that we have sunk eighteen ships, ten of them by subs, in the last few days so possibly he is again trying sea passage.

There has been an unfortunate affair between Russia and Poland. Germany suddenly stated that it had come across the fact that 10,000 Polish officers (I think that was the incredible figure) were massacred by the Russians in 1940. Amazingly Poland, without contacting Russia, appealed to the Red Cross for substantiation at which Russia immediately broke off diplomatic relations. Efforts are being made to patch the matter up by us and the USA but at the moment it is a distinct victory to Jerry to have put us at variance, blow him.

Out in America a coal strike has begun and Roosevelt has countered by taking over the mines. What will transpire no one can say. Over 500,000 miners are out, the reason being the usual one of wages. They are getting $7 a day and want $9. In our money they get £10 6s 0d a week and want more. Wish I got £10 6s 0d a week, although I recognise the cost of living is greater out there.

SUNDAY 9 MAY
Yes, Tunis and Bizerte have fallen, actually late in the evening of the 7th. Everyone is jubilant but again no hint of gloating. Jerry is bottled in the Cape Bon peninsula and is making, as yet, no attempt at large-scale disembarkation. Messages of congratulation have poured in from the King, Churchill, Stalin, Smuts and all the others who count and underneath the approval of us common herd is the wonder – 'where and when?' There seems a big opinion about that we will strike in two places and I'm inclined to agree. Jerry has been often reporting landing barges and convoys at Gibraltar and they are not there for nothing. On the other hand Churchill has said we will use Africa as a springboard to strike at the 'soft underbelly' and that seems an excellent reason for doing nothing of the sort. I still favour the shortest route, across the Channel with full fighter support and

as a help in the Battle of the Atlantic by cutting off the French Atlantic seaboard. Wonder if I'm right.

News tonight, merely the report that over 400 American planes raided Palermo today. Today is Italy's Empire Day.

FRIDAY 14 MAY
The tempo of the war is increasing, mainly by air actions. By yesterday not one Jerry remained in Tunisia, indeed in Africa, who was not in our hands. We have followed up by air attacks on Messina, Marsala, Cagliari and Naples while the Navy has just bombarded Pantellaria for 20 minutes. I should have mentioned that we captured von Arnim in Tunisia, complete with his staff, an excellent bag.

On Wednesday night our bombers made the heaviest raid, up to that time, of the war, dropping between 1,600 and 2,000 tons on Duisburg. Jerry retaliated last night with a raid on Chelmsford while we made a distributed raid on Bochum in central Ruhr, on Czecho-Slovakia and on Berlin, a raid even greater than that of the previous night. Over 1,000 tons on Bochum alone. Our losses were thirty-four on each night.

Today Fortresses made another raid on north Germany. We heard the droning while at work, dashed up to the roof but had difficulty in spotting them owing to the haze and height – so high it was impossible to see what type they were. But during dinner I saw thirty-five coming home, one of them with a smoking engine.

The Americans too have spring fever; they have just landed on Attu Island in the Aleutians, no details being released yet.

Churchill has just broadcast from America, it being the Home Guard anniversary, recalling the difficulties and short supply of the early days and leading up to the statement that as the Army goes overseas we will be entrusted with the defence of the country. Naturally many of us have realised that for months but it is as well that we should also realise that it is not a game. Yes, the tempo is certainly increasing.

Last night's raid was the longest for some time lasting 2½ hours, starting at 0140 hr. I could see huge explosions at Chelmsford (confirmed today that it was Chelmsford) and some time after it was over there were flickers from fires on the clouds visible from our post. I guess they copped it. Round here we had some excitement, eighteen dropping at various places around, but without flares; HE at Greenwich Farm and at Bramford but fortunately none in the town. Wonder if he will come again tonight. Somehow I don't think he will, or do I? Saw an interesting event last night. Towards the end a Jerry crossed the southern part of the town dropping six orange photo flares, equally placed and equal heights. Brilliant things and I guess he knows what our docks look like now.

MONDAY 17 MAY

I hear, reliably, that 1,000 houses were damaged in Chelmsford last week with forty-six killed and about sixty injured. Hope we get ignored here in Ipswich.

An excellent raid on the Ruhr last night,[5] a new one and I'm afraid I felt rather thrilled. Lancasters mined two big dams which control the Ruhr production and photos showed them both breached, one for about 100 yd. A power station has been washed completely away, and bridges too, while several other stations must be starved of power. The two rivers are in full flood, flooding a railway marshalling yard and sweeping away road and rail bridges and damaging hydro-electric stations. A ripping idea. Congratulations RAF on an effective raid.

There was a pretty good parade of the HG through the town yesterday afternoon, about 2,000 or more taking part. It was a glorious day and a bit hot for full equipment. In the evening we did our street fighting, house clearing demonstration in Cox Lane. It went down quite well but a roar went up from the crowd on one occasion. Stevens had been 'killed' by a bomb and was hanging out of the window, head downwards. A thunderflash landed just under his head so he gravely withdrew into the house till after the explosion and then resumed his 'dead' position without a smile. Everything went quite well, the Jerry prisoners looking quite effective. We marched them through the town afterwards back to the Drill Hall but there were no riots.

TUESDAY 1 JUNE

Still no news of anything much. As an indication of the scarcity they cited a Chinese victory as the chief headline on the wireless today. They are also releasing details of submarine encounters and defeats, one of them being that Coastal Command planes recently sunk for certain five subs in ten days. Another item was that in a recent convoy many attacks were made but not one ship was lost. Although these are excellent items of news it is a sure sign of scarcity in other directions when they are headlined.

Had my interview for the REME on Saturday. An interesting experience in which three captains of the Navy, Engineers and Artillery asked simple questions and, I presume, watched to see how I answered and if I was a suitable cove out of which to make an officer suitably to uphold the glorious tradition of our Army. As I don't think I proved any of those I fancy I shall get a note to that effect.

They started off by asking me about Magna, then went through some technical subjects, simple things like beams and bearings and the practical. I know I didn't shine electrically but I told them so, so it didn't matter. In a way it will be a blow to my self-esteem if I am not accepted but I don't much care either way. I don't want to leave home and the kiddies but if I have to must make the best of it. It should be better financially for me.

FRIDAY 4 JUNE
Jerry must know me and my birthday, blow him. I had often wondered if his Focke Wulf 190 could, or would, try the tip-and-run tactics on Ipswich and he chose 2 June to prove he could. A fine birthday present.

The 'cuckoo' went at 0525 hr and I decided to put my socks on 'just in case'. Trousers followed and so did a few bumps and sound of aircraft, then what I took to be MG fire. Guessed it was sneak raiding so we grabbed the kids and dashed downstairs during which we were urged by feeling the house shake. I dashed outside, grabbing my glasses, but it was all over. Some clouds of smoke and dust were rising over the docks district and then another bump as a delayed-action bomb went off a few minutes later and so did the 'Raiders Passed'. It was quick and a little disturbing when one thought of the little chance of preparation. Had he come over our way I guess we would have caught it.

Either five or six Focke Wulf 190s came over from the east, out of the sun, over Felixstowe Road district and hit houses in Hamilton Road and Myrtle Road, Ransomes & Rapier's and Cocksedge's and cannon-fire punctured our big waterless (and also empty) gasholder and 1 million cu ft pressure-type which was nearly full and was spurting spouts of flames. A total of eleven people were killed and seven injured.

On the other side of the balance sheet was one Focke Wulf 190 which was obliging enough to wreck itself. Part was festooned round Christopherson's crane on the wharf at R & R, the engine was thrown into R & R's workshop and the pilot was thrown out with half his head cut away, poor devil.

These low-flying raids are the very devil to deal with. The planes come out of the sea so low they cannot be picked up on radio-locators and they are over and gone before a gun can be trained, while the intervening buildings prevent sound reaching those in the path of flight. One result of these tactics is that the bombs ricochet and indeed Jerry is now fitting spikes to them in an effort to prevent it. That's what happened in one case here. The bomb hit Felixstowe Road at the end of Alan Road making a hole, then it jumped over the trees in Holywells Park about 250 yd ahead and landed in Myrtle Road, a flight of a third of a mile. One theory is that the plane was naturally unaware of this, proceeded on his course, dived into the river valley to cannon the gasometer, and the bomb bursting near his tail upset his stability and he crashed. It is certain that he hit the ground on the locks side of the river.

There was a mess at Myrtle Road, about six houses were destroyed and rubbish showered everywhere. Charlie Doe found a torso with a face cut off the head and covered it quickly. Osborne found an arm and telephoned the police who wanted a description of it. Tact! Showers of feathers came up to our district from the poor things' beds. I didn't go sightseeing. I went to see the ricochet but, when going past, there was a Salvation Army van and a food distributing van there. Poor devils. Sudden terrifying death in a matter of seconds but to give Jerry his due he was after a legitimate target here at any rate, except for Hamilton Road.

We all know that 'something' is brewing and one wonders if the signs are becoming apparent. There is a noticeable absence of planes around here, the RAF hasn't raided for a week, there are very few coaches standing by at the station and we in the local HG are having an ordinary colonel for district commander instead of the usual general. I wonder? Invasion barges are massing in the Mediterranean and the Navy has bombarded Pantellaria four times in the last five days besides heavy air attacks all over the Italian territories and a full moon is due in eleven days.

FRIDAY 11 JUNE
Pantellaria is fallen. Wonderful news. Must be unique too, the first fortress or island to be captured without soldiers and by air and naval bombardment. On Wednesday we had a thrill when Jerry announced that the island had refused to surrender and we

thought that summat was moving. Later we announced the same thing. Today's demand was apparently the third and when about 100 Fortresses arrived over the island they found the white cross laid out on the airfield and the white flag flying at the harbour – the arranged signals of surrender – and our troops took over early this afternoon.

Well, they took a pasting. The planes had been bombing heavily for over a week and yesterday about 1,000 planes of one sort or another paid visits. In addition there had been five naval bombardments on a cruiser scale. All the same, Malta didn't surrender. They found three Gladiators, out-of-date fighters, in packing cases in Valetta in the early days, assembled them, learnt to fly them and took on all the Italian air force which cared to come. That was Maltese spirit but after all I suppose there were Wops on Pantellaria. Quite an anniversary for Musso; his war is three years old today.

Our Air Force is still inactive at nights. Wonder why? Weather? I'd like to think it had some bearing on reorganisation ready for the big blow but I can't see any justification for thinking that.

SATURDAY 12 JUNE
Guess it must have been weather. Last night we sent the biggest number of heavies yet and again broke the weight record dropping well over 2,000 tons on Düsseldorf and Munster. Losses were forty-three.

After Pantellaria comes Lampedusa. We have switched our heavy bombing to there and have already called for surrender. She probably will by tomorrow.

2246 hr. Have just heard on the Empire news that Lampedusa has surrendered. And now, I suppose, Sicily.

THURSDAY 17 JUNE
Not usual to do this at 0800 hr.

Yesterday it was announced the King was in Africa with the troops. Suggests that he has gone to celebrate the historic occasion of a British and Allied invasion of the continent or something like that.

Had a mild thrill the night before yesterday. Listened to the Empire news and heard 'an important announcement' for the Netherlands. All excited I wondered if it had any bearing on the big question of the hour but heard warnings that the Jerry commander was to hold an unannounced inspection of identity and registration cards in public streets and in houses today followed a week later by a purge of 'hidden ones'. Gave one an insight into the efficiency of our Secret Service. Well, well, work now.

MONDAY 21 JUNE
The air war is again on the flow after a few days' ebb. We have warned the Belgians to get inland as far from industrial targets as possible as we intend to carry out an intensive campaign against those targets. News comes now that at the last raid on Düsseldorf over 1,000 acres were devastated and at Wuppertal another 1,000 acres. Think of it. Almost a mile long by half a mile wide. These heavy raids simply must cut down Jerry's output after a while.

Talking about output and reverting to input, I've been eating chocolate recently. Not remarkable perhaps until it is realised that a few weeks ago Dora lost the sweet ration cards and sweets, therefore, were just not to be had. I missed them quite a bit in spite of a penitent and sorrowful wife attempting retribution by mixing cocoa, sweetened milk and so on into a sticky mess which eventually hardened off into what were, rather dubiously I thought, called sweets. They weren't bad but when the cards turned up again last week from the butcher I thought the chocolate that evening was just perfect.

Went to camp at Levington Hall on Saturday till Sunday evening. Had quite a good time though a bit tiring, owing to being picked (by ballot they said) for guard duties. We did the exercises and went over the assault course and had good food all in rather warm and perfect weather, so feeling tired is perhaps permissible. Quite enjoyed the guard episode. There were five others and myself and having the awful responsibility of being 'corporal of the guard', had my first taste of responsibility and hearing my voice giving orders. Changing the guard every hour and a half meant no sleep but being in the woods made it a pleasant night.

Had my medical today. May be able to report at more length about it later on.

SUNDAY 4 JULY
Had an interesting chat with George the other night. I guess he could tell quite a bit if he wanted to about this war and what we are using but I'm glad to say he doesn't do so. If the Forces were as 'mum' as he is fewer secrets would leak out. He was also commenting about television during conversation and said we've

made a lot of progress in electrical matters and sets would be quite cheap after the war.

The Americans have now come to the rescue of the BBC. For weeks now there has been no news to report in the bulletins and now the Yanks have opened what appears to be a first-rate offensive in the south-west Pacific. They took a couple of islands off New Britain and have started a movement in New Guinea against Salamaua.

FRIDAY 9 JULY
Russia. I haven't mentioned it much lately. The situation, broadly, is that when the thaw set in and after Jerry had kicked the Russians out of Kharkov, both sides settled down to wait and activity was very low. Last week, however, Jerry started an offensive centred on Kursk and on a front of about 150 miles. He threw in masses of tanks and troops and a very fierce battle has been raging in which the Russians on the defensive have engaged him with artillery and minefields with results of big losses to Jerry. His only gain is a salient at the southern end which he is striving to exploit but the Russians have now brought out their tanks and their 50-tonners are engaging Jerry's 60-ton Tigers. I feel a bit sceptical about the phenomenal tank losses of Jerry's reported by the Russians, the total now is about 2,000 which is a helluva lot and which includes, I fancy, disabled and slightly damaged.

SATURDAY 10 JULY
It's Sicily. We invaded at 0300 hr today covered by the Navy and an air umbrella. It's not yet 2100 hr and there is as yet no official report of progress.

It is easy to say now that we might have known it would be there as for the last week there have been continuous day and night attacks on the airfield and the two ends of the Messina ferry service. For several weeks they've been intermittent though I haven't reported them here. For my part I think there will be no great benefit in attacking Italy herself; it won't lead anywhere and I don't see why Jerry shouldn't have the job of feeding and supplying her. We don't want the job.

Dora says this morning, 'How long will it take' and I plumped for 25 August. This is for record purposes and a little vanity. Poor old Aldy is not so confident. He hopes it won't prove another Gallipoli. He's true to his usual dismal form.

On the 10th of each month we are to have an official survey of the U-boat warfare which is to be the only official statement. This is to stop small items of information leaking out which may be pieced together by the enemy to his benefit. In today's, the first, it was stated that the thirty subs sunk in May had the effect of helping to make June the month with the lowest sinking losses so far in the war. One convoy crossed the Atlantic without even an attack.

Had a notification yesterday that I had been accepted as a fit and proper person to hold a commission in His Majesty's Forces as a result of a recent interview. At the same time it makes it clear that I may not be called upon to fulfil that exalted position. However, I still have an idea that I shall be so called upon.

SUNDAY 18 JULY
The Sicilian campaign is now eight days old. Seems much longer. The wireless news today said that one-third of the island is now in our hands but it may prove to be the easiest third. We, on the right flank are driving up the east coast towards Messina. In front of Catania we are being opposed by Jerries and fighting is fierce but progress is still being made. The Americans on the left flank are driving north and north-west and have been responsible for most (20,000) of the total 30,000 prisoners.

In a war like this one doesn't know how much newspaper talk to believe but I am beginning to think there must be some basis for the news that the Wops are not at all in love with the Jerries and will welcome their defeat from the fact that it is repeated so often. Substantiation comes from an appeal sent by Churchill and Roosevelt to the Italians. It has been broadcast time after time and is being showered down by leaflet, on Italian cities, including Rome. Briefly it calls upon the Italians to surrender at once to avoid needless bloodshed. As an urge we have just been told that Naples has had the heaviest bombing of any Italian town and for two nights our home-based Lancasters have been bombing north Italian power stations in an effort to hold up electric railway reinforcements going south.

Revealed today that we landed most of our equipment and troops by amphibian jeeps, which are 2½-ton lorries in a boat-shaped hull fitted with six wheels. Cute things, have the virtue that they can just waltz up the shore when reaching land by merely changing the drive from prop to wheels. Saves a lot of time which would otherwise be spent in disembarking or unloading.

We can organise sometimes and it seems that this is an example.

Mr Brown's War

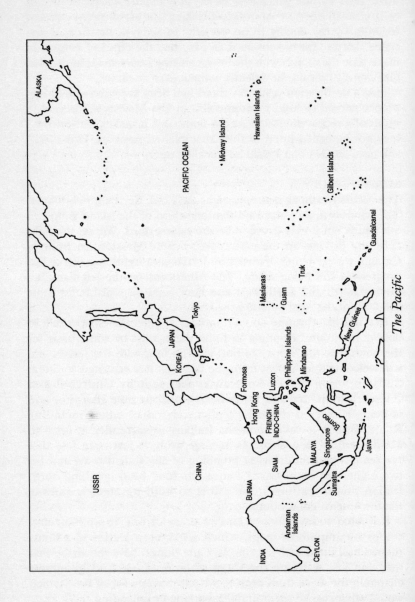

The Pacific

There has been in existence for some time, apparently, an organisation called AMGOT – Allied Military Government of Occupied Territory – and this has been put into operation in Sicily. Hope it works smoothly.

FRIDAY 23 JULY
News today that Palermo was taken by the Americans yesterday and, today, the western part of the island is in our hands. Now, I suppose, for the drive eastwards to turn the defence line which ends at Catania.

In Russia the Russians have been fighting fiercely for Orel just recently and all along the front they have been advancing. They are on three sides of the town and indeed it seems nearly surrounded. An outpost town has been captured and, as Orel seems an outpost of Kursk, there may be big developments soon.

Have just been listening to Jerry but was not amused. He had nothing of importance. This backchat between the countries is rather interesting. We both of us broadcast in various languages but there is a difference in that Jerry jams our stuff and we let him come through as clearly as he wishes. Confidence I suppose. In spite of his jamming, though, our news seems to get through and in spite of the death penalty for any luckless continental who is found listening.

Sometimes, if still up, I tune in at 2030 hr to hear Jerry. An announcer reads the news items, usually embellished with claims of huge losses on the part of Russia or us, wherever the fighting is. Often these are palpable lies but he hopes to catch the ear of some waverer I suppose. Then follows a comment on the news by William Joyce, 'Lord Haw-Haw' as the papers call him. A grating voice, that fellow has, just right for a renegade. He used to be a trade union official over here.

MONDAY 26 JULY
8 o'clock news. Mussolini has resigned!!! King Emmanuel and his new Prime Minister Badoglio have taken over. Badoglio says, 'the war goes on'. For how long? What now? Dora says 'Musso can stay in bed this morning'.

2230 hr. A day of grabbing at every available scrap of news from wireless bulletins to midday papers bought by other people. Briefly, Badoglio has declared a pretty strict martial law in all Italy, even forbidding more than three people congregating in the street.

Rumour says there have been riots which might account for it. He says, 'the war will go on' but for how long one can only guess. A new cabinet has been formed with not one Fascist in it. No one knows where Musso is but a report says he and his cabinet are under house arrest. All announcements to which such things are appended are followed by the Italian anthem and not the Fascist anthem and dates are once more 1943 and not the Fascist year 21.

And now anything may happen. Italy may drop out and then Hitler will have to garrison the Balkans himself while we obtain bases for bombing much nearer to southern Germany. On the other hand she may keep in but I can't see the troops finding any fresh heart to fight with. It may even be the beginning of the general rot. Everyone is excited about it all. I think we can all see big possibilities without being able to put them into any definite shape or words.

TUESDAY 27 JULY
The placards this dinner time said, 'Armistice negotiations reported proceeding'. Unfortunately it was a false report. Churchill made his expected report to Parliament this morning and made it clear that we had no approaches from the Wop government. As is usual, his speech was excellent. I took it as a plain warning to Italy to make the decision to capitulate now. He told them that Jerry wants Italy as an advanced battlefield to put off fighting on his own soil. If Italy agrees 'we must continue to make war upon Italy from every quarter, north and south, from the sea and from the air and by amphibious descent, etc. The only consequence – that Italy will be scarred from one end to the other. . . . We should let the Italians, to use a homely phrase, stew in their own juice for a bit and hot up the fire to accelerate the process.' As usual, too, he gave us warnings not to be over-jubilant. Jerry still has 300 divisions, that is about 4½ million men, and they are still well equipped.

First result of the crisis is that Jerry has taken over all the defence line in Sicily. Previously it was half Wop but evidently Jerry doesn't trust them.

MONDAY 9 AUGUST
Holidays are getting on. Soon they will be all over and we shall be just hanging on again, looking forward to a real holiday sometime. Wonder when and if at all? This war may take such queer and sudden turns one never knows. Last week I went to buy a beach hut

to put on one side till peacetime and we are allowed at Felixstowe again. I suppose we must be taking this postwar holiday seriously.

Took the boy for a tram ride today. Transport is quite a problem nowadays. In an effort to save fuel they only run trains and buses until about 9 o'clock. Rather hard in winter for the older people but as they find the blackout a little difficult to negotiate sometimes perhaps it cancels out. The local bus company runs several gas-operated buses here in Ipswich. It is quite a common sight to see a single-decker bus, and often double-decker too, hauling a producer gas apparatus behind it and it is also a common sight to see them stopped on the Woodbridge Road short hill. If they don't change gear at just the right place with a full load of people, they lose the gas and have to restart from a stop. That isn't always successful and then the passengers all get out, walk up the hill, and re-embark at the top. They don't seem to mind.

Naturally all this has made the push-bike very popular, especially as no petrol is allowed to the car owner who is not on essential work with it. The result is fewer cars on the road and more cyclists and the result of that is a dearth of cycles and an increase in cycle stealing. Am always a little apprehensive when leaving my bike anywhere, even if locked. Prices too are huge and have increased as well by purchase tax on new ones. I bought a second-hand 18 in cycle for Margaret at Christmas and had to pay £5 for it.

The railways run marvellously well, considering they move all the war goods needed. To help matters they appealed to the public not to travel this holiday and, in reply, they took just no notice at all. They flocked to main line stations and even encamped overnight at some London termini to wait for the next morning train. Still I suppose some of them wanted holidays more than I did and there are split-up families who want to meet again.

WEDNESDAY 18 AUGUST
Organised resistance ended yesterday in Sicily. Good going. Messina was the last place to fall and the Yanks were there first.

Yesterday evening we saw a homecoming of Fortresses, 136 of them. Many were going singly and only about 60 were in their squadron formation, suggesting they had been broken up. The target we learned today was Schweinfurt, the ball-bearing centre, which was interesting seeing that Dennis was going there one night earlier in the year and the trip was scrubbed owing to weather. A precision bombing job. Another force went to Regensburg, the

Messerschmitt factory. Both were deep into Germany and for daylight were the deepest penetration so far. They lost thirty-six in all.

Last night we went to Peenemünde, a Jerry research and development station. It was a heavy raid in brilliant full moon and another precision job. We lost forty-one, rather heavy. Wonder why that target? Possibly Jerry is developing something new to counter whatever it is we have to beat his subs with, or perhaps some new aircraft instrument or weapon.

He came round this way last night using fifty planes in all. Out of that he lost eleven. There were bombs at Kesgrave and Colchester but none on Ipswich itself, touching wood. Flak was heavier than of late but the searchlights were as usual no ruddy good.

MONDAY 23 AUGUST

I saw a Jerry plane shot down in flames last night without knowing it. I was on duty at the post and had been watching some very good gunfire but, being without a coat and a cold night outside, we retired inside the post. Soon I heard a sound we have not heard round here for years; the flat-iron-in-the-crankcase grumble of a Junkers 88. Going outside we saw there was apparently no notice being taken of him as he slowly went to the south-east of the town but soon some tiny lights which we thought were flares developed into an orange light which fell in a steep parabola, turned on another parabola and then went vertically. We heard this morning that it fell at Ewarton. Aldy had a good view, being nearer, and the tiny lights were the Junkers 88 and the night fighter illuminated by a searchlight. He heard the burst which set him on fire.

Still that air of expectancy about. A rumour today said that all leave is cancelled but it is only a rumour. All the same I saw lots of Yanks at 2 o'clock this afternoon, all going down Princes Street to the station. There were, however, still some in the town at 6 o'clock. So that proves nothing. A line of twenty Bren carriers, new ones, were being loaded onto trucks at the station this dinner time, with some 16-pounder guns as well and going over the bridge I could see some heavy tanks in the distance. I dashed to the roof but they were then moving through the station; I think they were Shermans. All that on top of other things keeps the old optimism at a high level.

Jerry, too, is feeling it. Last Saturday he offered an amnesty to all Frenchmen who surrender their arms and ammo by 26 August, next Thursday. They say they know they have big stores as the English have been dropping it by parachute. That's good news.

The French are finding a little backbone of a sort and are playing a war of nerves. They have suddenly become very polite to the Jerries, very affable and full of smiles instead of the previous blank looks. Since we have told them of things which may be dropped in the fields to them they have become suddenly very fond of long country walks. Jerry doesn't like it and has even made a few arrests but he can't do much about it. Apparently we have told them 'the hour of action is near' and that's the cause of it all.

Len and I have been house-breaking tonight! A house opposite him has been showing a naked light since this morning so at blackout we used a ladder and he took out the bulb – a bedroom light was the offender – after which he entered a back room and switched off a second one which was then discovered. The ladies round had become a little apprehensive so something had to be done and I don't suppose the owner wanted to pay a £3 fine.

The Russians have again taken Kharkov and are very bucked about it. Their summer offensive is going well and they are now threatening Ukraine. Good luck to them, but I wish I could somehow give them more credit for their claims. They now say Jerry has lost 1 million men since he started his abortive drive at Kursk on 5 July.

Another sign if we know how to read it. Any further intake into the Forces will be directed to the Navy or the Marines and not to the Army.

FRIDAY 3 SEPTEMBER
The war is four years old today and to celebrate it, perhaps, we landed on Europe proper this morning at 0430 hr. Under cover of a huge artillery, naval and air bombardment we crossed the Messina Straits and landed in the toe of Italy. It's a bit surprising that we made a frontal assault on the most obvious place and didn't even attempt any flanking move but perhaps Montgomery knows more about the game than I do. One significant thing is that the landing was made by the 8th Army and the Canadians and no mention is made of the Yanks, so possibly that flanking move will come after all and by them. There is practically no news of the progress except that bridgeheads have been established and are being reinforced.

As a support Fortresses have at last carried out a raid we have often speculated on – they have bombed the towns at the Brenner Pass such that temporarily at least the pass is blocked to reinforcements and supplies from Germany.

WEDNESDAY 8 SEPTEMBER
'ITALY SURRENDERS UNCONDITIONALLY (OFFICIAL)'
That was what greeted me passing the *East Anglian* today and a
paper-seller had just finished doing a similar placard in chalk on a
blackboard poster and was stepping back to examine it with
satisfaction. They say it's the best news of the war so far and I
agree. It's great.

Apparently the armistice was signed on 3 September but the
news was withheld until it suited us best to release it. Now, I
wonder why today suits us better than the 3rd??? Probably to give
us preparation time, possible the British 1st and the American 7th
Armies are now on their way to upset Jerry's defence line in the
north of Italy.

The terms have not been published but Badoglio has said that
hostilities have ceased instantly against the Anglo-Americans but
that any aggression from any other quarter will be resisted. I'm
darned sure we will be playing the Wop anthem over the wireless
within a week. It's pretty sure, though, that we will be fighting side
by side soon. We have dropped leaflets telling the Wops this is a
war of transport and urging them to upset Jerry's transport as
much as possible. It's estimated there are twenty Jerry divisions
still in Wopland, say quarter of a million. They will take some
shifting but they won't have had time to make heavy defences yet.
Probably they will defend the upper plains as a bastion.

We have urged the Wop fleet and supply ships to at once proceed
to British or neutral ports or if unable to do so to scuttle rather
than let Jerry get them. As an inducement we reminded them they
will be required to feed Italy with.

Have just listened to Jerry's news in English. At first the
surrender was not mentioned but later on he read a statement just
issued, at 2145 hr and we had it at 1645 hr. He sounded distinctly
annoyed, saying the armistice had been negotiated some time
before and calling it 'calumny and treachery' but that they had
been expecting it and had the military preparations already made.

Well, it's the beginning of the end now for Germany. She must be
feeling pretty down in the dumps over it. Rather a similar position to
that we were in in June 1940 but with less hope for them.

I've been writing this during the longest alert we have had for
months. It started about 2100 hr and it's now finished at 2315.
We've been watching some very distant flashes from due south and
south-south-east, and George and I have been speculating. He was

of the opinion we have started something over in France but somehow I don't agree with that. Soon perhaps but not yet.

By the way, we know now, possibly, why Churchill has kept in America. He went there after his broadcast and is with Roosevelt.

THURSDAY 9 SEPTEMBER
Things are moving once again in Italy. We have landed around Naples which explains why we blitzed the surrounding airfields on Monday, and Swiss reports say the Yanks (who have not yet been officially mentioned) have landed at Leghorn and Genoa. A Swedish report says the 'Littorios' have sailed from Spezia for Sicily which if true is relieving. All these rumours are merely rumours as yet; the only definite item being the Naples landing where we have already contacted Jerry. We have also landed behind the Jerries in the toe of Italy, the landing being at the instep. When the 9 o'clock news comes there may be more details.

Jerry's counter is to set up a quisling Italian government 'acting for Mussolini' and they have told the Wops to disregard Badoglio's orders and obey theirs. Jerry is awfully annoyed. Apparently Badoglio had been reaffirming Axis relations on the day he signed the surrender and they seem to think it was a dirty trick. So it was, but for Jerry to object is rather pot-and-kettleish.

Out in New Guinea we are making a big effort to kick the Japs completely off the island. His forces at Salamaua and Lae have been completely surrounded, 20,000 of them, by frontal and rear attacks and paratroops dropped behind. Only a matter of time now.

9 o'clock. The Yank 5th Army is at Naples and the sea was swarming this morning with ships of all kinds. There is still, however, no news of the 7th Army, nor is there any confirmation of rumours about landings at Genoa or Leghorn. Jerry says he is in full control of the northern part of Italy and rumour says he is at Genoa. The first part is probably true, especially as he quotes trouble with the Italians there.

FRIDAY 10 SEPTEMBER
More satisfactory news from Italy both in quality and portent. Our bridgeheads at Naples are firmly established and have repulsed five Jerry counters, and there are indications we have artillery ashore. We have also landed at Taranto, captured the place and have a fleet anchored there. The landings behind the Jerries at the toe are successful and the 8th Army have made progress there.

A strong Wop fleet has left Spezia for an Allied Sicilian base and Jerry has attacked it from the air at Sardinia. Up in the north Rommel is in charge and there are various reports of clashes with the Italians who have refused to be disarmed. Apparently we had 59,000 prisoners in Italy but most of them, quite naturally, were up in the north. Wonder what chance they had of release before Jerry took over?

THURSDAY 16 SEPTEMBER
More satisfying news tonight. At dawn today we resumed the offensive at the Salerno bridgehead and pushed Jerry back two to three miles. That's much better. We may indulge in a sigh of relief now. *Warspite* and *Valiant* joined in the bombardment and I guess that helped too.

The 8th Army was yesterday less than forty-five miles away and today Gen Clark said they would be in touch of Jerry in a matter of hours. A carload of war correspondents had the audacity to go ahead of the 8th and has arrived at the Salerno area. They report clear roads and no Jerries, so that's what Clark had in mind. Those correspondents have the cheek of the devil and lots more pluck.

MONDAY 20 SEPTEMBER
Churchill is home again safely, thank goodness. He's been away quite a time.

Sardinia has been evacuated by the Jerries. They were attacked by the Wop garrison and cleared off to Corsica where, reports say, they are again being chivvied by the Wops and the French there.

At Salerno we find things much easier. Jerry reports huge concentrations at Palermo, too big for reinforcements, so he is expecting further landings. May they come to him.

A peculiar war! The coastal areas of England which were closed to visitors recently are now reopened. Just as we all thought it meant an invasion of the continent. They say it was done because of the invasion exercise and may be reimposed at any moment. The sooner the better. Wonder if it is all part of a war of nerves?

Had an afternoon off on Saturday and we went to hear Boyd Neel. Afterwards we had tea at the Ritz (where my cup still had marks of the previous user's lipstick) and a young American sat at our table. Silly fellow, he told me quite unasked for he was on Fortresses, was stationed near Framlingham, his plane had a capacity of from 1100 hr till 0300 hr next day and that they were practising formation flying for night work but were finding difficulty in keeping station. Suppose I ought to have told him to shut up but I'm only human and he probably told lots of others as well. Actually a WAAF was also at the table and she started it by asking him what he was and where stationed.

SATURDAY 25 SEPTEMBER
Central Register sent to Reavell's yesterday to say I would not be transferred at the moment. They referred to 'recent correspondence' so probably it was one of the periodic comb-outs.

Russian news is good today. Smolensk together with Roslavl, an adjoining town, has been captured and the tail end of the line has crept along the shore of Sea of Azov to the junction of Crimea isthmus. Kiev looks like falling too, but still there is no mention of prisoners or booty. Jerry is pretty well back to the Dnieper now. If he hadn't made his defence line there I guess he will fall back to the Polish–Roumanian borders but I can't see him giving up the Ukrainian wheat growing area.

The Russians have done remarkably well to push him back all that way in a summer offensive but I'm still pig-headed enough to think that Jerry is honest for once in saying he is withdrawing according to plan. Certainly he is giving up huge areas of land and it has the same effect as if he were kicked out so I suppose it doesn't matter how he goes as long as he does go.

SATURDAY 2 OCTOBER
So many things to enter and not much opportunity lately. Have been out on one thing or another every night this week. Don't feel too badly about Tuesday night though. Went on fire-watch at the school but for the last time, thank goodness. Can't remember how much I recorded but just over a month ago Morrison, following some correspondence in *The Times* about what should be regarded as 'duty', made a vague sort of statement about Civil Defence work. In it he said that if wardens were within easy reach of their posts there was no need to sleep out on duty at night-time. Naturally we were jubilant and expectant although, in view of past contact with our local authority and our opinion of their brain capacity, we were not too hopeful. However, the group centre manning scheme, which was really fire-watching, has now been dropped and will cease on 7 October. In its place we are to sign on at the post at 2000 hr each night, we are on call and we are expected to do some sort of exercise each week.

SUNDAY 10 OCTOBER

Home Guard is getting rather prominent in the timetable lately. The new proficiency standard has been introduced by which we will be granted a certificate by the Army and which will be recognised by them as setting a certain standard of training and the OC is hot on getting us through. A batch of NCOs are being hotted up and all the others are being brought to the boil more gradually. I volunteered to teach map-reading, on invitation – an offer which was accepted – and I spent some time preparing stuff for it. Last Thursday, however, turning up with shining cap buttons and fully creased trousers, a large-scale specimen map for tuition and a lot of good intentions, I was a little surprised to find I was merely a looker-on while Sgt Hoskins did his stuff, the idea being possibly to bring me to it gradually. Naturally the OC doesn't know if I can teach and won't trust his men to a possible dud when the important proficiency courses are on and I can quite sympathise with that but time is so precious nowadays and the wife sees so little of me that I'm not turning up next Thursday. I suppose my self-opinion has received a blow.

Dennis should have been home on Thursday or Friday but hasn't arrived. Three reasons are possible, either he has broken the journey in London and is enjoying himself there, his leave has been deferred or it has been cancelled altogether owing to sudden military developments. I suspect the second one.

MONDAY 11 OCTOBER

Queer how naval news exhilarates. There was good news this evening about a weapon which has been whispered about but not officially disclosed. On 27 September a force of midget subs had the cheek to penetrate the Jerry naval base at Alta Fiord [Altafjord] in northern Norway and torpedo the *Tirpitz*.

For bravery, coolness and sheer cleverness I guess that exploit will take some beating. A base of that type would be guarded by minefields, nets and patrols of all types and merely to enter would be an achievement, so to torpedo the chief inhabitant is exceptional. Unfortunately three of the subs were lost but Jerry, some time ago, said he had taken prisoners so perhaps they were all able to surface. Hope so.

Air recce shows the poor old gal surrounded by small ships, possibly repair boats and current suppliers, while the usual patch of oil is present and indeed stretches for over two miles, so that's one more potential danger to our convoys removed. One day Jerry may decide it is better to use his ships rather than risk losing them in harbour.

SUNDAY 31 OCTOBER
Still nothing has happened. The news, as usual, starts off with the Russian progress and includes later on the information that it is raining heavily on the Italian front but that we have come up against the new German defence line. Hope, however, refuses to die down.

Had an airgraph from Cliff yesterday, the first we have had from anybody. Those airgraphs are a cute idea. The bloke writes his letter in a standard sized form, approx. postcard size, it is photographed to a much reduced size, a fraction of an inch long, I believe, the negative is flown to England where it is printed to almost its original size and posted to the addressee. The scheme saves no end of shipping as one plane can take about a million letters.

SATURDAY 6 NOVEMBER
Last Wednesday, the 3rd, we had it. Ipswich had its first real blitz and we had our share in Leopold Road though not the most serious. The alert went at 1845 hr as I was dressing for HG, so I turned up at the post for duty with a Sten. Possibly Jerry took it as a warlike gesture as he dropped some of his new flares, starting with 4 blues out to the east, and 4 yellow and 4 red simultaneously. Suddenly I felt a very strong premonition that I should go home. I gave way to it, handed the post over to Bertie and dashed home darned quickly. Dora and the kids were downstairs under the table so I put them in the dug-out with the bags and went off again, after opening all doors and windows, much relieved. Then things began. Guns opened up and I have a confused recollection of hearing a plane in obvious engine difficulties going north. By the time I reached the post again things were warmer with, I believe, more flares. I found a policeman in the trench in the road being dug for the next water main.

Then it happened. Down came a string – and such a string! – of incendiaries along all Leopold Road, across Colchester Road and on to the allotments. A marvellous sight! Leaping and dancing, intense white semicircles of light a few feet high with cracking and banging and smoke. I called down the post for the blokes to get on to the sector, grabbed my bike and dashed. When in the bombs I blew my whistle frantically but uselessly as no FG answered. Eventually one FG came out of Colchester Road. I snarled and swore at him, galvanised him into some sort of activity and entered Leopold Road. Miss Powell's bungalow was alight at the curtains though the glare of two IBs inside couldn't be seen against the glare of IBs in the road. It wasn't exactly a sea of fire but there seemed plenty about.

There was no water there so I dashed next door where I knew there should be a pump and found it, but no water. Some FG leader! Hope he does better now. Grabbing the pump I just stood and shouted for water and almost sang with relief as Cedric appeared with some. By the time Cedric appeared it must have been four, or possibly more, minutes and he was the first one I saw in all Leopold Road. That Fire Guard could be improved.

We dealt with Miss Powell's and George poked his head out of Mrs Mason's imploring a pump. I said I'd get mine, went after it and found the bedroom showing flames inside. What a feeling! It's one thing to deal with other people's fires and another to see one's own house in danger.

What had happened was that Dora had been down the dug-out when the IBs fell. The noise was terrific. I've heard people say it was like a plane crashing. She shut the door and then when they were down, opened it to find one burning in the hedge 3 ft away and decided to leave, being alone in the shelter. The kids followed obediently through the several bombs burning in the gardens to the house. There Dora found the glare from upstairs (thank goodness I'd opened the bedroom door or she might not have known it was there) and dashed up to find a bomb had hit a box of clothes in the bay window. Down she came for a sandbag and put it on and added a douche of water. It made little difference so she collected the kids and went. It's a darn disgrace that nobody was in sight in all the road. I went to find Dora and saw Harry's garage alight and out of hand. Poor old Harry lost a lorry completely, another lorry was damaged and the garage was in a mess.

And so it went on. The evening was crowded with incident, people finding IBs unexploded, someone wanted the fire brigade for his roof which I found was under stirrup-pump control, a shed suddenly flared up into a helluva blaze. While going about finding damage particulars and casualties (luckily there were none) the ruddy alert went again but nothing more developed and by 10.25 we closed the post and went home. I went indoors and found the electric iron red-hot!! Someone had switched it on searching for the light switch and not switched it off again.

Altogether twenty-nine houses in the road had been fired, but none seriously, leaving out Harry's garage. In Rushmere Road two houses were gutted upstairs, chiefly lack of water I hear. In a garden nearby was the IB container. It had held 500 and we had had the lot. Next day we assembled at daybreak, 7.30, and made a garden-to-garden search for UX. We found nineteen, about seventeen of which had the explosive tail, some of them dated 1936 and others 1937 and 1938. The density was quite heavy, each house plot having about six, some eight. Some houses had three inside. I hear we had two containers in the district, about 1,000 bombs. Our little affair was only part of the story. I hear 1,700 houses were damaged in the town altogether, 848 beyond the Norwich Road bridge.

Hope that's the last visit we shall have but somehow I fear it isn't. If we get more IB I fancy they will be the newer explosive type. The older type with a 2-oz charge made enough noise on Wednesday but the 2-lb charge will command a lot of respect. Still we hadn't better cross our bridges till we come to them. In the meantime we had better overhaul our resources, including the Fire Guard.

SUNDAY 7 NOVEMBER

So much has been happening lately. I can't do much more than briefly mention it. The Japs haven't been mentioned here much recently. Actually things seem to be moving, chiefly centred around their big base, Rabaul. As fast as they accumulated planes out there the Yanks upset them, destroying 100 at a time. Last week they made preparations for some sort of counter to the Yank advance and accumulated a fleet of supplies at, I believe, Rabaul. In swooped the American air force and sank seven supply ships and four destroyers. The Jap naval support forces were encountered offshore by naval forces of America and lost four more destroyers and one cruiser against damage but no losses to the Yanks. Then yesterday came the report that possibly a main Jap battle fleet was out as a force of nineteen cruisers and destroyers had been spotted steaming from Truk to Rabaul which may be the fleet's advance forces. Possibly they have been contacted as America reports two Jap cruisers sunk by air action.

The big news has come from Russia. Kiev fell on Friday and Stalin, in commenting on it all has made an interesting speech. He actually praised us, saying the Allied victories in North Africa and Italy and the heavy bombing of Germany were not a Second Front but something very much like it and recognised the help our supplies had been to him. He said that 'the Second Front in Europe which is not far off will considerably speed my victory'. He estimates Jerry losses for the past year at 4 million casualties including 1,800,000 killed, 14,000 planes, 25,000 tanks and 40,000 guns. Quite a lot.

Harris, Bomber Command chief, calmly said yesterday that 'we propose entirely to emasculate every centre of enemy production, forty of which are centres vital to his war effort and fifty that can be termed considerably important'. Sounds inexorable and grim to me and at the same time ominous for Germany and eloquent of victory for us from absolute air superiority. He reckons our air effort is containing 3 million Jerries in Germany to deal with us by fighters, ground staff and repair work.

There has been almost continual sound of aircraft today, mostly American origin. Yesterday afternoon there were Forts, Liberators, Thunderbolts, one Marauder and eight Lightnings about, and only two Spits. They will have to go a long way to produce something more beautiful than the Spit, bless it.

MONDAY 15 NOVEMBER

There's lots I ought to have recorded but Godfrey went into hospital on Saturday and that, with other things, has made time a little scarce.

Full details, as far as we can get them, about the 3 November affair over here are rather disquieting when one realises that if the attack had been concentrated on the centre of the town much more damage would have resulted. Jerry dropped 28 HE on Ipswich and 21 on inoffensive Bramford with a total of 9 IB containers on Ipswich and 5 on Bramford.

As a result of that night I drafted a few tips for a leaflet to be circulated to householders in the district and Maun said he would get them printed for me. The old blighter hasn't produced them yet and the affair will become so dulled in people's minds that the suggestions will lose their appeal and value if he doesn't hurry up.

In Italy progress is still slow, understandably in view of the terrain and wintry weather. Been cold round here too recently with a few flakes of snow on Sunday.

SUNDAY 28 NOVEMBER

Sunday again. Have had another week in which I have been out on ARP or HG every night except Tuesday but then I had to go down

town to Sanders. The war affects time in another additional way –
there being few toys about and we must make them, and Christmas
is only four weeks away.

Had an interesting morning today. Lord Bridgeman, the largest
noise in the HG, came down to review us and it's the first time I've
ever been to such a function. Turnout wasn't too good, there were
only 150 of us, but all the battalion went to Coplestone Road School
for the occasion.

There was quite a commotion at our school HQ where they made
us fall in in one company and split us up into provisional platoons.
Cobb and Mee fussed about putting us into correct order with the
tallest at each end and ensuring we knew the correct orders and
tightening all rifle slings.

Off we went, marching as well as we could to Coplestone Road.
To my surprise a band was waiting for us and played us in. It is a big
school with a large ground and they had put the band at the
entrance with the result that by the time the head of the column had
reached the other side they were marching to a different step from
what we were. In addition the conductor, the old so-and-so, speeded
up about 25 per cent as we were entering. The row of the band
made it almost impossible to hear orders, us being at the tail end, so
we went by instinct.

Eventually, when all five companies had assembled Col Howes took
over. I said before that Bridgeman was the biggest noise but he isn't.
Col Howes just stood in the centre of the foreground and merely
opened a cavernous mouth and shouted, without apparent effort,
but what an effect! A clear roar that could be heard everywhere.

Bridgeman arrived soon after, received the company commanders
and then addressed us with some good sound common sense. The
fact that the invasion was not so likely now was due to our presence
and we could not say that we would not be needed. The Major, for a
wonder, congratulated us on our marching and bearing. I must say,
from the bearing of the other companies as they arrived at the
school, we deserved it. Bridgeman's speech was, of course, one in
the eye for Citrine, the TUC idiot, who recently said publicly that
the HG was not now needed.

We had SW and a group meeting this week, and there were some
criticisms of 3 November from the authorities. Apparently we didn't
report enough about the fires we had. I fancy someone is
looking for scapegoats and who is fairer game for that than the
wardens? Putting two and two together I fancy it wasn't our post

at fault so much as CI, but all the same they say we sent nine
requests for fire services and we only reported one fire because
only one got out of hand.

SUNDAY 12 DECEMBER
Jerry came round here on Friday night but not to Ipswich, thank
goodness. He seemed after 'dromes inland judging by the flares but
the searchlights picked up quite a few for short periods. Even our
big chap at Rushmere found one, for two seconds. Guess the crew
had heart failure. I saw the biggest blanket of red tracer I've ever
seen go up over Felixstowe on one occasion. The sound, when it
arrived, was a continuous rumble. It got the plane, apparently,
though I didn't see it fall. One Mosquito brought down three
planes, all Dornier 217, by himself.

We've been very lucky. Godfrey went into hospital on 13 November
and came out on Friday. All the while he was there there were only
two alerts and only on one occasion was there gunfire – one shot. Jerry
kindly waited till the chap came home before resuming his visits and
I'm glad he did. Should have been worrying a bit with him up there
during a noisy raid. When the alert started he gravely asked me if Jerry
had any more fire bombs. A little rashly perhaps, I said yes, so he
wondered if he was going to drop them on this house. Although
apprehensive he wasn't too scared while the rather considerable
gunfire sounded and Jerry dived and roared overhead.

Flu is about rather badly and deserves inclusion here because
probably overwork and war mixing of populations is the cause.
They are using Service doctors to help the civilian force. Hope we
escape it.

We have our exam next Sunday for the new proficiency exam,
HG of course. We've been training, twenty-four of us from all the
company being the chosen few, for some weeks now. Hope we pull
it off, there are only twelve of us going at first. Some apprehension,
even trepidation, has been caused by reports that the examiners'
severity in getting five rounds off in 20 sec on a rifle and over the
Sten 'instinctive handling' clause. However, must do our best I
suppose. I managed the five rounds quite easily last night but it
will be another matter under actual test conditions.

MONDAY 27 DECEMBER
Boxing Day, yesterday being Sunday, and an ecstatic feeling of
nothing to do. The whole of the week is a Home Guard holiday;

can't think who had the brainstorm which resulted in that decision but it's one with which I am in sympathy for once.

I'm glad that the unofficial truce was again observed this Christmas. Every year, just before the holiday some bright bloke hops up in Parliament and asks for a truce to be declared for a day or so and always the answer is that we intend to pursue the war to the discomfiture of the enemy no matter what the day. All the same, nobody has yet raided during Christmas, though I'm not too sure about 1940 when the London blitz was on. I've an idea the Manchester heavy raid was on Christmas Eve.

On Thursday night we visited Berlin again to the extent of 1,000 tons. Germany has now had its second 100,000 tons of bombs from the RAF. During daylight on Thursday the American air force went to the Pas de Calais area after 'military installations'. The force sent was the biggest so far, 1,300 bombers and fighters with British support too. Not one plane was lost. The 'military installations' have not been officially disclosed but the papers all say they are the rocket-gun installations being erected for bombarding us. Seems as if Jerry is in earnest with his rockets, if so as a commentator has said, it is an admission of the defeat of the Luftwaffe.

All sorts of wild rumours are going round about these rockets, chiefly from neutral sources. Some say they are huge things of 10 tons and 45 ft long with light alloy wings. Others say the final HE remaining for explosion on impact will be bigger than our 8,000-pounders. Rather interesting.

Scharnhorst is sunk. News came this dinner time and when I heard the headlines I dashed outside to warn George next door who was in his garden. No details yet but it has been released that she was attacking a Russian convoy when she was sunk off the North Cape by units of the Home Fleet. Good news. Now Jerry has not one ship of battleship class available for service. All the others are being repaired, which says something for our Silent Service and the RAF.

A bit of a bombshell on Christmas Day. Eisenhower has been appointed C-in-C of the forces on the Second Front. Sounds peculiar but I suppose Churchill knows what he is doing. The *Sunday Express* even quotes 'a reliable source of American information' which says the forces attacking on the Second Front will be 73 per cent American and 27 per cent British. Still, we know the *Express*. George suggests it may be because we are not too popular in France and the Yanks may be hailed more as liberators than we would be and be given more support. Maybe but I rather fancy if the jelly-backs want to do anything for themselves they will do it, no matter who arrives.

NOTES

1   The name given to the special force commanded by General Orde Wingate which operated behind the Japanese lines.
2   The Maquis, the military branch of the French underground movement, taking its name from the shrubland of the Mediterranean coast.
3   As an engineer engaged on war work, Richard Brown was exempt from conscription. However, this exemption would have been periodically reviewed.
4   Dido class cruiser – possibly HMS *Diadem*.
5   The famous Dambusters raid, 617 Squadron, led by Wing Commander Guy Gibson.

1944

Richard Brown like the rest of the population positively hungered for the opening of the Second Front. Picking up on every possible indicator and making bets at the office, he predicted that the landings would be between Brest and Cherbourg. Within months he was to be proved almost right. D-Day, Operation Overlord, finally came on 6 June and the Allies invaded France.

In retaliation the Germans unleashed their unmanned flying bomb, the V1, on the British Isles triggering another wave of evacuation from London. Three thousand V1s came over in the first three weeks. They were followed in September by the even more dangerous V2, the 14-ton rocket against which there was no defence.

In the months that followed fighting on the continent intensified and the Germans resisted fiercely but were unable to prevent the inevitable: Paris was liberated in August, Brussels on 3 September five years to the day since war was declared. There had even been, in July, an attempt on Hitler's life by his own generals. A plot which misfired badly and brought a terrible retribution on the plotters. At the same time the Russian armies were sweeping across eastern Europe and in October British troops landed in Greece after the Germans had withdrawn. As the Allies advanced the resistance fighters rose to lend their support and the noose tightened on the 'Master Race'. Alas a Pandora's box was opened in the liberated areas. Who would take control? The old regime or the new left?

The Allies did not quite sweep all before them in 1944 and there were hiccups; the attempt by airborne troops to safeguard the Rhine bridges went badly wrong at Arnhem and at the end of the year Field Marshal Gerd von Rundstedt mounted a dangerous counter-attack in the Ardennes with twenty-four divisions. In addition there was a renewed spate of heavy raids on London and the provincial cities in response to the massive air raids on Germany.

In Italy the campaign which had virtually ground to a halt before Cassino at the Gustav Line early in the year was to be reopened in strength in May. The Germans were pushed back and on 4 June Allied forces entered Rome.

As it was in Europe so it was also in the Pacific – inexorable advance bitterly resisted. The Japanese were slowly driven from their conquered territories and India was made safe at last as the 14th Army turned to the offensive in Burma. But there was still a very long way to go.

On the Home Front there was little respite as 1944 opened. Mr Brown put in 72 hours' HG and CD duty in January and worried about the clash of interests. It was also another trying winter bedevilled by shortages, a flu epidemic and a lack of fuel, exacerbated by miners' strikes.

Jubilation at the advances made as the year progressed could not hide the fact that after five years the British people were still being daily affected by the war. Ipswich, being on the east coast, was in the flight path of both the V1 and V2 and had its fair share of alarms and explosions; Mr Brown complained of constantly disturbed nights.

But by the autumn the war was to all intents and purposes won and in September the blackout became a dim-out, street signs started to reappear and the tank traps were removed. On 10 September it was announced that Home Guard parades were no longer compulsory and in November the HG was stood down, rather to Richard Brown's regret.

The tremendous raids on Germany had an effect but took their toll. One of the casualties was Richard's nephew Dennis, lost over the Channel on 30 July; it was October before his family was informed.

SATURDAY 1 JANUARY

New Year again. Wonder what it will bring? By the next New Year quite a few problems will have been solved and questions settled, I guess.

Wonder if anything is happening in France? We have been heavily bombing the coast, chiefly the Pas de Calais area and in the last few days it's been super. We even went there at night just before Christmas and the Yanks sent 1,300 bombers and fighters. On Thursday they exceeded even that in a force which went to south-west Germany and then with Marauders at the French coast again; well over 2,000 planes were used. What a total! Again they went yesterday to the 'military installations' as the wireless announcers call it with an emphasis in the voice. Den came home yesterday and remarked that obviously that's where the invasion will be. Hadn't even thought of it myself. Must be slow, but I can't see why we shouldn't be foxing Jerry all the same.

TUESDAY 4 JANUARY

It's about time I said something about the Russian affair. This time last year they were still fighting in Stalingrad, from memory I believe it was relieved in February, and today they crossed the Polish border at one place. I guess Jerry's goose in Russia is cooked.

How long before we start cooking it over here? Montgomery was recently taken away from the 8th Army in Italy and appointed in command of the British armies for the Second Front. Yesterday he arrived in England to take over. The wireless broadcast a record of his farewell in Italy and everyone, apparently, accepts the idea of the parting.

I wonder! When Jerry came here last November a big contingent of the 8th Army was up Whitton way. If it is still there or not I don't know but I hear on pretty good authority that Felixstowe is full of them. I suppose I'm not blabbing military secrets when I say Den casually remarked 'it's an open secret the majority of the 8th are in England'. I suppose they will be the spearhead and we must have seasoned troops in that position but what a difference between fighting and learning the art in the desert and then switching to the cold, muddy, desperate fighting in France. I suppose it will be in France. It seems then, that Monty's transfer is merely a transfer of scene, not of command.

Berlin had two more 1,000-ton packets on Saturday and Sunday nights. Losses were twenty-eight and twenty-seven. I think the last four ops have all been on Berlin.

To return to the subject, I suppose the chief question in everyone's mind is – when? Candidly, seeing this is a diary I may as well admit and record it; I feel just a little apprehensive for the local surroundings. I quite expect visits here from Jerry, though not necessarily on a big scale, but so many incidents such as certain ships in the dock, 8th Army around here, and Jerry's tendency to experiment on us, rather point to visits. I've mentioned to Dora that it would be advisable to keep bags packed as completely and conveniently as possible and I intend to get the respirator census done as conscientiously as possible. Beyond being prepared we can do no more.

SUNDAY 16 JANUARY

Now I've started I don't feel much like writing. Suppose I'd better get going though. It's getting, once more, to the stage where it feels heavenly to be able to sit down and do nothing. Last week consisted of a full day ARP on Sunday, three evenings on HG, one on alert duty, two on visitors and today we had a full morning HG. There's still a lot of expectancy about regarding Home Guard mustering. I fancy, from sifting all of it, that there may, probably will, be a skeleton muster at HQ but the majority will continue at work until possible raids by Jerry, I mean paratroop raids. We in the Warden's service won't muster till Jerry gets in the vicinity.

Peculiar weather about here recently. Cold snow-promising weather one day, mild and warm the next and a June day, almost, on Friday produced the thickest fog ever for these parts on Saturday. Last night it froze. We were apprehensive about marching but were lucky enough to find the roads in the town reasonably free.

SUNDAY 23 JANUARY
Went to the second and last (thank goodness) of the training lectures at Argyle Street today. Hours were from 1015 hr to 1800 hr without a break for lunch. It's all been a waste of time except for about two lectures. It emerged this afternoon, however, that which I had suspected, that we will probably get gas. A new series of weekday evening lectures is starting now. I suppose we need them. Chiefly they are incident control, rescue and IB control. Then, I believe, we hand it all over to the fellows.

On Friday, possibly Thursday, we made a landing well behind Jerry lines facing the 5th Army on the west coast of Italy. We haven't said yet where it is but Jerry says it's only a few miles from Rome on the plains. Resistance was amazingly light, we have established the bridgeheads and captured a port. Just before we staged an offensive which possibly drew up Jerry's reserves and now the roads and railways around and approaching Rome have been bombed to uselessness.

SUNDAY 13 FEBRUARY
Salerno beachhead was a name which became famous in this war and will be, I think, immortal if only by reason of what depended on it. Anzio beachhead will be another and for the same reason. It's the one I mentioned a little while ago, or did I? On the beaches a few miles below Rome. Things looked a little serious earlier in the week; Jerry countered heavily time after time and it was evident that we had had to give up a little ground. Even so it is still about ten miles deep and about twenty long. Naturally we have control of the air and of the sea but early in the week the weather changed to

northern gales, snow and rain and almost stopped flying and then some sort of indescribable uneasiness came over us. Jerry was pushing hard with all he had and the continual reports of bad weather coupled with the expectation that the 5th Army would link up. . . . Jerry interrupted that.

FRIDAY 18 FEBRUARY

To continue with the Anzio beachhead, the situation has been static all this week. Jerry has been attacking again but has been beaten off after the few days lull which enabled both sides to get a breather.

Further down the coast, at Cassino on the 5th Army front, a Benedictine monastery stands on a hilltop, literally. Jerry used it for OP and for light artillery to our discomfort as it commanded the road to the north-west. We objected and tried to ignore it, then sent leaflets warning any Italians there that we would have to shell it. Next day lots of Fortresses bombed it. It's a big pity as the interior was a wonderful example of marble and ornamentation but couldn't be helped. Naturally it created worldwide interest.

Did I report the ten divisions trapped in Ukraine? So few opportunities for writing that I forget. Anyway they have now been liquidated with 52,000 killed and 11,000 prisoners and lots of booty. In addition 20,000 relieving troops killed and 300 planes, mostly Junkers 52, shot down. The Russians gave them the opportunity to surrender but they refused, thinking they would be rescued.

SUNDAY 20 FEBRUARY

On Tuesday we made the heaviest attack of the war. It was on Berlin to the extent of 2,500 tons and over 1,000 bombers were used. Losses were forty-five machines. Naturally I expected a retaliation on London last night but we had the wettest day for some months and it didn't materialise till Friday, usually the day for activity round here. He sent about sixty planes and rather more than usual reached London. Reading between the lines I guess he did some damage, chiefly with incendiaries, but we say the fires were soon dealt with. Unfortunately only three were brought down and they were over their own 'dromes by our intruder patrol. Perhaps better results next time.

The Second Front is, I suppose, a week nearer than it was last Sunday. We may even be on the brink of it. Don't think so, though, although fresh pointers keep cropping up. Last Sunday we, all the CD services, went to the Regent and the Public Hall to hear a lecture by a military major on 'Security'. It was probably intended to impress us not to spread news of anything we may see or hear in the near future. We all had to turn up in uniform, pass through an avenue of scrutinising police at the entrance and had to listen to just nothing more than a suggestion that we should hold our tongues. I put in 72½ hours in January and can't spare fine afternoons like that.

Another more significant pointer is this new series of lectures they are giving us senior wardens on incident control. They tell us that in the event, if things turn out as seem likely, the police will be used for convoy work and as Jerry will probably bomb us – maybe cascade raids – incidents will be plentiful and we shall have to do everything off our own bat. The Home Guard arrangements to turn out and help us are being perfected too, probably to the same end. I hope I shall be able to acquit myself to satisfaction if it ever becomes necessary but hope it won't. There's lots to learn and lots more of common sense needed and of an adaptability to circumstances. Even more than that we shall want a higher standard of cooperation from the wardens.

We had an officers' and NCO's meeting of the Home Guard last Thursday at which we were given a few details such as the code word for the action at an anticipated raid and at the event. The authorities seem to have an estimate of the probability of diversionary raids by Jerry at Second Front time. Wonder if he will? At the preliminary warning the OC wants a platoon of men to mobilise and doesn't know who. He seemed to prefer us in No. 9 but can't have us because of our wardens' work if Jerry blitzes us at the same time. Taken to its logical conclusion we should always be on call for wardens' duties seeing that Jerry would be liable to blitz at any time and to that extent we are valueless to the HG. That suggests that we could be disbanded but the OC would be in a bit of a flat spin as I can unblushingly say that we are his best platoon. Quite a situation. Of course the real position is that we were enlisted for use if Jerry invaded and that situation has now changed.

Am now buying a pair of binoculars from a chap at work. They wanted adjusting, a matter we have attended to, and are now quite good. It's quite fascinating to see planes gliding about with a new value of colours. George has bought my field glasses. I was sorry to part with them. They've given me wonderful service and I've spent many happy hours with them but they've gone to a good home. Queer how one gets attached to such things.

SUNDAY 5 MARCH
The moon is now within a few days of full; in four weeks' time the April moon will be near and it's quite possible the Big Event will be launched then. I fancy March is too unsuitable for weather and May will be leaving it rather late so it's something of a thought to realise that five weeks from now we will probably be using the new Forces programme and breathlessly, almost, listening to the hourly news flashes. It will be a grave time and we certainly won't have it all our own way to begin with. All the talk of it being over within a month is just piffle.

Let's have a prophecy. I think the venue will be (still think so) between Brest and Cherbourg in order to extenuate Jerry's communication and supply lines and make them more vulnerable. If we strike down southwards, having our backs to the sea and being able to use sea power to edge down the west coast, we will cut off Jerry's easy access to the Atlantic and have him only on our front. Eventually I fancy, the line will stretch from the end of the Pyrenees to Ostend, bending back perhaps to clear Paris, reaching that condition by about the end of the year. The RAF will continue night attacks on German centres and towns while the USAAF will support the daylight actions and the Army.

Wonder what surprises we have for Jerry? Can't prophesy any of those but I have faith enough to guess that we have some.

SUNDAY 12 MARCH
It was stated this week that America, three weeks ago, approached Eire with the suggestion that they should close the Jap and Jerry embassies in Dublin which are hotbeds of spy organisations. Now after three weeks de Valera has flatly refused, sheltering behind the virtue of neutrality. The *Express* points out that the spy service has already cost lives and that we are fighting for Eire too, so what the hell. Wonder what the reply will be? Hope it's to the point. One recalls the Irish boat which saw a U-boat and soon after contacted a British destroyer but didn't relay the news under the pretext that it was really nothing to do with her. Soon after she was sunk by another sub.

The Russians are doing marvellously. They are now striking southward and south-east at the western end of the front bounding the northern Ukraine, the object being to cut off Jerry in the Dnieper bend. It seems they are likely to achieve the object. Jerry has a long way to go, the main railway link with Germany has been cut and their casualties are heavy. It seems they are losing all their ability.

TUESDAY 14 MARCH
Cheers! Churchill in Parliament today said that the closing of traffic between this country and Ireland was the first of other measures being taken to isolate Southern Ireland in the coming difficult times. Rather strong to talk deliberately of isolating a neutral country but worthwhile. As he says, if we suffer a military defeat through leakage of information and because of spying we should deserve the greatest censure and America, too, expects us to take the greatest care of her armies while over here. Wonder how much has already been said to Jerry agents about our aerodrome positions and planes by the Irish labourers over here? There are crowds over here, a wild lot too by reports, and they regularly go home each seven weeks for a short stay in order to avoid paying income tax over here on their earnings. Den said the traffic at Stranraer was very heavy at weekends. Glad we are taking care of such an obvious leakage and wonder what the next steps will be.

Yesterday morning, I hear, there were considerable troop movements around here. Even Aldy wondered if zero hour were approaching, even his fearfulness couldn't contradict his own eyes.

SUNDAY 19 MARCH
A good day. Awoke to a rain shower, gloried in it, specially as there was no parade. The weather cleared later and am afraid I spent most of the time till sunset looking upwards with those new glasses. There were plenty of planes about of various sorts.

Week before last I heard Grayson say he had had enough coal the day before to last the Works till the end of the day. Appeals to some string-pullers in the government departments had resulted in a delivery of 5 tons 9 cwt which would last him till the next day. After that it would be helping to overload the grid. Adverts in the paper implore us to think before switching on a light or a fire. The present ruling on coal purchase is that no one may buy more than 4 cwt and no one may buy coal which would bring his possession to above 5 cwt. Coke is unrationed but there is none to be had in the town. Using it sparingly we may have enough to last till summer but lots of it is dust. The fuel situation certainly is getting serious but if we have nothing worse than that to endure we won't be so badly off. Most of Russia had no coal at all for domestic consumption during the 1942 winter.

I will merely state the fact without any comment and say that recently the shipping losses figures included that we have lost fewer ships than Jerry did U-boats in February and that we are losing fewer than 1 ship in 1,000 in convoy.

SUNDAY 26 MARCH

Those Russians! Today they reached the River Prut, boundary of Roumania and the starting point, one of them, from which Jerry invaded in 1941. Marshal Koniev is the commander and he has the honour of being the first marshal to beat Jerry back to where he started from.

An interesting broadcast tonight. It was a recording made by a BBC van in Jugo-Slavia by the patriot forces there under Tito, the first of its kind from enemy-occupied Europe. Plucky lot those patriots, a pity they had difficulties in the shape of internal friction. Gen Mihailovitch took up the job soon after Jerry occupied but he seemed to slow up in enthusiasm and some reports even suggested he had been won over to the Jerries. Now Marshal Tito has taken over the leadership and is making a job of it. The movement has grown to such an extent that he has even been fighting pitched battles and winning them.

THURSDAY 30 MARCH

The government was defeated on Tuesday and it has created a peculiar situation. The defeat itself was negligible both in size and importance, the voting being 117 to 116 on the question of whether women should have equal pay with men teachers in the government Education Bill. Considering the voting strength is 605, of which 150 are on active service, I think the whole thing is a storm in a teacup but, custom is custom, and there arose the question of whether the government should resign. Churchill has overcome the question in this way. He says that such important events are about to occur that there must not be a shadow of doubt about the support of Parliament so at the next sitting they will be asked to reverse the vote as a vote of confidence. Queer that the whole constitution can be threatened by a chance vote but I suppose it's one up on the totalitarian countries that we have a flexible system of government.

I don't believe I reported the leading-up events of this affair so here goes. Some months ago a daring exploit was accomplished in Burma. A chap named Wingate took a decent-sized force of men, penetrated the Burma jungle and moved about behind Jap positions for three months. He was supplied continually by air and was continually in touch with HQ. The event was recorded and commented on as an exploit but nothing further.

Now, about two weeks ago came the resulting action. A huge air armada of planes and gliders took off from India, landed 150 miles behind the Jap front, developed and enlarged an open space into a landing field, and a big army has been flown there and is now upsetting all Jap ideas on warfare. They are in big danger of having their supply lines cut. No imagination, those Japs.

FRIDAY 31 MARCH
We caught a packet last night. Between 900 and 1,000 bombers went to Nuremburg and we lost 94, the biggest loss so far. This evening between 8 and 8.30 there was that heavy roar again. Tonight I suppose we are showing Jerry we can take a loss of 94 but I wish they wouldn't go out on moonlit nights. George and I wondered if the Second Front is really near and they have targets which must be visited before it opens and time is getting short.

Our officers in our company have a 'highly important' meeting tonight, possibly to get their orders for eventualities. It's a bit interesting to note the various reports which come to hand over the affair. Some time ago we were told there would be a platoon stood by at the preliminary code word (shhh!) for an anticipated Jerry landing and No. 8, I hear, was eventually chosen.

EASTER SUNDAY 9 APRIL
Had our Second Front details on Thursday, HG I mean. At a certain time we start mounting guard at a certain, at present secret, Vulnerable Point. Fourteen men and two NCOs per night for three of our platoons while one platoon, the remaining one, the platoon given the position of honour which I need hardly say is our platoon, will be the 'lying-in platoon', which means that at certain intervals, possibly four weeks, but always on Saturday, we hold ourselves at some HQ ready for instant movement to any threatened position, supposedly being used against paratroops.[1] By that means there will always be a platoon ready for use to deal with any eventuality while the rest are being mobilised. When this all starts all training is

suspended except for special training. Hope it doesn't clash with any use we can be in any air raid which may materialise.

Today is the anniversary of Jerry's walk into Norway. Four years ago – longer than it seems. Now we are, presumably and possibly, on the eve of an invasion of our own. Shall we try to picture what this wartime town is like? Let's. Suppose we ought to start at home. Hope I don't miss things out.

The most obvious sign of war indoors is perhaps furniture. Our carpet, for instance, is showing signs of wear but it will just have to last – a new one is almost unobtainable and, if it were not, would cost about £30 for a pre-war £5 quality. Our particular furniture looks good (touch wood) but there again new stuff is not obtainable in the ordinary way. The only new is 'utility' furniture and may only be sold by permission of the government who issue permits to newly married or bombed-out people. As in lots of other cases this has rocketed the price of second-hand stuff. The cause is that a wise government has closed down all the factories not absolutely essential and put them on war work.

The fire is small, very small, supplies being restricted. They won't let anyone have more than that amount of coal which would bring up the stock to more than 4 cwt. The miners have been striking to such an extent that over a million tons of coal have been lost and I suppose they have been making stocks of coal to take overseas when we do invade. Industry must have the coal which is available and it has been rationed.

Food is adequate, good in quality, but does not include some of the pre-war luxuries. Things like ice-creams, cream, cream cheese, bananas, good quality cake, cake icing, white flour have disappeared and sugar, butter, meat are rationed. The amounts are, roughly, per head, ½ lb sugar, ½ lb bacon, 1s 2d worth of meat, 2 oz butter, 4 oz margarine, 2 pints milk, 2 oz tea, 2 oz lard and 4 oz sweets per week. Eggs are approximately 30 per year issued singly at certain times. Each person gets 24 points per week to spend on anything he chooses so long as his demands are not huge enough to be refused by the shopkeeper. As an illustration rice is 4 points per pound, sultanas, etc. are 8 points, prunes 6, tinned fruit about 8, luxuries like salmon about 16 or 24 points per tin. Clothing, too, is rationed and this has resulted in certain unusual sights, for instance one sees usually immaculate people in shirts of a different pattern from the collar. Housewives spend lots of time in cutting down and it is the rule, almost, for youngsters' things to be made from rejected grown-up things. Sounds rather poverty-stricken but the results are really worth the effort. I've been wearing a mac for work this winter which had been retired once.

Curtains are beginning to look shabby. Curtain material has to be bought from rationed material otherwise we would be wearing peculiar clothes. It was the thing, at one period when blankets could be bought ad lib, to make dressing-gowns from blankets.

Newspapers are smaller. The *Telegraph* is six pages, except Saturday when it is four. The *Express* and similar are four every day. *The Times* varies from eight to ten pages. Paper is naturally scarce and books are scarce though I suppose it is only in comparison with the pre-war flush. This book,[2] for instance, cost 4*s* 7*d* and kiddies' books are extortionate.

Everything which can be saved is saved. The dustman collects salvage one week and 'dust' the next, but there is seldom any refuse. Salvage includes paper, rubber, metal, bones and string. Last year we had, like every town did, a book salvage drive in which all books given were sorted, valuable ones used to replace bombed-out libraries, useful ones sent to the Forces and others scrapped.

Wood is scarce and cannot be bought unless for house maintenance or bomb damage repairs. Lots of people collect sticks from the country for fire-lighting but the most scheming arises when making toys at birthdays and Christmas. The kiddies seem to have lots of toys but they are usually home-made and lots are war-like, aeroplanes, tanks, tommy-guns and so on. I suppose I was wrong in saying books are scarce as we buy books for presents as a substitute for toys.

Almost every house has its air-raid shelter, either an Anderson corrugated steel one sunk in the garden, a home-made one like ours in concrete and wood, a Morrison steel shelter in a room, which is 2 ft 6 in high and can be used as a table, or a concrete one built in sections in which people sleep. They have saved lives and are not used for storing garden tools.

Blackout too is another respected and useful adjunct to the house. Sometimes of heavy curtains, sometimes of wood frames with thick paper, sometimes of solid wood shutters put up either indoors or outside, the latter an unpleasant job when it rains.

And then the respirators. Everyone has one and periodically they are inspected by the wardens, effectively, to make sure people know where they are I'm afraid. We have taken the gas danger very lightly and are only now thinking a bit more about it in view of what may be coming. At first we used to carry them everywhere but nowadays they are left at home to conserve rubber and because the danger is not so great.

Almost every house, too, has its wireless. It is almost an essential in wartime. We get news services at 0700, 0800, 1300, 1800, 2100 and 2400 hr, war commentaries, etc., but not very good music programmes. A parallel programme serves the Forces with an even more frequent news service. There again there is scarcity in supplies of radio sets. New ones are almost unobtainable or rather very scarce as the radio industry is overworked on other things.

I nearly forgot earthenware and glassware. Conditions are a little easier now but at one time 'crocks' were just not obtainable. People advertised in the local paper for tea services and cups without saucers were often on tables at teatime. We were more fortunate, being reasonably careful with washing-up, but our patterns are rather mixed. Now all crocks are white, there being no patterns at all, but no one asks or expects such luxuries as patterns, being only too glad to get the articles.

Let's go outside into the street. At first it looks like a pre-war street unless it happens to be one where Jerry has 'been' and there may be a house missing here and there but it's not evident. However, there are no bulbs in the street lamps and of course no lights at night. The blackout is not very bad though, unless we go cycling or motoring on a rainy moonless night and then it's worse if we wear spectacles to get smeared with raindrops and distort the lights of oncoming traffic. Some towns have 'starlight' street lamps, bulbs of a fraction (one-twentieth I believe) of a candle power, but that's only outside the 25-mile limit from the east and south coast. A great help to the night travel is the white line, a never-ending series of white dashes, about 18 in long, about 4 ft spacing, and say 4 in wide, running down the middle of the road. It changes to a continuous strip at bends and comes to a stop altogether at a road crossing and I've been quite a distance on a really dark wet night with that line as the only thing in existence, seemingly, as I kept my cycle lamp on it and just followed it home, easing away as the oncoming traffic drew near. It's a great help that line, and on all the main roads. In the town, in order to save labour in repainting it has been replaced by a series of 'cats-eyes', small cast-iron squares let into the road surface containing a pair of glass beads set in rubber, facing each way, which reflect one's headlamp.

Going down our street we see other wartime measures. Some

gates have green plates affixed reading 'Air Raid Warden', or they are screwed to the wall against the front door. Other houses have a big letter C or A or whatever company the Home Guard who lives there belongs to; it is an old scheme, now unused, which was intended to facilitate rapid call-out. Lots of houses have cards in the window signifying the occupant, probably a lady, has joined the Magna scheme and a G or FA or R shows if she specialises in Gas, First Aid, or is a Rest house. At about every thirty houses is a white enamelled steel plate, 2 ft square with red letters, showing which Fire Guard assembly point it is and a house may have a detachable label of FG showing the occupant is on fire-guard duty in the street that night. We have quite a few notices in the streets, of one sort or another.

Down at the corner on a piece of wasteland is a large tank of water with a statement painted on of the capacity, from 5,000 to 10,000 gallons and how far the next one is away and where it is. It is static water for fire-fighting and if a large one, there is a lifebelt hanging up in case of accidents. In the town, if Jerry has 'been', cellars and basements of demolished houses are used for static water storage.

There are not so many private cars about and owing to petrol shortage those we do see are probably on business. The ordinary motorist using his car for pleasure just is not allowed any petrol and his car is laid up, others have petrol coupons allowed to cover their needs. Cases of petrol waste sometimes appear in the police courts. The Army car and lorry is, however, very numerous especially the lorries. Now and then we see convoys of about a dozen go by, some trailing anti-tank, AA, or field guns, some merely moving troops, others huge tank transporters, each using thirty-four wheels and tyres, catch the eye as they dash along. At some places on the bypass road they have cut a path through the islands at the crossroads to help this traffic and the tanks on 'the day'.

Motorcycles are almost completely non-existent. Almost every one one sees is an Army DR and they are not numerous.

Public conveyances are well patronised now private cars are not running but they stop about 9 p.m. both on account of blackout and owing to shortage of labour even though there are lady drivers and conductresses. One often sees a lady driving a double-decker tram through the town.

There are lady postwomen too, ladies serving in the shops and lots of them at workshops like ours and even in the foundry. They are more at home, though, on machine work rather than in a dirty foundry. Ladies also run bakers' carts and milk carts. Talking of milk carts there will only be two seen in this street we are walking in, one from the milkman, or dairy to whom this street is allocated, and one from the Co-op which was allowed to keep some of its own customers wherever they were. Whereas people dealing with just anybody had to change to the milkman allocated to the street. All this was to save or economise in distribution labour.

As we get into the main streets we notice the big percentage of people in uniforms. Here in Ipswich are British Army, a few naval, Air Force, American air force in plenty, airborne troops, British women's services – WAAF, ATS and a few WRNS. In restaurants a mere civilian like me feels out of place with the overwhelming preponderance of khaki and blue but we make up for it by displaying a badge in our buttonhole of the Civil Defence service or Home Guard to which we belong. Incidentally the service in the restaurant is not pre-war standard, the cleanliness being a bit below par and the waitresses overworked. Labour shortage again.

In the main streets there are several shops shut down. Sweetshops, jewellers (who just can't get any supplies at all), confectioners, clothiers and others spread their goods in the windows and even shut off some windows, suggesting a shortage of goods. On the whole, however, essentials appear plentiful enough although the prices of clothes are a bit staggering and the windows are by no means empty. In fact it is only by searching that we see any shortage at all. The whole policy of the government is to discourage spending, except on essentials, and to encourage saving so that the war may be run as economically as possible. Wages are high and they don't want them spent any more than necessary, to keep inflation down. Very wise too.

Here and there we see a blue noticeboard displaying the fact that there is a public air-raid shelter and giving the seating capacity. Now, however, most big shops have a spotter who goes to the roof at the alert and gives a warning when enemy aircraft are in the vicinity, at which all assistants go to the basement and customers are expected to do so as well. Almost every shop except the largest, and even some of those, display notices that they close from 1.00 to 2.15 p.m. another indication of labour shortage. They open, mostly, at 9 a.m. and close at 5.30 p.m. in summer and 4 p.m. in winter. As most firms work from 8.30 to 6 p.m. this is a thundering nuisance as it means that we do almost no shopping at all and must leave it all to the wife. However, it is merely an inconvenience and is taken as a necessary war evil.

EASTER MONDAY 10 APRIL

To continue. There are not many advertisement hoardings about. They were well-made things with sheet zinc covering and now they've been pulled down for the sake of the zinc and because there's not much paper allowed for printing adverts. Rather a blow for the advert bloke but an improvement to the town or rather that part of the town just outside the centre.

There are several bridges in this particular town, over railway and river, and each has dozens of cast-iron sockets in the road at one end, fitted with covers of course. They are sockets for hunks of steel girders made from, I guess, 10 in × 5 in joists which are stacked on the pavement or in a nearby recess, and which have to be illuminated with red lamps each night and are intended to be used as a tank-trap in the event of Jerry invading. The bridges themselves were mined too but nowadays no one expects either apparatus to be used and their chief use is, I suppose, to act as a reminder of the war.

As we get out into the side-roads and streets again and in the minor main roads, we notice something which looks strange and is not yet easily identified until suddenly we notice a dog jump into someone's front garden and realise that there are no railings to be seen. There were many gardens fenced with various types of iron railings and gates but some time ago these were all commandeered for scrap by the local authorities and taken away. The result was that some who could do so put up a wood fencing but others just left it and the result is a more free-looking, more pleasant street.

We eventually reach the dock and pass by. We have to pass by because we can't go in unless with a permit. An easy way in which to obtain a nice safe lodging, free, for the rest of the war would be to wander round the dock with a camera, assuming one could get a film from somewhere.

Works are similarly taboo. Ours, for instance, and I suppose it is typical, is a closed camp. There is barbed wire round it at the back. There is only one office entrance guarded by a receptionist who only lets in a visitor after taking his particulars and issuing a pass, and only one works entrance, guarded by a gate-keeper who also keeps the big gates shut until they are needed open. There is plenty of work about, of course, although some is restricted by lack of coal, and all work is somehow related to, and essential to, the war effort. If it were not it would not exist. Periodically officials from the Manpower Board arrive and try to annex just a few more men either for the Forces or for other more important jobs, leaving them to be replaced by women, but by now that has been just about worked out. Compared with pre-war treatment the chaps in the Works are pampered today. They have the tea wagon each morning and afternoon, a Works Council which acts as intermediary with the employers, concessions in time such as leaving off early on pay-day so as to draw money and be off at the usual time, are allowed to smoke all day and somehow get away with a slightly lower standard of work. I merely state this as a fact, not that I am opposed to any of it except the last item.

Nearly everyone in the town does some sort of spare-time job either in Civil Defence or Home Guard. There are wardens, Special Police, Home Guard, Fire Guard while the youngsters are only too eager to join the ATC. I should have included, of course, first aid people, rescue services, repair services (gas, electric, water and sewers), NFS, decontamination squads. There are scrimshankers, bound to be, but everyone up to fifty years of age is roped in for something unless unable to by reason of health or special circumstances. Even women, either single or married, provided there are no children under sixteen, are bound to do some sort of job if only for half days, and some even carry on their husband's allotment when they go into the Forces.

Talking of allotments, most people have one or cultivate the garden for vegetables. An enormous amount of food must be grown in this way to help out our rations and quite a lot of trouble is taken by the authorities to help in that way. Radio talks rarely refer to flowers nowadays. There are shows held to stimulate interest and adverts in the papers tell us what to do and when to do it.

Yes, the newspapers help a lot nowadays with the adverts. They tell us plainly nowadays that we must save fuel and think before we open a switch or light a gas-tap. They incite us to save all we can in War Savings, tell us how the Red Cross can help in various ways of the war, give details of gardening procedure, give cooking hints, salvage hints, hints on how to save clothes and materials and even how to do one's own cycle repairs to save shop labour in doing it for us.

Another national economy stunt is to institute feeding centres in most of the towns where one can have a respectable lunch for about 10d or 11d. It saves rations and saves time and transport for thousands who would otherwise have to go home long distances and, when applied to school kiddies, is a means of allowing their mothers to go out to work. There is, too, an exchange in Ipswich where anyone with good quality clothing which is still in good condition but too small for the kiddy concerned may exchange it for some other article brought by someone else.

Well, that's a short, and I fear an inadequate, impression of life today as we wait impatiently for the Second Front. Somehow I fear I've missed a lot; perhaps it is because of its very commonplace nature. If so I may add it later.

SUNDAY 30 APRIL
This morning there were a few bumps and George told Dora that possibly the rumour was correct – the 'rumour' being something printed in his Sunday paper to the effect that a neutral source says the Second Front opened this morning. Am surprised he took it in and when I spoke to him later he told me too, but he seemed quite willing to believe it. Perhaps he knows something he keeps to himself, wisely, just the same as I know it couldn't have been this morning. All the same I listened in at 1 o'clock just in case. Yes, I don't think it will be till next weekend.

Everyone speaks knowingly of tides, moon, time of year for most favourable landings and weather in the Channel. Personally I think that, seeing that landings will have to keep on until several ports are taken, it doesn't matter much what conditions are reigning as, however favourable they are, they must change.

We opened the ball by forming the first lying-in picket last night at the Battalion HQ at Woodbridge Road Drill Hall. Guards were also mounted at bridges and other vulnerable points in the town by us HG – our company's job is Spring Road viaduct. Our first taste of ops. We assembled at platoon HQ in full battle order and wasn't it hot with the greatcoat!!! after which we cycled to the HQ. Being mobile we had our bikes. It says something for HG spirit among us that Fred was able facetiously to hold up lines of imaginary traffic when our OC arrived on his bike.

Arriving there we each drew a palliasse and two blankets and the thirty of us prepared to live for an evening in the lecture room. Quite an experience but I took a sheet just in case. We had the use of the miniature range till midnight, I turned in at 0030 hr and lights out was at 0130 hr of which I was only dimly conscious. Awake again at 0520 hr, we had a cup of tea, dismissed at 0615 hr and slowly, very slowly, cycled home in a clear fresh spring morning. I had not expected any interruption but wondered if it might possibly come and there wasn't an alert either, for which I was really pleased. I should feel lost and a shirker if an alert occurred and I couldn't lend a hand.

SUNDAY 14 MAY
Naturally no news. The Second Front will just keep out of reach until patience and expectancy are stretched not quite to breaking point and I suppose we are not there just yet. Small convoys of six and twelve lorries are continually passing our Works and that's only one road in the town and now and then we hear larger ones, sometimes of tanks, on the by-pass. The roads in the town are displaying Army direction signs with mysterious word diminutions and arrows. DID POL says one and ORD CRS. Suppose they know what they mean but it all looks very businesslike and efficient. Scopes went to the Midlands during the week and says every town seems full of Americans. I suppose something will happen some day.

Quite enjoyed myself today. Fired twenty rounds through my Sten and ten through Fred's rifle. There is a camaraderie in the platoon which one doesn't get anywhere in peace life. It's a sort of mass friendship I would never have experienced in peacetime and I suppose it's useful too. Two and a half years we've been in it. Seems like two and a half months, or does it?

WHIT MONDAY 29 MAY
I can remember several occasions on which we could have called it Wet Monday but that's not true for today. It's been hot with not a sign of a cloud and we've cycled out to find Debach aerodrome. Undoubtedly it is an American Liberator station. We were stopped at a road halt by an American in greeny khaki with peaked field cap, green sunglasses and a large half-smoked cigar, who inspected our identity cards very courteously. Quite a lot of similar chaps were about with the short American rifle and several Jeeps, trucks, cars and a concrete-mixer passed us manned by Negroes, also adorned with white-rimmed green sun-glasses. Several planes were about the dispersal points, all Liberators, and mostly the new aluminium colour. The runways were huge, the first I'd seen. The one they were using had a slight rise in the middle so it had a horizon.

Soon a squadron of about a dozen came over low, circled and peeled off one by one to land. They touched down about a mile or more away from us disappearing as they did so, coming up over the horizon of the runway a few seconds later and then trundled to

their dispersal point. Three had an engine stopped but they took
their turn and had no preferential treatment. Later ten more took
off and this time they were quite close.

SUNDAY 4 JUNE
I don't believe there ain't never going to be no Second Front. Went
on lying-in picket last night, the second time. The Civil Defence
authorities have, I hear, restricted our activities to once a month or
thereabouts on account of being wardens and might be wanted on
other business. I've never been perturbed about a duty before and
I suppose I wasn't over that one either but as all the signs and
portents of the coming (?) Second Front come nearer I wondered
if it might open say on Thursday and by Saturday Jerry might
decide to interrupt any convoys in the Ipswich district and on our
bypass road in particular. In that case I didn't want to be
marooned at Battalion HQ listening to the bangs and doing
nothing about it. However, as Saturday came I felt better,
reckoning that the two occurrences would not coincide on that
night and went off without any qualms to speak of.

   We had quite a decent time, lights out at about 0020 hr and up at
0500 hr. Slept quite reasonably but twenty-eight men in one room
with no ventilation at all owing to blackout makes one appreciate fresh
air in the morning. Once more I quite expected to hear good news this
morning. Yesterday evening George and I were saying it was a matter
of hours. My last hope now is that tomorrow is full moon.

   The Americans made their first shuttle service flight Friday to
Russia. They bombed Roumania then carried on to their own
prepared 'drome in Russia. It was arranged at the Teheran
Conference.

   We just had a ten-minute daylight alert, the first for months.
Recce I suppose. Incidentally it was the 968th in Ipswich
according to George Young.

MONDAY 5 JUNE
Things move quickly. We entered Rome yesterday evening.

TUESDAY 6 JUNE
Today is, at last, the Day. There is a general sense of release of
tension in most people. It didn't come with the metaphorical
flourish of trumpets some of us expected though, in fact it crept in
on us. Like this.

I had a confused idea at about 0600 hr that planes were about and again at 0630 so resolved to get up in time for the 7 o'clock news in case things had happened. Accordingly I woke up at 0703, as to be expected, and was just too late to hear the beginning so went back to shave without more concern. Then at the 8 o'clock news came the announcement that we had told the French we would warn them before an attack was made in the particular towns concerned. 'The warning may be only an hour before the attack,' we said, 'and when it comes take only the luggage you can carry and get into the country a mile from the town. Don't get on a road and don't congregate.' Nothing much there.

Then followed a report from Jerry news that we had landed paratroops in Normandy in the Havre district, that we had bombed Calais, Dunkirk and Havre, and that their naval forces had attacked Allied landing craft. No more than that.

Going to work with Cedric we both asked the question everybody asked 'Is it?' I reckoned it was. Green said it was only a Jerry report and probably one of Churchill's feints. Hatherley had been on HG duty all night at Colchester but none of the troop could sleep owing to the noise of aircraft for hours from about 0300 hr. Our spirits and hopes rose. Then came the thrill. Miss Youngs came with news that they had heard an 11 o'clock news bulletin in the canteen which included Eisenhower's statement that D-Day had begun.

After that, speaking for myself but I think I was typical, I could settle to nothing. Work was a darned bore and what I did contained (!) mistakes. We went in the canteen for the midday bulletin and I left early to hear the 1 o'clock. News is scarce but briefly what we know is this.

Last night the RAF used 1,300 planes and dropped 5,000 tons in north France. Both records. The invasion fleet contained 4,000 ships and several thousand smaller craft. The air forces have 11,000 planes on which to draw and have sent 31,000 Allied airmen over France today between midnight and breakfast alone. The landing was the largest ever attempted anywhere, was made with far fewer casualties than expected and is proceeding well. Fighting is now proceeding in Caen, ten miles inland, and landings have been made on the beaches with much less loss than expected. Naval losses also were low, thank goodness. Battleships were there too, to bombard coast positions, and they say we landed many secret weapons. Resistance by Jerry has been light but, I fancy, only naturally so.

The stage is set, one hopes and believes, for the final action. Today is historic and we are privileged to live it. If only I could write and describe it adequately I would be more satisfied but I suppose there is so little upon which to draw for information. There are only impressions. We've just had an hour and a quarter news bulletin commencing with a talk from the King asking for general prayers and a series of dispatches from correspondents who tell us what they saw but naturally few facts of the sort we are itching for. Possibly they will come later. Then they finished with a short service from the studio, a simple impressive service.

Now we need fine weather and it looks as though it will disappoint us. Indeed the invasion was planned 24 hours earlier and postponed due to the weather. A week ago it was hot and cloudless. Now it is cold, people have fires, a west-north-west wind is blowing a light rain, rain we have prayed for for months without response is now falling as though set for a wet spell. Hope it won't be too bad for the lads out there. We have had favours from the weather and we've had ill luck in some actions because of it. Hope it's all for the best now.

THURSDAY 8 JUNE

We've captured Bayeux, our first town, and Caen is being bombed into submission. The Luftwaffe is more in evidence and lost 114 planes. Am afraid we must go by Jerry's reports for the strategical picture as we are not giving anything away. There have been tank battles, indeed one paper says the fighting has been the heaviest of the war, while the radio says we have completed the first stage of clearing the beaches, are in the second stage of engaging Rundstedt's tactical reserves and must await the third stage of meeting Rommel's strategic reserves. Incidentally I wasn't so far out in my estimate, made years ago, that we would land between Cherbourg and Brest.

We are having an excellent radio service now. After the 9 o'clock news we get a daily series of reports from correspondents, soldiers back wounded, eye-witnesses and commentators. It's full of interesting cameos and word pictures.

Churchill, good old cautious common sense, is warning us against over-optimism. Natural enough. Green says it will be touch and go with us but I feel more optimistic than I did before it happened. Fighting will be terribly heavy but with other landings keeping Jerry guessing we should pull it off. All the same I suppose Salerno and Anzio were touch-and-go at one time.

SUNDAY 11 JUNE
In general things are going well in France. One good sign is that we have set up a fighter airstrip or aerodrome and transport planes are taking away wounded.

There are fantastic stories being told, some obviously authentic, others not quite so acceptable but possible. Six of our men were captured and found themselves with 100 Jerries. Soon mortar shells were dropped and they told the Jerries their position was hopeless, to such an extent and to such purpose that they surrendered to the six. One of our gliders snapped its tow rope on D-Day and turned 180° in the following reaction. They continued their journey and landed in England and, when an Air Force fellow came up, surrounded him with 'Achtung you . . .' He asked them where they thought they were and eventually a disappointed crew took their place at the end of the queue waiting to embark. And so on and so on. There will be books about it all afterwards.

Jerry flooded the low land to a huge extent at the base of the Cherbourg peninsula but now the Yanks have captured Isigny they have control of the sluice gates and can drain it.

One piece of interesting news is that we knew quite a bit about the beaches but there were some soft spots we were not sure about. A few men were taken there and one night they crawled about, instruments which they carried recorded their course and they took samples of the soil, which told us lots about the ground our tanks would have to negotiate.

FRIDAY 16 JUNE
Fluttering in the dovecotes today. News released that Jerry is using the pilotless aircraft in attacks on this country. He started it on Tuesday night causing a little damage and again last night and today causing, to read between the lines, a lot of damage.

The news was given in Parliament this morning. Apparently the planes are really winged bombs. They are smaller than a Spitfire. They are probably rocket propelled seeing that they have a light at the back by night and leave puffs of smoke by day, coinciding with a pulsating roaring noise, and one description is that they are like daggers moving handle foremost. They fly low on a straight course and may be radio-controlled. Advice is that when the engine note ceases and the light goes out, explosions may occur in five to fifteen seconds and cover should be taken immediately. Counteraction will be by gunfire at the moment and the alert will sound as a warning as usual. Morrison emphasised that we must not give Jerry any hint of how successful his aim is so he will only state that there has been a raid on southern England if they fall anywhere below a line from the Wash to Bristol Channel. So we are southern England. Probably for the same reason Big Ben is not now broadcast direct but from a record which will be synchronised with it.

Effects here are chiefly among the ladies who, after all, have the responsibilities of the kiddies and there is a fair-sized morale effect in the weapon. I fancy, for my part, that we won't see anything of this new weapon round here in Ipswich, at any rate unless we become an invasion centre. Accuracy with a weapon like that is necessarily low and would be reserved for a big target. Also we know little about it but I fancy the bomb load will not be more than 1,000 lb, plenty I know, but not a matter of tons as we some of us expected.

If the alert goes tonight I guess our household for one will get up pronto and so will all the street. I'm not suggesting there is the slightest panic; that would be absurd and in fact I fancy the wife thinks I'm too unconcerned about it but one can sense an air of readiness which was about on 3 September '39. It's a new weapon and anything may develop from it. After a month I suppose it will be relegated to its proper place in the perspective of attack.

WEDNESDAY 21 JUNE
Good old RAF. They've done it again. When the pilotless plane came in the picture we all wondered what to call them and the best the radio could do was refer to them as 'those things' but now the RAF have turned up with 'doodle-bug' and doodle-bug it shall be.

We have had a fair amount of success in shooting them down by fighters but some get through. Stories get through of the damage done, stories I would like to record but had better not and, even allowing for exaggeration, the damage is fairly heavy. Saw a picture of the doodle-bug today and it looks an interesting ingenious design.

Good news from the Pacific this morning. The Americans said the Jap battle fleet was assembling east of the Philippines and at midday came the news from Japan that a naval action has started. Nimitz, the Yank C-in-C, welcomed the chance of action and I hope he is justifying his optimism. I think he will.

Last Sunday the Americans completed their drive across the base of the Cherbourg peninsula. Yesterday they reached the defences, penetrated the outer ones, and are now 3½ miles from the town. No one can say the Americans can't fight.

THURSDAY 6 JULY

Churchill made a newsy speech today re the doodle-bug. He said that up to 6 a.m. today they had fired 2,754 doodle-bugs and had killed 2,752 people with 8,000 in hospital. The tone was that it is a dangerous weapon and to be highly respected. He didn't advocate general evacuation but would assist the evacuation of any whose presence in London was not essential and the deep shelters would be available for use.

Something like a rout is in progress in Russia round Minsk way. Whole battalions are surrendering. Richard, anything may happen out there.

Rundstedt has been sacked from his command in France being superseded by Kluge, I think. He is described as being more of a yes man to Hitler and the announcer said Montgomery might be pleased with the change.

SUNDAY 9 JULY

Last week, Friday I believe, we started a big offensive round Caen and today comes the news that Caen is taken. Another example of cooperation in that the prelim barrage was a visit by 450 heavies of the RAF dropping 2,000 tons on tank and troop concentrations followed by naval bombardment too, after which the infantry went in. Jerry is reported as being dazed by the weight of the bombing and the artillery support. No wonder. We hear of amazing things nowadays, such as *Rodney* bombarding at 18-mile range, another wonderful thing not adequately appreciated being that the Luftwaffe can't interfere. Poor old Goering and his boast that not a bomb would fall on German soil.

Doodle-bugs about still. We had a 'cuckoo' at 1 o'clock Friday while I was coming home and rumour says it was one of them. The radio says we are now bombing 'rocket' sites so there is more unpleasantness coming our way. Can't credit that the enormous concrete structures such as we took at Cherbourg are for rockets, at any rate intended for England, but we speak of using 12,000-lb bombs 'which can penetrate the structures'.

Was on picket duty again last night. Quite enjoyable experiences in a way if it were not for the fact that our sector, our post area rather, is a little denuded of wardens should anything occur. I hear Maun is a little worked up about it and intends appealing to Argyle Street about taking his wardens away. I can quite see his point and am in sympathy to an extent; if anything big crops up it is exasperating to have thirty wardens from the group 1½ miles away and unable to come and help but all the same if Jerry puts his dirty feet on our immediate part of the island I consider it my duty to try and discourage him.

THURSDAY 20 JULY

I hear that Fish has laid Green two pints that we are in Paris by the end of August. Poor fool. Everyone knows the three forces have done wonderfully well – even to land in France was an achievement – and it's just lunacy to lead us up the garden in the news reports and then let us down with a bump.

Jerry says a bomb attack was made on Hitler today. Thirteen of his staff were injured but he only suffered slight burns and bruises. Glad he wasn't hurt. We don't want him martyrised or there will surely be another war after this.

SATURDAY 22 JULY

A sense of excitement and speculation about since Thursday. The attack on Hitler had more behind it than appeared at first. Reliable news is scarce and difficult to get but Jerry has broadcast that the attempt on Hitler's life was part of a plot by a small clique of German army who have been 'suppressed'. So far they have published the names of only two, a Colonel something who planted the bomb and General Beck. A Swedish report says even some of Hitler's bodyguard were in the plot or revolt and that an SS detachment is tackling an army force at Munich. A significant fact is that Himmler has been placed in control of the home army and I guess he will unearth any plot there is going.

I think they can kill each other as much as they like as long as they do do so and as long as they don't pack in with their experienced army still in being and ready to organise the next war years hence.

FRIDAY 28 JULY

A little more rumoured in the press about V2. It's supposed to be a 90-ton rocket-propelled bomb, the bomb itself weighing 10 tons when it lands. One Stockholm rumour even suggests they are capable of reaching America and that thousands are ready in Denmark. How much there is in rumours only Jerry and our intelligence know but there must be something if only on account of the frequency with which we are bombing the rocket sites, using 12,000-lb piercing bombs. The size of the bomb would account for the size and heaviness of the launching ways.

Sent up a suggestion to the Air Ministry yesterday for countering the doodle-bugs. It's probably in the w.p.b. by now but one never knows.

There's a complete rout in Poland now. There seems to be no holding the Russians. Warsaw is now almost in the front line and East Prussia is very near now. It's possible, I suppose, that Jerry is retreating voluntarily but even so the morale effect must be huge and he's losing many men too. A map of the line is now well away from Russia itself and on Polish territory. Good lads.

In Normandy the picture is changing a bit. After our much blazoned attack last week we have stopped, being held by the ruddy after-effects of the ruddy weather and by Jerry's dispositions. He has twenty-five divisions in Normandy, eight of them being armoured. Six of these eight are facing us at Caen while the other two are facing the Americans who, on Wednesday, made a thrust in the direction of the armour. They are doing well, some claiming a breakthrough, but the only pointer is that 4,000 prisoners have been taken and that the fighting is so fluid that there is no definite line in the area. Our holding action will help them a lot.

SUNDAY 6 AUGUST

The weather is improved; there's been a continuous north and east wind all the week which merely brought low cloud from the sea mist until it suppressed it, presumably at the coast on Thursday, and it's been sunny ever since. We've been to Pond Hall yesterday and today but with the restrictions of movements it's not so enjoyable as last year because the best spots are closed and there's lots of people about. However, the river was beautifully calm. I've had a swim and enjoyed myself. I fancy we don't fully appreciate our surroundings in Ipswich. It's taken a war to make me, at any rate, discover some really beautiful spots, places that many other towns would care to own.

There's an amazing situation in Brittany, the kind of thing we have never dared to hope for. The Yanks have reached Brest and the mouth of the Loire and I suppose it's only a matter of time before Brest, St Nazaire and Lorient fall into our laps. Reporters say there's a complete disorganised rout in the German army. The Jerries are getting eastwards just as they can, in carts and even with wheelbarrows. Groups are met on the road just without any order at all and the tanks are so far ahead they've almost lost touch, our tanks I mean. They've no need to bother about mines and tank traps, concealed positions or anything else. Prisoners are so numerous that they are in some cases going to our lines under their own officers under honour to report at the cages. The doughty Jerry is reduced to that.

MONDAY 7 AUGUST
Up again last night for 10 minutes at 2330 hr. These raids are of a totally different nature from the old type of plane raid. In 1940, '41 and so on, we had plenty of time, though we didn't waste it, to get up and ready before the planes came droning over singly and unopposed and we knew that if nothing developed within say half an hour that it wasn't Ipswich that time unless a lone bloke peppered us. Then last winter he would come over more concentratedly and we were out for only about one or two hours instead of anything up to six or eight. Now it's doodle-bugs and nobody ever seems to think of plane raids, in fact there hasn't been one for two months.

Churchill said he couldn't promise us more than 1½-min warning and that's about right for here too. Last night was pretty typical; the alert went, I was out of bed, so was the wife, instantly started dressing. By the time the alert had finished its 1 minute I had put on socks and uniform, glasses and picked up the odds and ends I leave out for picking up rather than waste time putting them in uniform pockets beforehand. Straight downstairs, put on shoes, tin hat and coat if cold, and go outside buttoning up my uniform and shoes. By that time last night the searchlights were swinging round in circles about twice and then reversing, which sign, I've decided, means 'OK in this area'. Sure enough in 10 minutes off went the 'Raiders Passed'. Twice I've heard, and once seen, the doodle-bug go over while dressing. Hope I don't hear them stop.

The 9 o'clock news has just said that Jerry is countering with four armoured divisions towards Avranches in an attempt to split our forces. He is using no air cover and our Typhoons are playing havoc with his tanks and he is being mauled and held. It's good news we are getting now.

Jerry in East Prussia is now using all his civilian male and female labour to dig defences and he is rushing up all the reserves he can in an effort to delay the Russians.

TUESDAY 15 AUGUST

Big news tonight. We've made another landing, in the south of France this time. Not many details yet except that it's from Marseilles to Nice, was preceded by heavy air attack, there was no air opposition and feeble ground opposition. Good progress has been made. I was dimly conscious of previous news items that the Riviera coast had been bombed heavily in recent days but had attached no importance to it, actually had thought it was south of Bay of Biscay coast.

Am afraid I was a little prejudiced still. They played the 'Marseillaise' this lunchtime and Maitland Wilson's address included 'Remember 1918', and my opinion was it would also be necessary to remember 1940 and throw the 'Marseillaise' into the dustbin. Still I suppose they are trying once more.

An air record today, over 1,100 RAF heavies and 1,000 American heavies with air support have been pounding Jerry airfields. Wonder why? They were chiefly in Holland, Belgium and that district. Are we strong enough for yet another landing? Eisenhower said, 'Let's make it a record week', and it seems they are.

MONDAY 21 AUGUST

Have just heard Montgomery say in a radio address to the Army that the end of the war is in sight. So it jolly well seems. The news is good everywhere but I don't expect the end to come before next spring. May be wrong and hope I am, but we are a long way from Germany yet, although it does seem that Green will lose his two pints of beer over the fall of Paris.

The German 7th Army is now decisively beaten in the Falaise pocket. We didn't close the bag as soon as we'd hoped but there's been terrific destruction of Jerry's transport and tanks and the good work goes on. Naturally the weather has turned completely 'bluddy' again. A north gale is raging today and there's been no flying at all from this country. All the same we'll manage.

There's a French army fighting in France now. We saw pictures of them at the cinema this afternoon. It must be a thrill for the French civilians to see their own men back again, in tanks bearing the cross of Lorraine, even though they are Shermans.

Jerry says there is a revolt in Paris and says it is an armed rising which will soon be put down. The Paris police have been reported to be joining the insurgents. They are strong near our southern landing in Haute Savoie district. They are also reported to have surrounded and taken Vichy which may be a little optimistic but it is a fact that Laval had moved the Vichy government to some place nearer the Swiss border. Wonder what he feels about it? Also poor old senile Pétain? And Weygand the poor fool? To say nothing of the know-all French generals who advised Pétain that England would have her neck wrung in three weeks, way back in 1940. Switzerland is giving passage to badly wounded Jerries but says she will intern lightly wounded men.

WEDNESDAY 23 AUGUST
'Paris is liberated!' That was the headline in today's midday news. We are getting on. When they had made the announcement the 'Marseillaise' was played and I turned the radio up to full blast, just to celebrate and to let non-listeners know something had happened.

The full story is that on 9 August a general uprising was declared by the underground movement in Paris and 50,000 armed patriots assisted by several hundred thousand unarmed rose to the occasion and to such an effect that by yesterday all Jerry resistance had been overcome and Paris was theirs. I'm glad it was done by the French and not by us or the Americans. It shows the individual French are not all jelly-backs.

Well, it all seems good. George tells me of a fellow at his place who has bet 1,000 Churchman No. 1 that the war will be all over by 31 August. An optimist but it's a sign of what lots are feeling. I suppose we can't be blamed for wondering when we blackout if it will soon be for the last time. Close on the heels of that thought comes the unconscious, unspoken hope that by that time we shall not have caught a stray doodle-bug. There's always that very possible chance; there was one at Bealing the other day but one realises that Ipswich is a big place. They are sending them over in larger quantities today and last night; someone commented it was to get rid of them before we capture the sites. I don't think that that event will be long now.

SUNDAY 3 SEPTEMBER
Five years of war. Five years is a big slice out of one's middle age but, on the other hand, it doesn't seem so very long ago since that

Sunday morning when we heard Chamberlain make his historic announcement and George and I got on with our shelter building. We've been through quite a bit of various experiences since then: excitement, torpidity, apprehension, concern, relief, gritting of teeth, tightening of belts, patience, expectancy and now, delight. Patience, I think, has been most exercised but I can't say that fear, fear for the outcome I mean, was ever experienced except for a few days in the Dunkirk period perhaps.

Yes, Jerry is running. He is taking any transport he can find to get away back to his Fatherland, even bicycles with flat tyres and where he can't get those he is legging it on foot. He is short of transport, petrol, ammo and food and, most important, of accurate news of our strength and whereabouts. He is also short of von Kluge, the newly appointed chief of the Normandy fighting. He is reported as having committed suicide or, alternatively, as having succumbed to a heart attack after his army's defeat.

Casualty figures have been published for the five years' fighting. Haven't seen them in print but from memory the total Empire casualty figure is 928,000 including 246,000 killed. That's a low figure compared with the last war figures and with the Russian results of this war but it's a lot all the same.

On Friday night Jerry sent two of his new pick-a-back[3] planes over here. They caused little damage and no casualties but it's the first time he's used them over here.

WEDNESDAY 6 SEPTEMBER
Revealed today that Gen Patton's spearhead made a recce into Germany and withdrew. Naturally he can't make a full-scale attack without full assembly of force and I guess my forecast of mid-October won't be far out.

There is terrific fighting for Brest where Jerry is fighting savagely. He has refused offers to surrender and has been bombed very heavily. From descriptions there won't be a building left standing. Hitler has ordered the commander to hold out at least four months. The Channel ports are being attacked too.

The Secretary for War has made an announcement on the future of the Home Guard. We are to parade voluntarily now, all compulsion being stopped from next Monday. Wonder how that will affect attendances? It will show those worth keeping.

THURSDAY 7 SEPTEMBER

An air of excitement everywhere. A sort of jovial restlessness, caused by the announcement this morning following the HG relaxations of last night. On Monday week, the 18th, the blackout will be lifted almost completely. Lights will be allowed to be screened by ordinary curtains, street lamps will go up, cycle lighting and car sidelights will be normal except the reflectors must be matt white, CD forces will be allowed reduced duties, only 12 hours per month instead of 48, and some of the personnel dispensed with except in London and some coastal areas. In the event of an alert all lights must be put out or blacked out. It is not clear yet, although the wireless report seemed clear enough, if the blackout will be relaxed here or if it does not refer to London and coastal areas but anyway it's good news and some people seem to think it's all the better considering the inferences. If the government can take such a drastic step as to lift the blackout, the almost total defences of the country, except for the Navy, in 1939, what must they know?

That combined with the HG relaxations has set many people cock-a-hoop. The war is nearly over, they say. Jack Watt told me I could chuck my ruddy warden's uniform away now. Didn't say if he had done so with his. Green wonders if he will get a strength of a section at a platoon parade. Rolfe asked me what the blazes should I do when the war ends to amuse myself.

All the same I can't see it so close, although I'm not so cautious as poor old Aldy who says he will still keep his blackout up. I shall keep to my estimate of mid-October before we assault the Siegfried Line and the final declaration at March, the earliest.

The Battle of London is over! So said the radio this evening, referring to the flying bomb attacks. It was an amazing statement. The battle started with intelligence of something developing eighteen months ago, April '43, followed by being located at Peenemünde, and the sites were put up on the French coast, 100 of them, all of which we smashed. Over 8,000 have been sent of which 2,500 reached London. Some dived into the sea but some reached Norfolk and Northampton. At the end of the period, i.e. just recently, 75 per cent were being brought down and only 9 per cent reached London. The record bag was on 28 August when 101 were sent over and we destroyed 97!!!!! Apparently those which came in over here on an east to west course were launched from Messerschmitt 111s. They fooled lots of people besides me. Casualties were 4,700 killed and injured.

SUNDAY 10 SEPTEMBER

We had our last ordered Home Guard parade this morning. I found it a little impressive. We started by parading in clean fatigues as we heard we were going to the Odeon. Was privately rather pleased at being marker for our platoon seeing it was the last time under such circumstances. Major Cobb then put one or two things to us. Seeing next Sunday's marksman's badge effort would be voluntary he asked each one of us if we preferred to keep it on and we all agreed to do so. Then he put it to the proficiency badge class – would they prefer to carry it on or drop it as battalion HQ were not too keen on it. They all said drop it, for which I shall be spared an evening's tuition this week. Following that the marksman's badges which had been won were presented with special comment on Charlie Doe, our platoon sergeant, who had won it at the age of sixty-seven. Good old Charlie, we were all pleased.

Eventually we landed at the Odeon, all the nine companies of the battalion. A band played us in, our band, and eventually we were addressed by Maj Barnard, batt. 2-in-C, Capt Collett, the adjutant, and Col Tempest the boss of this sector. Barnard put it to us would we prefer the batt. to go into cold storage or to continue training, probably chiefly shooting, and we mostly, about 80 or 90 per cent voted for training. The dissenters were chiefly the new heavy weapon company who, poor devils, were in a peculiar position. They can't fire their Smith guns or the 2-pounders and they haven't rifles.

We were also informed of plans for the eventual 'Stand Down' order, that we would then pack all our equipment in separate labelled bundles to be stored at HQ and available for quick collection in event of necessity or of a peace parade. Hope that is not put in force, once in store not many will get them out again and I'd like to see a peace parade.

Col Tempest addressed us chiefly showing how we had been useful in releasing troops for the present show and complimenting us by saying that there was no invasion of England because there was a Home Guard. I came away with a mental picture.

It was those three, with another regular officer on the platform, standing at the salute while we in the auditorium, about 800–1,000 of us, were at attention to the playing of 'The King'. The table on the stage with the Union Jack (unfortunately upside down) draped on it, the four officers in the usual peculiar shadows of the footlights, those lights vaguely round the screen space, the back curtain with a design of dark blue and yellow flowers and the general orange-red colour background and the heavy dark green side curtains, the subdued lights in the body of the hall, the overshadow of the circle upstairs and the rows of stiffly-at-attention part-time soldiers. Seemed as though we really were standing down then. Outside in the car park we formed up as a battalion and marched off as companies to the accompaniment of the band. I think we made a reasonable show.

We in A company are doing one parade per month, mostly shooting.

Heard tonight we will probably not have the blackout lifted in Ipswich. Am not surprised and think it best.

SATURDAY 16 SEPTEMBER
Rumours about everywhere concerning V2. The general trend is that there have been, as one chap put it, 'large lumps on London'. Don't know what the truth is but I think it is fairly conclusive. I won't mention the places I've heard, after all one must make an attempt at discretion although with everyone talking of it it's a bit of a farce to keep quiet in an unimportant diary like this, but the craters are supposed to be large. The wireless and the newspapers are quiet about it, not a whisper has come through, which is as it should be – we don't want to encourage the blighters, but I guess they will release it when Jerry obviously knows. There's a sort of soberness in people's comments and no joking to speak of. After all, when you can't even hear the ruddy things come until they explode, that is if you are in the area concerned, it must be a bit nerve-racking. I suppose they arrive at the speed of sound or if still on a trajectory even higher.

We had an alert this morning just before dawn. Quite a surprise for lots of people. With all the relaxation in blackout coming tomorrow and the doodle-bug coast captured we have been led to believe the doodle-bug threat is over but this morning I saw five and heard another. They had probably been released from Heinkels, I guess.

We had a group meeting on Thursday and as a result of the experience obtained when the doodle-bug dropped in Maryon Road, Mr Maun suggested each post area should adopt a permanent incident officer, who should turn up at every incident, no matter if it's his night or not. It was generally agreed and I was chosen for our post. Guess I'd better work out some scheme now and have a post meeting and put over what I expect to do under some circumstances. It might not be popular but it's necessary and would save people running around in circles if and when the time comes.

Tonight we put the clocks back an hour and double summer time ends. Shan't we miss it when the war is over? I love it and have had many arguments on the subject with Green who quotes hypothetical farmers who dislike it. Blackout gives way to dim-out tomorrow for this town, although there won't be any street lighting till we get a master switch. Can't say why we should be allowed it and Colchester is not.

Was pleased to hear the Russians are so near Warsaw they have captured Praga, a suburb on the other side of the Vistula. The Poles in the city on the other side, in Warsaw, are still holding out after forty-five days' fighting, marvellously holding out.

Leaving the best news till last the Yanks have broken into the Siegfried Line in four places and at one of them near Aachen have broken through it on a 9-mile front.

SUNDAY 17 SEPTEMBER
It will be a memorable day for us. We saw the finest sight we, stuffed away from the front line as we are, have seen this war. It was the 1st Airborne Army making an attack on Holland. Like this.

Going to Bromeswell around midday I had dinner at 11.30, at the open French window, alone except for my binoculars. Was a little surprised to see Martlesham excel itself by putting up forty-seven Thunderbolts each with two long-range tanks, when I decided to go outside to investigate a roar which was becoming louder. Then I became excited and shouted for the wife and the kids to see what was coming. Dakotas pulling Horsa gliders were coming over in droves. They were slowish, fairly well spaced and seemed to fill the sky for about twenty minutes. A lot can pass in twenty minutes. I counted about 90 pairs and then gave up but estimated a total of 150 to 200 pairs. Margaret, energetic soul, counted 368 planes including the fighters. Then followed a streak of Mustang, about twenty, a few Marauders at high speed and I went to finish dinner.

Within ten minutes they were at it again. Halifaxes towing Hamilcar tank carrying gliders this time, about fifty of them, then another 100 or 150 Horsas towed by Stirlings chiefly. There were a few twin-tailed gliders too, strangers to me. A wonderful sight. Speculation was active as to where they were going. My guess was to Holland, they were going east-by-north to land above the Rhine outlet and turn the flank that way.

Very little news has come through but I was a little out. They landed around Eindhoven and Tilberg over the Dutch frontier with Belgium and around Nijmegen between the Rhine and the Maas. We guessed it was the newly formed airborne army in action, a combined British and American force, and it was.

What now? Shall we hear another roar tonight as glider supplies are taken over as after D-Day? Will there be fighter cover sent this way and shall we see Tempests and the Gloster jet-propelled craft? There'll be a rush to the windows I guess at the sound of aircraft tomorrow and tonight.

9 o'clock. No details yet of the landing but it sounded as though we only saw a small part of it go over. They are about twenty miles from our spearheads at Tilburg and Eindhoven. Hope they do well.

The Americans are now twelve miles inside Germany at Aachen and are in the outskirts of that surrounded city.

MONDAY 18 SEPTEMBER

It happened again today. At 12.15 I saw the first pair of Dakotas pulling Horsas and we went on the roof of the Works to see the beginning of the stream. All through the dinner hour they went droning over and for some time after I was back at work. As an estimate I should say there were 750 and possibly 1,000 pairs of planes. An amazing sight. The sort of thing one knows one can only see once in a lifetime but hopes to see again tomorrow.

Yesterday was the first day of the dim-out and about 8.30 the alert went due to doodle-bugs. The radio said many had to sit in the dark in London because they had destroyed their blackout. Many people thought they might as well black out as usual if the alert's still going but Sidegate Avenue this evening looked cheery with a few houses in full blaze of light behind their curtains.

SATURDAY 23 SEPTEMBER

The battle around Arnhem is going to be one of the most decisive battles of our campaign. The facts of the airborne landings are that they landed at Eindhoven and Nijmegen the first day and Arnhem on the second. It only penetrated my thick head yesterday to appreciate from the map that the Siegfried Line ends at the Rhine near Arnhem, hence the import of the landings.

SUNDAY 24 SEPTEMBER

The Arnhem force is still virtually isolated but a patrol crossed the river from the 2nd Army and made contact this morning. Was a little disturbed to hear the announcer read that 'it relieved a situation which had been giving some concern'. We used 1,500 gliders and tugs yesterday to fly supplies and reinforcements and Jerry's air force was out to engage but he lost twenty-six to our fourteen fighters. Today's 'wicked weather' as a Brussels correspondent put it, will prevent any air activity at all I guess. Those brave blokes have been at it for a week now but have taken over 900 prisoners I note and sleep can't have been very plentiful.

Went to Landguard today and probably the last parade of the sort which we shall have. The weather was cold, blowy and drizzly at first turning to rain which made us pack up early, and spoilt a record in which we had always had fine warm weather for our trips to Landguard and Bromeswell. The elements were perhaps sorry to see the last of us there and showed their sorrow.

Came home quite satisfied in a personal way. They tried to get us through the marksman's badge and I fancy three of us, myself included, obliged. I suppose it was a bit of a wangle, although quite above board according to rules but they gave us two chances to improve our grouping and three attempts at application. After all our best scores on other occasions had been counted so there's no reason why these should not be included.

We are to have company photos next month, a march past parade preliminary to stand down on 29 October and a 'smoker' on 4 November. Shall be sorry in a way to see it all go but it would be a bit useless to keep on, I suppose.

WEDNESDAY 27 SEPTEMBER

Our chaps have been withdrawn from Arnhem. They came over the river on Monday night, about 2,000 strong out of 8,000 who went there. In addition about 1,200 wounded were left and it is understood Jerry is looking after them.

We've been listening just now to two reporters who were with them and they gave a thrilling story of constant shelling, mortaring and sniping for the whole nine days, concentrated on their area of 900 yd × 1,500 yd. At the end rations were down to one-sixth and they were drinking rain-water. They didn't say a great deal of just how they came away, how they walked clean through Jerry's lines and got across the river but that seems a huge achievement to me.

And now to bed a little early. Those doodles have been over every night for the past week or so, sometimes twice, usually twice in fact, about 8.30 or so and about 4 a.m. Usually we see or hear about four in this district.

SATURDAY 30 SEPTEMBER

Dover, Folkestone and nearby towns have today been hung with flags and they have been rejoicing. For over four years they have been subjected to long-range shelling from Jerry guns on the Calais and Cap Gris-Nez districts. Just when Jerry felt like it and sometimes when a British convoy was passing, he would lob shells across in an indiscriminate manner. Flashes from over in France would be followed by shelling warnings in Dover and people would anticipate the shells which would arrive in a matter of a minute or so. Now all that is over because the Cap Gris-Nez guns have been captured intact and Calais is almost captured. Yesterday the commander of the Calais garrison was asked to surrender but he refused because Hitler had ordered him to hold out. He did, however, ask for an armistice which was refused under the unconditional surrender terms but a 24-hour truce was proclaimed for the French civilians to evacuate the town. It expired today and the fight is on again. Soon it will be over and Calais will be ours for harbour clearance.

SUNDAY 1 OCTOBER

Calais fell during the night. Last night we had an unbroken night's sleep. Quite an event for recent times. There have been alerts every night since 16 September mostly more than one during the night, and once three or four times. All for doodle-bugs of course. Fortunately they have all gone inland (touch wood) though not so fortunate for the poor blighters who catch the packet but the country is lightly populated and, I fancy, casualties are relatively light. One dropped at Ardleigh and killed four people, another hit a barn on the Colchester Road at Dedham and damaged the nearby house. One came to rest UX in some trees at Bergholt, another landed the other night at Woolverstone and shook the house even at that distance.

Put up my marksman's badge tonight, looks good. Godfrey was quite interested while I was sewing it on. There are only nine in our company and six of them are in our platoon.

WEDNESDAY 18 OCTOBER

Figures published tonight of our casualties since D-Day totalling 104,000. Heavy but light. They include 20,795 killed.

We've found complete sets of maps of England in Brussels, left behind by Jerry. The whole of the country was covered and road maps made of each town. His invasion plans were also found and in connection with that the maps were kept up to date till the end of 1943 when, presumably, he thought that invasion of England was at last off.

His scheme for invasion was a parachute feint landing in the Midlands, a landing aimed at London, on the south coast in Brighton district and the main force was to have been through Devon, up over Salisbury Plain in a left hook to the rear of London. Thank God he didn't try it. I should have said the scheme also intended blocking the Tyne, Humber and ports in general on the east coast with block ships.

I'm not sure if I recorded that Athens was liberated last week and the southern chunk of Greece is now free from Jerry. He properly mucked up all the port facilities but has left Athens itself untouched. The Greeks are feeling a bit relieved, although the food situation is sticky owing to the port destructions and the fact that Jerry took every bit of transport he could lay his hands on but unfortunately their political feuds have flared up. There was fighting in Athens on Sunday. Pity they can't compose themselves in a little better manner.

Those ruddy Jerries have now started a systematic cold-blooded extermination of Poles in one of the concentration camps with their blasted gas chambers. The survivors of the Warsaw affair are among them. Makes one subscribe to the view that the only good Huns are dead ones. Really, they are a foul crowd.

SUNDAY 22 OCTOBER

Had this morning what was possibly our last Home Guard parade before the finale. We paraded for photographs as a company by platoons and officers and NCOs. I suppose I came out like a grinning gargoyle or frowning fat-head.

On Friday the Americans made their biggest landing so far. They landed on Leyte Island in the Philippine Islands and now have an army of 100,000 there. The Japs are being taught lessons in strategy. The Yanks by their heavy attacks on Formosa and on Luzon probably led the Japs to think an attack of some sort was intended there. Anyway the Leyte landing was made with such ease that it suggests they were caught on the hop. Naturally resistance stiffened later but too late to prevent the biggest airfield falling into American hands. Didn't realise the importance of the place till I saw the map today. Firmly held it will cut off Japan from most of the empire she has stolen or at any rate it will make communications very hazardous.

Thought we might be in for a packet yesterday morning about 0500 hr. The alert had just gone and the wife and kiddies had entered the shelter when I saw a light approaching in the sky. There was no noise. It was one of those doodles which had been hit and was going along under the influence of a continuous flame. It was approaching us looking as though it would pass by only a little to our left – and the damn thing went out. I had already called out to George next door who had not yet emerged and couldn't have been aware of it coming so I yelled again for him to be careful. After a pause there was a flash to the north-north-west and that was that. It had glided to a village called Barking near Needham.

Good Christmas news released recently. All kiddies under eighteen will have ½ lb of sweets extra on their ration and everyone will be entitled to ½ lb extra sugar and margarine while the meat allowance for the week will go up from 1s 2d to 1s 10d. Dates will also be available at one point per packet of 6 oz.

Lots of people are taking advantage of the blackout concessions. It's quite pleasant to see the curtained windows all aglow with light. Took some getting accustomed to though. I suppose about one house in twelve or perhaps twenty are doing it, but all lights go out on alert. We are still blackingout, it's easier.

About three weeks ago I put up two boxes in the sector, one at my gate and one in Sidegate Avenue at G—'s place. I go along every evening, perhaps I've missed three times so far, but have only had results one night. The object is for people to drop a note if there is any variation in the number of people sleeping at any particular house, to help the rescue party in case of necessity. Hope it's never used.

SUNDAY 29 OCTOBER
The day we were to have been 'stood down' in the Home Guard. Then came the surprising cancellation of everything. I heard, as we all 'hear' these things in wartime, it all arose from the suggestion of

a stand-down being put to Eden who agreed to it in Churchill's absence in Canada. When Churchill returned he was furious and wasn't going to have his army stood down like that. The King would do it properly when the time came. Now, in the 6 o'clock news I heard the stand-down will come next Wednesday.

Tirpitz has been hit again by at least one 12,000-pounder. She was lying in Alta Fiord [Altafjord] after the last air attack and thought she had better be getting home when the Russians started moving along Norway. Accordingly she crept out in a dark period which occur in those latitudes with no moon and fetched up at Tromso where we found her this morning.

Fighting in Holland is fierce now. We made another landing, this time on Beveland Island which joins Walcheren and our heavies have been bombing the guns on Walcheren. Jerry seems to be pulling out of that part of Holland but slowly so as not to give our Typhoons the chance of strafing big columns of transport. He is also countering heavily on the eastern flank of our salient. There seems plenty of fight in him but insofar as the weather is keeping our planes grounded it is helping him. It has been really foul. For the last two or three weeks we have had rain some time in almost every day.

The Russians are still doing well. They have taken Petsamo and Kirkenes after entering Norway, cutting off the escape route of any Jerries in Finland. Also there is one of the fiercest fights, even of the Russian sector, taking place in East Prussia and Jerry is using his Volkssturm, his Home Guard.

Had to turn out this morning at 0515 hr in a really filthy night. It was pouring down and as dark as pitch although the moon had only just set. One doodle crashed pretty close too but don't know where.

TUESDAY 31 OCTOBER
Received first intimation of Dennis's passing yesterday. Came a bit of a blow. Hope we get to know the exact circumstances.

Cologne had another terrific hammering last night. Over 4,000 tons went down at the rate of 100 tons per minute, it following the heaviest of the war on Saturday morning and four Mosquito attacks in between. We used 850 heavies and didn't lose one of them. That sort of news brings Dennis to mind. Wish we had news of him.

MONDAY 13 NOVEMBER

Tirpitz is sunk! Hooray! News came this morning that twenty-nine Lancs went to Tromso yesterday morning and 'hits were made with 12,000-lb bombs'. Now this evening the Air Ministry reports that she is capsized and sunk.

Excellent news, both in the fact and in the inference. A big threat to our Atlantic shipping is finally removed and our Fleet out East may be reinforced with the units which are now released. I amused the kids no end recently with a coloured yarn of the adventures of the *Tirpitz* and now they will be tickled at its conclusion.

This evening happened what we had been mildly expecting – the alert went before, just before, we left off work at 6 o'clock. Nothing further until on the Woodbridge Road and then the 'cuckoo' sounded. Soon came the throaty growl and the darned thing came sailing along on a reciprocal course only a few hundred yards away. Arriving home I found the kids having their tea <u>under</u> the table and eating more owing to the fun of it. It was the first doodle the gunners have let through in this direction for weeks.

The Japs have had a reasonable victory in China and chased the Americans out of their last land airbase suitable for attacking Japan. Pity.

THURSDAY 16 NOVEMBER

Still no news of Dennis. Wish they'd buck up and write.

We found a Jerry convoy off the southern part of Norway on Sunday, 'we' being a surface force of two cruisers and three destroyers. The convoy consisted of eleven ships including escort; nine were sunk and one driven ashore.

The Russians have made such progress in Hungary that Budapest is seriously threatened.

Yesterday we started a new, a big, offensive in south-east Holland towards the River Maas and Venlo. It has developed into a big affair involving six armies and is going pretty well. Wish they'd do something for the Dutch, poor devils, things are bad for them. Probably, though, we are getting food to them in small doses by parachute or other means. Can't see us deserting them completely. A lot of the difficulty is caused by their own patriotism. We called on them for support and the Dutch railway workers struck. Things didn't go as well as we had hoped but they still kept out on strike to hamper Jerry, knowing they were making their own supply problems difficult. Heroism that.

SUNDAY 19 NOVEMBER
We heard re Dennis on Friday. His plane collided with another in
heavy cloud over the Channel on 30 July. A naval vessel went to the
rescue, searched an hour and a half and only found one body –
Dennis's. They buried him at sea, twenty miles north-west of [Le]
Havre at 0930 hr the same day. Decent of them to tell us all
particulars. Although they must have thousands of similar letters to
write they made it sound a very personal letter.

So that's how it was. Poor chap. A pity he couldn't have been
spared having gone so far through the war. Shows the damnable
nature of war too.

SUNDAY 3 DECEMBER
Again lots has happened. Naturally the most prominent is today's
event, the Home Guard stand-down.

It's been a rather impressive day I suppose. Wasn't aware of it at
first, merely went along to parade as I've done many times but by
now I've come to the conclusion we must have been appreciated by
somebody.

We paraded at 0845 hr and marched to the Regent Cinema,
the whole battalion, where the miniature shooting cup was
presented to the winning team, B Company, and the shield for
the stretcher-bearing competition to the sector winners, our
platoon. Major Howes, our CO addressed us and so did Gen
Deeds. I was pleased they spoke plainly and appreciatively but
with no fuss and without ladling out absurd compliments. The
9th Battalion went to the Odeon.

Following that we marched to the park and formed up as a
Battalion on the grass before the Mansion, eventually marching away
following the 9th to the march past at the Cornhill where Gen Deeds
took the salute. We went along Crown Street to Hyde Park Corner,
along Westgate Street, Carr Street and so up St Helen's. Five bands
played us along at various points. Can't say much of what I saw at the
saluting base. Like the others, I suppose, I was concentrating on
marching, listening to orders and keeping position.

In London representatives from all units in the country, 7,000 of
them, marched past the King. We sent Foster, a good bloke. I
suppose we did do a job of work. We were ready if needed for
active service and in a negative sort of way we did it when, around
invasion time, we did those pickets and guards. They released a
great many full-time soldiers who would have had to do the job in

our place and enabled the Army to concentrate wholly on their part of the war.

So now it's all over, although only being stood down we are not disbanded and are liable to recall at any moment. There are 1,631 on the strength of our battalion, in addition 245 went to the Forces, and I suppose the 9th had similar strength, and I also guess that our platoon wasn't far off being the keenest and most conscientious of the lot. We turned out at almost full strength today, thirty-five out of under forty.

Now we concentrate wholly on ARP duties. We started the one-night-in-six rota on Thursday. Six nights will seem a helluva gap but I guess we won't complain. We all turn out at trouble.

SUNDAY 10 DECEMBER
This is getting a once-a-week affair now. Naturally the reason is Christmas preparations. Presents are so scarce that once again I'm making things and this year it's a helluva programme. A workbox for Margaret, five small aeroplanes, six book-ends, a 'spill' holder and extensive preliminary polishing experiments. I usually know what it is to be thoroughly tired just before Christmas. Squealing eh? Must be that chill I picked up from somewhere.

Last Monday week, 27 November, there was a whacking great explosion in Lincolnshire. An RAF bomb dump went up and caused a lot of damage. It was 90 ft below ground and the report said that hundreds of people were killed and enough bombs for hundreds of major raids on Germany were exploded. Eventually it was officially stated that 4,000 tons went up, a big enough figure certainly, but only enough for one raid and only fifty-three people were killed. Goebbels, the opportunist, said he had scored a direct hit with a V2. He would. He didn't say though how it penetrated 90 ft. Our statement said that sabotage was not suspected.

Last Sunday commenced the big event of the week in the shape of trouble in Athens. Political friction has flared up, a left-wing group called ELAS (don't know what it stands for) is fighting the government forces. We are backing up the government and take the view that the arms were given to the Greeks to fight Jerry and not to be used for political ends. Having kicked him out the weapons ought to be surrendered and political squabbles settled by the vote. Yesterday the ELAS leader said be would abide by the orders of Gen Scobie, our leader in Athens, but his followers say they won't and fighting has again flared up. Wonder how far it is Jerry-fomented?

The Russians have now made two big thrusts each side of Budapest and the city looks like being taken soon. Excellent strategy those Russians are capable of. It might even now mean that the main thrust into Germany from that side will be by the Austrian frontier in spite of the mountains which Uncle Joe has avoided up to now.

Details of V2 have been released this week. It is more of a jet-propelled affair than a rocket, but what's in a name? It is 47½ ft long and 5½ ft dia. with 2,000 lb of explosive. Range is approx. 200 miles. Rumour says that London is having between one and eight each day. Some chaps were awakened about 5 a.m. the other day by a wallop.

Have been outside this evening in a south-easterly gale and rain with no moon. Doodles were coming over to the south and I saw five either shot down or explode on their own. Three of them were within 6 miles.

TUESDAY 19 DECEMBER
Big news. Jerry started a counter on Sunday which he has now developed into the biggest counter-attack he has yet launched. He struck at several places, which developed into three main thrusts on a seventy-mile front from Aix to Trier on the Luxembourg frontier. By tonight the general position is that he has advanced on all the seventy-mile front and has penetrated anything up to twenty miles or more. His air force too is being used and he has lost a few hundred planes.

An order of the day from Rundstedt to his troops has been captured which described it as a last effort. Certainly it may be. He has naturally the surprise effect of being able to concentrate on a front of his choosing and it will undoubtedly be a very heavy attack. Indeed it has been described as the heaviest European battle of the war. News is difficult to obtain as there has been a shut-down on all official sources.

One or two at work are a bit dumpy about it, but my opinion is not by any means similar. I think it is an excellent idea. As the *Telegraph* puts it, Jerry has come out of his concrete and our job will be easier. Aldy says that's all very well, provided Jerry isn't pulling one over on us, provided he hasn't something up his sleeve against which we have no counter. He would.

TUESDAY 26 DECEMBER

Boxing Day. We've had a good Christmas, plenty to eat except sweets and seasonable weather. We've had three days' unbroken sunshine and heavy frost, been freezing all the while. This morning, after a heavier frost than I can remember, the trees looked wonderful against the blue sky, as white as though covered with snow.

Good old Churchill. He's a wonder. He turned up in Athens yesterday, Christmas Day, and has today opened a conference between the opposing parties. He's there with Eden, the Greek archbishop is chairman and after opening the affair our chaps are leaving the Greeks to come to some decision – we hope. I'm almost despairing of the ruddy chumps doing anything of the sort but Churchill may have some influence. At his age, he was seventy a month ago, there are not many people who would travel so far at such a time.

Yes, we've celebrated this holiday by today having no blackout and availing ourselves of the dim-out relaxations. Only curtains everywhere except the kitchen, where there are only flimsy affairs. Seems a lot of hope for the future in that.

NOTES

1   It was anticipated there may be some offensive move against England at this time to hinder preparations for a Second Front.
2   Refers to the small bound notebooks in which the diaries are written – twelve in all.
3   Junkers Mistel composite aircraft: a piloted Messerschmitt 109 or Focke Wulf 190, pick-a-back on an unmanned, explosives-laden Junkers 88, which would be released when near the target.

1945-6

By the end of January the last Germans were cleared from the Ardennes 'bulge' and the Russians were ninety-five miles from Berlin. Early in March the Rhine was crossed at Remagen, General George S. Patton's US tanks raced ahead of the infantry and the British and Canadians pushed south from Holland. Meanwhile the Allied air forces pounded strategic targets and harried the retreating Germans at will. The V1s and V2s continued on their destructive paths until the launching sites were overrun. The last V2 fell on England on 27 March.

Sadly President Roosevelt did not live to see victory in Europe; he died on 12 April and was succeeded by Harry Truman two weeks before Russian and American forces linked at Torgau on the Elbe. It was over. On 30 April Hitler committed suicide in his Berlin bunker.

Richard Brown reported every detail of the last battles and political wranglings in the dying days of the war and it seemed an interminably long wait until Victory in Europe on 7 May. The end of nearly six long years of war in Europe was celebrated with much rejoicing and lots of street parties somewhat muted by the fact that Allied forces were still engaged in the Far East.

Throughout the summer the airborne kamikaze suicide attacks on the US fleet caused many casualties but the Japanese navy was to all intents and purposes a spent force after the April clash in the East China Sea. US forces landed everywhere in the Pacific, island-hopping towards mainland Japan. The battle for the island of Okinawa was the most fiercely fought and more than 12,000 Americans lost their lives in the eighty-one day campaign. In Burma the lines were less clear and the war was expected to last another two years.

At home life gradually resumed some kind of normality; the lights came on again and on 17 May Mr Brown took the ARW sign from his gate. With some irony he reported that war in Europe had ended but the nation was nevertheless in the grip of escalating shortages and further tightening of belts. There is a gap of four weeks in the diary when his daughter was seriously ill and he was unable to vote in the General Election. To his disgust the result is a landslide for Labour, though Churchill is still personally popular.

When the first atomic bomb falls on Hiroshima on 6 August and, as Mr Brown notes, puts a new and terrifying complexion on the future of warfare, it really is only a matter of days before the Japanese agree to unconditional surrender. Victory in Japan was celebrated on 15 August. The Japanese formally surrendered on 2 September 1945.

SUNDAY 7 JANUARY

News just released that when Jerry made his attack on the Belgium–Luxembourg frontier on 16 December it was followed next day by the appointment of Montgomery as commander of the front down to the apex of the salient which incorporated the American 1st and 9th (I believe) Armies. He guessed Jerry, or should I say Rundstedt, would aim at the Dinant crossing of the Meuse and raced a British force there to hold them. The British reached the bridge first, crossed it, and stopped Rundstedt four miles away.

And now Rundstedt has struck again, this time in the Saar district. He has made about twelve miles progress and there are hints that we may have to evacuate Strasbourg. Naturally, the weather is still bad, foggy and snowy and with ice-covered roads. The Tactical Air Force can't do much, possibly that's why he has struck now, and transport is hampered by the roads. The Strategical Air Force, however, is doing its stuff, although the frost has not yet completely disappeared here in England, and is continuously bombing Jerry's supply roads, lines and bases.

This air attack is a big event but we are too close to appreciate it. We want a Wellsian time machine to allow us to see it in the perspective of five years hence. As it is we hear the Forts droning round before light, at about 0700 hr, later they roar over with the sustained, threatening, labouring note of a box of thirty-six machines, and we know they are off after assembling. Soon a more hasty, obviously single-engined growl follows and Martlesham sends up its quota of sixteen or thirty-two or more Mustangs which circle perhaps once and off they go. Later some race over westwards, we see if they are still in fours, and they have an 'in-a-hurry' look as they dash for home. Then out of the cloud, sometimes so misty that they use their searchlights or wing lights, come low-flying Forts in groups or wings of twelve – if there are no losses and if some haven't peeled off at other 'dromes on the way. Stragglers follow, and these sometimes have a stationary prop or the bomb doors may be stuck open, some circle Debach and land and then silence shows another op has been accomplished but we don't know what it was.

Budapest is still surrounded by the Russians who are making it another Stalingrad, clearing it house by house. Jerry has 80,000 men inside with 2 million civilians. He is trying to relieve the city but his attacks are being held. On the rest of the huge Russian front things seems fairly static.

In Italy things have been stabilised now for some months on a line running approx. east–west at Ravenna. Weather again has been atrocious there, holding up everything with torrential rain and now frost.

I don't believe that I reported some months or so ago that the Americans landed on Mindanao Island in the Philippines. They met almost no land opposition and have things well their own way. The Japs now say the Americans are shelling Luzon, the largest island of the group. Perhaps another landing is being made.

We've quelled all organised resistance by the ELAS in Athens. A sad business that; can't say how it will develop. Now there is a regency things may be easier. Seems queer; nobody seemed to know the king was unpopular.

FRIDAY 19 JANUARY
Warsaw fell on Wednesday. I heard a remark this afternoon that not one civilian male was found there but I don't know the circumstances. Possibly they were conscripted for labour in Germany – we'll hope so. There have been some damnable atrocities by the Huns in this war. I haven't made much reference to them but if only a tenth are true the only safe Jerry is a dead one, true enough.

The Russian drive is sweeping on. Three armies under different generals are thrusting along the line from East Prussia to Czecho-Slovakia. One correspondent professes to see in them a thrust to clear East Prussia, another into the industrial district of Silesia and a third on the centre aimed directly at Berlin.

MONDAY 22 JANUARY
Great news yesterday and today from the Eastern Front. The news is issued in 'Orders of the Day' from Stalin; there were five

yesterday and five today, issued like latest news from a newspaper. They are read out in order on the news at 9 o'clock and give a thrill of excitement as they move the line in the mind's eye further and further westward. Tonight the Russians at the nearest point are only 165 miles from Berlin. Considering they were in Warsaw only a few days ago the advance is phenomenal and my, usually valueless, opinion is that it is not so much an advance as a follow-up of an orderly retreat by the Germans to a prepared line on the German border or on the Oder. That doesn't detract any from the excellence of the Russian achievement but the chaps at work are generally reckoning the war will be over in a week or so. Perhaps that's not literal nor do all of them think that way but that's the idea. Queer how some people and some newspapers go up in the air at a victory and down in the dumps at a setback.

On our front things are going well in our little offensive from the south tip of Holland. Our fighters have had a record bag behind the Ardennes bulge on the retreating Jerry transport. They've bagged 880 vehicles since breakfast, the highest so far. Our offensive is aimed at destroying Jerry against the River Roer, not a huge-sized effort but the intensity is huge.

Armistice terms to Hungary published today. She will pay £75 million in six years, £50 million to Russia, the rest to Czecho-Slovakia, payment to be paid in kind. Sounds a reasonable amount. Perhaps they've realised huge payments only damage the recipient.

SATURDAY 27 JANUARY

Jerry says the Russian spearheads are at the border of Poland and Brandenburg which is only 100 miles from Berlin. The Russians have not yet claimed it but it's probably correct. They have made another thrust in Silesia and taken more towns. In cut-off East Prussia they are closing in on Königsberg only ten miles from the outskirts.

The big news is really – weather. The frost still persists. I put my thermometer out of the window at work this morning and it showed 22°F. Fortunately it's been dry these last few days although the side-roads are still icy from the last snowfall and now it's snowing again.

They've been appealing for economy in gas and electricity recently but the economies were not sufficiently forthcoming so now in some parts of the country the current has been cut off to household consumers for a half-hour or so in the morning for the past three days. Someone in the *Telegraph* has recalled that the big three-month frost of 1895 started with a thunderstorm on the same date which followed the same path as one we had recently. What hopes! Hope the similarity ends there. I don't mind snow for itself but I don't like cycling on frozen roads and in the 1895 affair the Thames froze. The whole northern hemisphere seems in the grip. New York is registering 30 degrees of frost today.

FRIDAY 2 FEBRUARY
Almost without doubt the Big Three are now conferring. A report from Cairo says that one of the points brought forward by Stalin is that they cannot countenance a Fascist state in Europe (Spain) in the after-the-war conditions, which may become a hotbed of future conspiracy. In other words Franco must go. It has my whole-hearted sympathy. Good old Joe.

There's been some bumps early this morning. Another came just now, a double bump typical of a rocket which made both the wife and I think one of the kiddies had fallen out of bed. They don't have the same effect as doodles or an orthodox plane raid insofar as, there being no warning and no expectation or alertness or turning out of CD personnel, nobody takes much notice except the poor devils in the immediate vicinity.

Last night we sent 1,400 planes to drop 4,750 tons of bombs on the railway centres through which are passing the troops and armour Jerry is taking from the Western Front to the East. Berlin is being mined, barricaded and defended. The Berliners will be tasting what they expected to dole out to us soon, I fancy.

WEDNESDAY 14 FEBRUARY
Marshal Koniev's strategy is keeping everyone guessing and he is threatening strongly from over the Oder towards Dresden and is only seventy miles away. In support the RAF went to Dresden last night, 800 Lancasters dropping 750,000 incendiaries and HE. That was followed by 450 American heavies in daylight today. I guess the Russians could see the glow.

Dresden is apparently a big railway and distributing centre for Silesian coal among other things. It may even be possible that Zhukov will keep his armies on the east bank of the Oder as a threat to Berlin, locking up many Hun troops there while his pals outflank the city.

I saw in the paper that the Americans on the Western Front have put up a huge sign facing the Jerry lines saying 'Russians stop here! We are the Americans'. Irrepressible.

U-boat activity was a little greater last month and losses were up a bit but still lower than 1943. Jerry is using that 'schnorkel' which allows him to run his diesels under the surface through ventilating pipes so he is harder to spot.

SUNDAY 18 FEBRUARY

Interesting news re de Gaulle. He had been invited to meet Roosevelt at Algiers as the latter was on his way home from the Crimea Conference, but de Gaulle refused on the grounds that the decisions of the conference needed consideration. It was obviously, the commentator said, an illustration of de Gaulle's disappointment at France not being represented at the conference. What the hell! Does he think France has done so much that she is on a level with the Big Three? Sounds like sulks to me.

We went out yesterday alone – the first time since last Whitsun. We walked to Martlesham and back, tea-ing at the Black Tiles. I saw forty-seven fighters on the field and I don't suppose they were all in view and certainly others were aloft. There wasn't much effort at dispersal either. Darned good sign.

SUNDAY 4 MARCH

Jerry's retreat west of the Rhine is now a rout. The American 9th linked up with Crerar's Canadian and British yesterday; they reached the Rhine above Düsseldorf. The 1st has reached it above Cologne and is only two miles from that city. Jerry has blown three bridges near Düsseldorf but has left others, over which he is retiring, urged, when the weather allows, by the TAF. There are not many Germans left west of the Rhine now.

Gen Zhukov has now made a big 60-mile advance today towards the Baltic coast in Pomerania. He is only a few miles from the coast and will cut off lots more Huns in what is left of East Prussia.

Yesterday morning at 0500 hr the siren went. The first time for over five weeks. I got up in case of anything new and heard a doodle as the alert died away. This morning at 0300 hr the alert went again. Again I got up and was glad I did. Soon came the sound of a plane, to my astonishment very, very much like the old Junkers 88. Then another different note came in and then came sounds of gunfire and a wallop. The flash was to the south-west and could only be one thing – a bomb. The first plane raid since last June!!!

One wonders now what will happen. There is only a dim-out, the Fire Guard is stood down, business premises are not fire-watched, the balloon barrage is disbanded. There has just been a second plane visitation, nothing on Ipswich, touch wood, so I expect an announcement on the blackout tomorrow. Actually people are playing fair and not many lights are showing. It was like old times to see the ack-ack bursting in the sky and to get near my emergency dropping zone once again.

The bomb I just mentioned, this morning's one, was a pair of bombs on Seymour Road, probably dropped by a fighter-bomber which is reported to have machine-gunned a car on the Nacton Road. There was some damage, nobody was in his shelter and eight were killed. Osborne went down and said he'd rather have a fire any day than another job like that. Pretty rotten sights I believe. I suppose being the first of its kind for some time, people were getting a bit blasé. Certainly the killed were mostly in their beds.

I fancy he must have trying for the Stoke Bridge. Wonder if it's all an organised recce? It was fairly general and six were shot down, and two more over the other side by intruders. There have been a few gliders seen around and several Stirlings and there were certain soldiers in the town for the past week. I still fancy that landing somewhere north of the Rhine mouth and possibly so does Jerry and he's looking around.

THURSDAY 15 MARCH
Yesterday for the first time we used a 22,000-lb bomb. Ten tons!!! Makes one almost shudder to think what will be used in the next war. It does, however, make one think with pride of the Lancaster which can carry it, the only plane in the world, including the Super-Fort. The bomb was used against a viaduct and it hit it too with the obvious result. Today it was used again against a second viaduct.

Peace rumours again. From Stockholm comes a report that suggestions of peace terms from Hitler, against Hitler's own wishes though but overruled by the others, have been turned down by the Allies. Peace was to include the continuance of the Jerry war against Russia. What a crowd those Huns are.

SUNDAY 18 MARCH

Dora went blood-donating this afternoon. I think that's one of the most satisfying of the war jobs. You know that when you get home and survive the slight thrill of excitement and the feeling of self-satisfaction at having watched the sticky looking stuff trickling into the 'milk' bottle this time, that you have done something tangible for some badly wounded combatant. It's all accentuated by the callous way in which the blood is stacked, like milk, in bottles in wire crates and just dumped. Each one is, however, carefully graded and classified.

Jerry had us out three times last night. The second time, at 0245 hr, I heard what I took to be, in my sleepy state, a crashing plane and didn't realise till I was downstairs that it was a doodle, darned low. Opening the front door I saw it disappearing westward after going almost directly overhead. The vibration shook a half brick down the chimney of a chap down the street. Don't wonder at it with nearly 1,000 hp going over with an open exhaust and no expansion.

WEDNESDAY 21 MARCH

Grub. Food. Meat in particular. It's annoying that with the war going so well, due to finish in a very few weeks in some people's opinion, the food situation is getting a little serious. I reported a few weeks ago that the government had miscalculated a little and food was getting scarce. Now, owing to drought conditions last year in Australia their cattle supply is short and they won't be able to help us. America was expected to be able to help but they have now announced a 12 per cent cut in their rations due to similar causes. Sounds awful, but that brings their ration down to 5⅓ oz compared to our slightly over 1 oz per day. Five times our ration!!!!! Sounds like we are underfed but we are not. Some American has also said that we have 700 million tons of food stocked in the country. That's been stated to be false as it's all gone, or going, to the liberated countries. Queer that we are warned we may have to pull in our belts just now. My chief reaction to rations is that I would just love about a hundredweight of milk chocolate and guzzle it all at once. My idea of peace conditions is (almost) simply unlimited chocolate. As it is suppose I must be grateful for my 2 oz per week. Never mind. Some day.

The Japs had another smack yesterday. The American carriers caught them at anchor in their bases, the Jap navy I mean, and damaged fifteen or seventeen ships some of which may be sunk. One of them was a Yamato, the 45,000-tonner class. They also had

200 planes shot down and lost 275 on the ground. Shore buildings were also hit. The Americans had one ship badly damaged but she is getting home under her own power.

SATURDAY 24 MARCH
Yes, it's come. Monty crossed the Rhine at three points last night and the final big battle, we believe, has begun. No big details yet, the news was only released at the end of the 1 o'clock news. In fact one wonders at times like these why we get all het up and excited as all we know is that the three crossings were around Wesel at the top end of the Rhine, that a big RAF bombing preceded it, that the Navy came in with something new in river crossing technique, that the 1st Airborne were dropped over there in support and our ground forces have linked up somewhere at one spot with them. Churchill is at HQ with Monty and has sent a cheering message to the troops. Good old boy. He has lots of courage.

9 o'clock. There are four bridgeheads and one has penetrated to three miles from the river. This morning 1,300 gliders and 200 parachute droppers went out from Britain. Pity they didn't come from this district. We shan't see the sight I expected to see tomorrow morning. Or shall we? The armies concerned are the British 2nd holding three bridgeheads and the American 9th holding the fourth.

Saw my first doodle in daylight today. It was at 0700 hr and went streaking across the sky with a bluish silver streak behind it, against a clear blue dawn sky. It was about three or four miles south going a little north of west on the same course as another we saw during the night. There are about three, once five, alerts each evening and night for the last week or so. Chiefly doodles though once planes came over.

WEDNESDAY 28 MARCH
'Disintegration Follows the Great Collapse' says today's *Evening Standard*. 'Montgomery's Tanks racing into Reich at Will' says our local *Star*. Yes, it's good news. Everyone asks everyone else when he thinks it will all be over and the general opinion is that anything may happen at any time. Our cabinet is standing around over the holidays 'in case'. The American cabinet is doing the same and this, together with a misquotation of Eisenhower's, caused a big upheaval in New York yesterday when a rumour went flying round that it was all over. Today Fish offered to bet Aldy three to one in

large Players that Hitler would be captured, either dead or alive, by a month's time. Not being taken he reduced the time to 48 hours but still nothing doing.

Tonight the radio says our TAF in their forward flights report that Jerry's retreat to the Weser is now a rout. Prisoners are reported but not many killed. Most places they seem to be surrendering very quickly, only too glad to get out of the war excepting, that is, the paratroops on our northern flank.

EASTER MONDAY 2 APRIL

The Ruhr is surrounded. A whole army group of approx. 100,000 men is surrounded. Yesterday four columns were less than 200 miles from Berlin. Today one of them, Patton's, is 90 miles from the Czecho-Slovakia border.

Jerry is pulling out fast from north Holland and the transport crowding the roads is being strafed heavily in the Falaise Gap.

That's the position and people are going about saying, 'Yes, this is it at last'. Soon we may hear that Jerry is packing in.

SATURDAY 7 APRIL

Chief news today, to me, is that there has been a naval clash in the Pacific. American recce forces spotted a Jap battle fleet near Japan, in the Inland Sea I believe. Carriers raced to the area and planes found them when only about fifty miles from Japan. They attacked and sunk the *Yamato*, 45,000-ton pride of Japan, and two cruisers and three destroyers and shot down 200 Jap planes. The *Yamato* sank from three torpedo and eight heavy bomb hits, rather obligingly for such a ship. Japan has a lot to learn in shipbuilding. The Americans lost three destroyers and seven planes.

We are only a dozen miles from Bremen and Hanover and progress is still good though stiffish on our left flanks towards Holland. There are nine more bridges over the Rhine than Jerry ever had and we have four bridgeheads over the Weser. We certainly do move.

THURSDAY 12 APRIL

Last night a spearhead had reached the Elbe. Today the American 9th Army is there at Magdeburg and they have also crossed the Elbe at an unspecified point. They are thus less than sixty-four miles from the outskirts of Berlin.

Himmler, not Hitler be it noted, has issued an order today that the officer who surrenders a town to the enemy shall be sentenced to death. The general who surrendered Königsburg is sentenced to death by hanging in his absence and, due to that absence, it's being taken out on his family though in what manner is not stated. Those Huns are a lot.

War correspondents have been telling us tonight of some of their experiences and comments. They've seen some of the released slave workers trudging along the roads. Altogether Jerry, blast him, took and uprooted 12 million foreign workers, Russians and Poles and some French, to work in his ruddy factories and our advances have released over a million. Some looked fit and well but the majority didn't. Some had been looting shops for food and clothing. They present a big problem to our chaps. They want feeding and their release leaves the Jerry farms and food production untended which will further restrict food supplies. Those correspondents have also seen some of the atrocities. I don't mention many in this diary and they don't say a great deal about them. Their comments are restrained, even tonight when they said they had seen the remnants of a Dutch scene. The damnable Hun had found he had trouble in transporting a batch of sick Dutch workers so he shot them with tied hands, some beside the graves they had dug. Others had died purely from torture. At another place corpses were stacked, neatly, blast him in his orderliness, and others had just fallen in groups. The witnesses say they can't print the tortures from which lots had died. Tonight's commentator had seen some of this and he also found the Hun civilian in the overrun territory anxious to be friendly. Thank God, he says, that no one will play ball. The 'no fraternization' order is sound common sense.

FRIDAY 13 APRIL
Roosevelt died last night. It's sad news but on reflection not surprising. His photos taken at the Crimea Conference showed him to be worn and tired and ill and, bearing in mind his affliction, it is a tribute to his courage and stamina that he should have taken on the presidency for four periods. One could feel that his life might have been spared for a little longer if Stalin had agreed to leave his country for once in January instead of expecting a sick man to go to Russia.

He died from cerebral haemorrhage very shortly after complaining of a headache. I'll guarantee the thoughts of almost everyone in the Empire are with Churchill today hoping he will be spared some years yet.

Exciting reports this afternoon that we are only fifteen miles from Berlin but there is no official confirmation.

SUNDAY 15 APRIL
The *Express* headline today says 'Any Minute Now!'. A bit exaggerated perhaps but yet it may not be. As substantiation they say that organised government is ceasing and that yesterday our cabinet received very important news which has not been released, and cessation of hostilities may literally be at any minute. Well, let's hope they are right. The only visible pointer in the same direction here is that outside several churches are notices that a service will be held in the evening of the day hostilities cease.

It was rumoured from Stockholm yesterday, and now reasonably confirmed, that Jerry has split his government, one half looking after the north of the country, the other over the southern half including the redoubt which is now probably accepted as being in being. Rundstedt is in charge, militarily, of the south and the north is handed over to Busch. I'm talking of the Western Front of course. Obviously they fear an early link-up between Patton and Koniev, now only 100 miles apart.

THURSDAY 19 APRIL
More POW camps have been overrun with the expected results. Was pleased to hear that Bader, the pilot with two artificial legs, has been released. We don't hear a great deal about conditions in the POW camps except that food is poor but a concentration camp, a big one, was overrun recently and there were pictures in the paper this morning, the first of their kind, of some of the mentionable and allowable scenes. A whole heap of dead bodies was one scene, a prisoner in pyjamas (they all wore only pyjamas) hanging from a low gibbet, and distorted dead being laid out in a big grave. All these things are being watched by German civilians. The American commander had forced them to see some of the Gestapo crimes and he also made them dress in their best clothes and dig the grave and inter the bodies. A ghastly job but from what we could see of the spectators there was no sympathy in their faces; merely an expressionless matter-of-fact air of inspection. Cheers, anyway, for the common sense of that American commander.

Spain has agreed to prohibit the landing of any Jerry plane in her country. Up to now there have been daily civil plane arrivals and this new rule cuts out any chance of escape for Hitler's pals by that route.

By the way Eisenhower last week laid it down that V day would not be until all major pockets of Jerry resistance had been wiped out.

FRIDAY 20 APRIL

I believe we really must be getting near the end of this war – yesterday we removed the Cellophane from the glass in the French windows. I had hung on to that last protection in face of mild but sensibly non-persistent suggestions from the wife that it looked bad, looked dirty and that we couldn't see properly down the garden. My reply was invariably that the room is our refuge room during an alert and it ought to be the last thing to go. It was the last. In fact there's such an air of certainty that there will be no more air attacks that I wouldn't be surprised if George and I start demolishing the shelter at the bottom of the garden at Whitsun. I may be an ass but to me it's symbolic to be able to see the garden and the new things growing in it clearly once again.

And now today comes news that dim-out is to be abolished on Monday. It being double summer time and not dark till after ten I fancy street lights will not go up till 15 July when single summer time comes back but I shall at any rate be able to have the kitchen light on without feeling a little self-conscious at the light it throws on the next-door wall. It's only half covered with flimsy curtain and strictly speaking should be blacked out, but I don't feel like it and haven't done so for a month.

So once again the lights will go up, except for a five-mile strip of coast, and best of all, the light will be ceremoniously switched on above Big Ben by the Speaker and will remain on while Parliament is sitting as in the old days. The war does seem nearly over.

The last pocket battleship, the *Lützow*, has been sunk by Bomber Command in Swinemünde harbour today. She couldn't stand up to 12,000-pounder bombs. And today is Hitler's birthday too.

The Russians are only seventeen miles from Berlin suburbs. There is speculation as to when and where the Russians and Americans will link up and some apprehension as to whether they will recognise each other's tanks but I don't anticipate much trouble from that. It's probably newspaper talk.

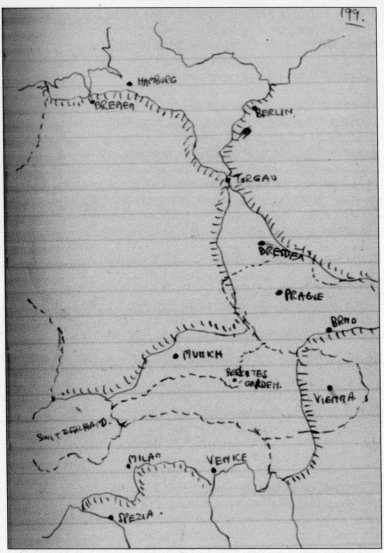

Map of the Torgau link-up, April 1945, from book 11 of
Richard Brown's diaries

WEDNESDAY 25 APRIL

Berlin is now surrounded, Hitler is inside, half the city is captured, most of it is in flames. In a general way I suppose, Jerry stated heavy reinforcements were arriving from other parts of Germany and our Typhoons found them riding two abreast and played havoc with them. He is also using the underground railways to take the Russians in the rear – the Russians have countered by beating the assault, taking field-guns downstairs and firing along the tubes.

Monty is around Hamburg and is in the suburbs of Bremen.

Arrangements have been made to drop food to the Dutch and the Jerries have been warned to leave it alone and not to fire on the planes. We are dropping 'F-Rations', a pre-digested food suitable for people on the verge of starvation, a good idea I think. Just another of those marvels of modern science.

Down in Italy things have been moving for a few weeks. I ought to have referred to it before. We broke the long lull by a heavy offensive and Jerry cracked. That was about two weeks ago I should say. We took Bologna about four days ago and now have advanced to the Po and yesterday we crossed it. Ferrara and Spezia are also taken and Jerry seems generally in a bad way.

Patton has now struck south to clear the bog-like area west of Bohemia and north of Austria. This morning he was only about thirty miles from Austria and he is now threatening Munich. At the same time the French are going along the frontier of Switzerland and are past Lake Constance.

Pétain has crossed Switzerland into France and has given himself up for trial. Poor doddering old idiot! What an ignominious life he has had during this war.

FRIDAY 27 APRIL

The Russians and Americans met on Wednesday afternoon and the news, according to plan, was released this evening. Dora and I were at the flicks watching a picture on Chopin's life and they interrupted to flash the news on the screen. There was a lot of applause. An historic event, Richard, and I think it symbolises Jerry's defeat more than anything else.

We've finally cleared Bremen today, finding a destroyer, eight subs and several midget subs in the docks but very little shipping.

The Wop patriots have done a fine job of work. Risings have cleared Jerry out of Milan, Turin, Genoa and a dozen other towns.

Jerry is in a complete rout, so fast that a bombing mission today had to be cancelled because the Army had got there first.

Milan radio today speaking for us announced Musso's capture. It had been rumoured and now presumably is correct.

Goering yesterday asked permission to resign leadership of the Luftwaffe owing to severe heart trouble. Our paper today says he has bunked with his wife and 5 million sterling. This war is, to quote Aldy, getting comic.

TUESDAY 1 MAY

A general impression that the papers are only waiting for full arrangements to be made before they are signed. Churchill spoke in Parliament and said that although there is no great news to impart there probably would be before the week is out. Instructions are being issued to all local authorities telling them what to do on VE Day to signify 'Victory-in-Europe' day. Shops are asked to cooperate to the extent that grocers are asked to remain open for one or two hours after the announcement, milk distributors are asked to operate and, although street lighting will not go on, floodlighting and bonfires are allowed. All this because it was stated some time ago that two days' holiday would be national, VE Day, VE Day plus one and, later on a third day.

Yes, it's as close as that. I suppose I ought to go into eulogies over this being a day within sight of the cessation of hostilities but I just can't. There's nothing to go into rhapsodies over. It's all come so gradually, people for weeks have been saying, 'This is IT. Jerry won't last long now', that we are just sliding into peace conditions. The abolition of the black-out came by steps, stand-down of various services has been by steps too. There is nothing to suggest a sudden stoppage. It's real, though, for all that and there will be celebrations all the same.

More food for the Dutch, 960 tons yesterday and more today by 400 Forts and Lancs as well. The Yanks took 800 tons and us over 1,000 tons.

The *Mirror* today published a photo of Musso, his mistress and two other men hanging upside down suspended by the feet from a framework.

Dachau concentration camp has been overrun. A hundred yards from the gates outside was a train of fifty trucks filled with bodies dead from starvation. They were from Buchenwald and had been kept there for three days without food, water, sanitation or attention of any kind. Those who had tried to get out were shot and still lay there by the trucks. In the camp were many, many more bodies of those who had been just mown down by MG fire as the Americans drew near. That sort of thing, and we've heard a lot of it, lots which I haven't recorded because one just doesn't want to, illustrates to me what we have been fighting. 'Evil things' Chamberlain said at 11.15 on 3 September '39. Though we didn't know what he meant we know now and we Britons only just escaped similar horrors.

WEDNESDAY 2 MAY
Fine news to start the page with. The Germans in north Italy have surrendered, the treaty being signed on Sunday to take effect at noon today.

Hitler is reported dead and Admiral Doenitz is the new Führer. It was given out on the Jerry radio last night that he had 'fallen' yesterday (Tuesday) but had appointed his successor on Monday.

Today came the startling news that the siren system came to a halt at midday. The ban on bells, hooters and works buzzers is lifted and the sirens are now dumb. They will not even be sounded at the 'Cease-Fire'. This evening I had instructions to let the fellows know there would be no more signing on on duty nights and I went round to tell them with the greatest pleasure. For the last time I have put my cycle in the shed making sure that I could get it quickly in the dark in the event of an alert. That's a fine thought.

There's also good news from the Pacific. The British have made a landing on Borneo and on the Burma coast.

FRIDAY 4 MAY
This evening between 1810 and 1820 hr Jerry plenipotentiaries met Monty and agreed that all enemy troops in north-west Germany, Holland and Denmark would surrender unconditionally at 0800 hr tomorrow. Another big slice taken.

The American 7th passed through the Brenner today and linked up with the British in Italy.

Amazingly good news. Today's paper said there is chaos in north-west Germany. Jerry has been trying to 'Dunkirk' to Norway and our planes have played havoc with his shipping. Up there the war turned comic again on Wednesday. We came across two divisions who wanted to surrender to us but as they had not been fighting us we didn't accept it and sent them packing to the

Russians whom they had been fighting. There is a distinct
preference on Jerry's part to surrender to the British rather than
the Russians where they have a choice. Makes one glad the
Russians are in Berlin.

Everyone is saying, 'When will VE Day be?' My prophecy is that
being very close now and since in the last war it came at 1100 hr
on the 11th of the 11th month, this time it will be 5 o'clock on the
5th of the 5th which is tomorrow. Wonder how far out that will be?
Mrs Osborne had a brainwave yesterday and suggested that as a
celebration we should give all the kids of the street a feed on the
day after VE Day. She and the wife have today been canvassing the
whole street, 100 houses, and met with an excellent enthusiastic
response, both in cash and offers of help. Harry is lending the
tennis pavilion and courts, rather weedy but all the better for us.
Last time I went there was to collect UX and burnt out IBs.

I feel I'm not fully appreciative of the present trend of events.
They are mighty events, we are living in history, experiencing
historic events and I, indeed everyone I encounter, merely take
them almost as a matter of course. There is no jubilation, merely a
feeling of satisfaction – but that I suppose is how it should be.

Wireless news was given today for the first time since 1940
without giving the identity of the announcer.

MONDAY 7 MAY
It's happened. This morning at 0241 hr Greenwich time Jerry surrendered unconditionally. The announcement will be made
tomorrow by Mr Churchill, bless his heart for bringing us to this
stage, and the King will speak at 2100 hr.

All U-boats have been ordered to stop hostilities and all German
ships have been ordered not to scuttle. They know well enough
that they'll want all the ships they can find to get food in.

There was a fly in the ointment. Prague was, and is, the scene of
trouble. SS troops have refused to surrender and are still
committing atrocities.

Rumours have been flying round all day at work. It was to be
announced at 6 o'clock, the King would speak at 9, it wasn't to be
announced owing to the Prague business etc. I don't think anyone
felt like work and to make it worse no one could operate the
canteen wireless to get the correct programme at 4 or 5 o'clock.

Well, it's definite now and celebrations of a sort will be on
tomorrow. There is a strong feeling that there ought not to be

much owing to our men still fighting in the Far East but there will sure to be jollification of a sort. There's lots of bunting and flags hung out of private houses and round pubs. I've just used two of my precious half-inch dowel rods for our kids' flags. Hope they duly appreciate my sacrifice but we must unbend somehow.

SUNDAY 8 MAY

VE Day. The day we didn't bother to think about for four years but to which we have been looking forward for the past few months. I'm sure I don't yet quite realise what it is. I know there is no more chance of hearing the alert, no more 4-hour duties in the post, no more light patrols, we <u>know</u> that every plane we hear is Allied and there won't be any more huge fleets of Forts assembling and climbing with the busy looking squadrons of fighters going up later on, but there seems only a partial realisation of the deeper meaning. One looked at the photos of the foul damnableness of Belsen or Buchenwald and said within oneself with somebody or other I've forgotten 'There but for the Grace of God am I' and indeed my family and many, many other families. 'But for the Grace of God' and the guts of our Services and leadership of Churchill, we could add I suppose. We missed all that by a very small margin, without knowing it at the time, and that's at the back of most people's minds although it's rarely spoken of. We were spared the horrors of a German occupation and all the dangers of underground movements and the churches today were, I believe, well attended. Sounds rather serious but it's a very, very true reflection.

Had a quiet but interesting day. Churchill made the official announcement of peace in Europe this afternoon at 3 o'clock. At 4 we went to a short service at church, at 8.30 started the most interesting wireless programme of its kind I've heard, including a fifteen-minute speech by the King, until ten to 11 o'clock. I'll record it tomorrow, perhaps, and go to bed.

FRIDAY 11 MAY

Yes, an excellent programme and suited to the occasion. For half an hour there were tributes to the King from each Service, Navy, Army, Air Force, Merchant Service, Fire, Civil Defence, Police, Home Guard and ending with an East End woman who had been bombed-out. No swank, just a sensible matter-of-fact covering of what they had done. It was answered by the King's speech and then the mike went to the various armies, to Eisenhower, Monty,

Bradley, their men, to Whitehall, Buckingham Palace and various parts of the country.

Martlesham went a bit wild, sending up flares and there were bonfires in most directions. The crowds in the towns were gay but orderly, I hear.

Next day, VE+1, we were busy. Mrs Osborne had had the idea of the kiddies' party and we went to it for the final preparations. There were quite a few of us working. We fitted power to the pavilion and moved a piano and a radiogram there and fitted an aerial. The pavilion was decorated with fairy lamps and Christmas decorations. Tables were laid on the grass and we built a huge bonfire. George and I made an effigy of Hitler and slipped inside two rounds of blank .303. I also made an excellent Jerry flag. We ran him to the top of the pile on a wire.

About eighty-five kiddies came and, I believe, most of the grown-ups in the street. There was a conjurer, an entertainer, races and then the bonfire. My .303 went off beautifully, so did the thunderflashes which had somehow been left behind when the HG equipment went in.

There were several other similar street parties in the town. Most people thought of the kids. The town is well decorated with flags but I don't know what floodlighting was done except that we floodlit our name REAVELL on the Works and painted the VE white. Cute idea.

Did I record that Goebbels's body was found in Berlin by the Russians? He had taken poison with his wife and family. No definite trace of Hitler has been found but the Russians have four charred bodies which they are examining. Himmler has disappeared but is suspected of being in the mountains. Goering is captured by the Americans, looking very well, 'pink, plump and in good health' as one report put it. He has been talking very freely, derogatorily of Hitler, saying that he suggested to Hitler it was time he stood down and Goering took his place. Hitler flew into a rage, arrested him, he was rescued by his faithful Luftwaffe staff and guarded ever since. Sounds just the heroic stuff one would expect him to invent. He also said his Luftwaffe was unbeaten until petrol ran out. Kesselring is taken too and he's been talking as well.

SATURDAY 12 MAY

U-boats are coming in. Twelve have surrendered so far. They were ordered to surface, fly the black flag and steam to the nearest

English port. Surface boats at sea were ordered to British ports too but there's no record of any arriving. I nearly put !! there. The E-boats were supposed to steam from their bases to Felixstowe on Friday, under escort of course. It was cancelled, because of fog officially, and today it's been postponed again. Wonder why?

The Lancs, Forts and Liberators have been bringing home the prisoners of war. They've brought 60,000 so far. There's a bit of a thrill seeing a batch of about twelve sailing over at about 2,000 ft and knowing who is inside. Good idea too. Relieves the food position over there for one thing.

The Channel Islands were found to be pretty badly off. Although the kiddies had been receiving most of what was going the adults were very poorly fed. There were no cats or dogs anywhere. A relief convoy of sixty ships went there today with food and clothing.

I didn't say before that we are now having weather forecasts again. The first was on VE Day. The announcer said we had bad news from an old friend – the Depression. He was found between the Azores and Ireland, stationary. A comedian tonight said that when he arrived at Broadcasting House he asked why a piece of seaweed was hung in the hall and was told it was because they had resumed the forecasts.

Naturally everywhere there is a kind of effervescence of relief, good humour and fun, but no over-exuberance or excitement. There is still the Japanese war and until that is over there won't be terrific rejoicing.

WEDNESDAY 23 MAY
I said before it's a comic war. It is. We've won it, therefore our rations are being cut down. Sounds odd but there's reason in it. Food shortages are reported from most parts of the world and there are countries like Holland to see after.

Actually we won't be doing so badly. It's reckoned that we will get 2,800 calories per day and the French just under half that. It's said that an adult needs about 3,000 to be healthy. There was some talk a little while ago that we would have to feed Germany but it's now been stated that she will have to feed herself. No food will be sent there unless epidemics develop which would threaten us and as their labour shortage promises to become awkward they may have a tough winter this year. Darned good job. They would have given us a far worse one.

There are still twelve U-boats at large in the Atlantic and our convoys still have escort on that account. They may not have received the surrender signal (?) and they may be fanatics.

Churchill resigned as Premier today, ending the coalition government after ten years' life. The Labour Party don't want an election till the autumn; they say a July one will be too hasty but Churchill says the government cannot function well while an election is so long ahead with all the friction which has developed and I agree. The *Mirror* this morning calls him cunning and a hypocrite. Party politics may be healthy for a nation and we are always being told so but I can't see why; attacks like that make me want to vomit – all over the *Mirror*. Fish this morning went around making sure he was on the register 'that's two votes for Churchill' he said when he found he was.

THURSDAY 24 MAY

Himmler committed suicide today. The news has just come through. Nothing had been heard from him for some time and he had disappeared. On Monday, however, he was stopped while in civilian clothes, a black patch over one eye and his moustache shaved off, by a routine examination of civilians passing a certain point. His papers showed he had been discharged from the army but as no discharge papers had been issued after a certain date he became suspect. It was not until yesterday as the interrogations became more and more intense that he owned to his identity. Today he was being medically examined for carrying possible poisons and the MO told him to open his mouth and felt inside. Himmler bit his finger and then crunched a phial of prussic acid hidden there. The doctors jumped at his throat to try to stop him swallowing but it was too late and the old sinner died. Pity. He ought to have been handed to the Russians or Poles. That's another gone. They are being accounted for one by one.

The score so far is Hitler, almost certainly dead. An official statement today says the Russians have found that he was in a bad mental state during the Berlin siege and his doctor gave him a shot of injected poison and his body was burnt. Goebbels poisoned himself too. All this sounds like a penny thriller. Goering is in custody and will be tried, we suppose, eventually. One paper said next November and the Russian papers are getting a little snorty about it all. Streicher, the Jew baiter, has been captured. Only Ribbentrop remains unaccounted for.

Over 550 Super-Forts attacked Tokio last night dropping

750,000 incendiaries on an industrial district. All 4,500 tons of them! Three-quarters of a million! Equal to one a minute for nearly two years!! And I suppose it will get worse still. The Japs tried a half-hearted attempt at peace terms a week ago. No wonder! Some say they will be broken by the end of the year.

WEDNESDAY 30 MAY
So much has happened and there's been so little opportunity, time, or indeed, inclination to record it. Margaret has been queer, I suppose she's been seriously ill, and is still showing temperatures of over 104, and there's been lots to do.

One outstanding item is that William Joyce, 'Lord Haw-Haw' as he was nicknamed and as he was often announced by the Jerries, has been captured. The British 2nd Army took him somewhere up in north-west Germany near the Danish border. He was ass enough to speak to a couple of British officers in a wood, out of bravado I suppose, and they recognised his voice. When challenged with his identity he admitted it and went as though to pull a gun but one officer beat him to it and shot him through the thigh. There's lots of satisfaction over the event and the papers make a lot of it. Most people hope he will be tried for treason and our dismal Jimmy, true to his type, has a story that Joyce being a naturalised German cannot be tried. The Army don't like him a bit. He wasn't a traitor so much as a ruddy renegade and I wouldn't like to be in his shoes.

SUNDAY 1 JULY
The longest by far that I have left this precious diary. Reason, of course. We've had Margaret seriously ill, the peak day was 5 June and now today we are at Clacton giving her a little recuperation and the wife and I a little change and, perhaps, recuperation too. It seems that I can hope to make up a little leeway in these entries.

The most outstanding event of the moment is the General Election. It comes on Thursday, the 5th and, being here, I shan't vote but I don't suppose anyone will mind that. It's a queer election. A kind of metamorphosis, in which the government officials who have been working together for over five years are now calling each other names. Admittedly the Labour Party started the 'calling', with the Liberals following the lead in a hesitant sort of manner and the Conservatives answering back. For four weeks there has been one official of each party giving a twenty-minute talk on the radio, Churchill starting, and ending last night.

There is a very pronounced, probably a complete, Allied superiority in the air in the Pacific and the Jap has replied in two ways. By far the most important are his suicide attacks.

At first they were a bit serious. He loaded a plane with bombs or HE in the fuselage and packed in a pilot who had determined to crash his plane on a target. The first ones were arrayed in ceremonial robes and a religious service preceded his take-off. Now he dispenses with the robes and his quality has deteriorated, a little due to the best ones having done their stuff. The chief attacks were on the Allied naval concentrations at Okinawa to which we have countered by having a screen of AA ships, and probably carriers, on the interception routs.

TUESDAY 3 JULY
At least I think that's the date. We are still on holiday and am a bit hazy.

The general strategy of the attack on Japan is unfolding. Naturally the Americans took the major part but we are now getting in as well. They started the counter-attack on New Guinea and then hopped on from island to island but they leapfrogged to the Philippines, the Marianas, the Ryukus and the general position now is that practically all New Guinea is freed of the Jap, Guam (I think), Saipan in the Marianas which is being used as a base for Super-Fort attacks on Japan proper, the whole of Leyte, Luzon and Mindoro in the Philippines and now Okinawa in the Ryukus. Okinawa was an achievement. It was attacked on Easter Sunday 1 April and being only about 400 miles from Japan proper was audacious. All the same the Jap, although he fought stubbornly, was eventually kicked out and the Americans now have another base very close to Tokio.

Now we are attacking Borneo. About four separate landings have been made, in Brunei Bay in the north-west, Sarakan in the north-east, another place in the north and, recently, at Balikpapan in the mid-east. That, with one big exception, is the general picture. The big exception is Burma. I ought to have reported it before and I ought to apologise to someone about it. Wonder if I can cover the history of it?

It all began early in 1942. The Jap, with his gift of Indo-China, pushed us out of most of Burma and then the monsoons made him halt. He paused and sparred for a time and made plans to take India which seemed quite a possible project, especially with Jerry reaching out a little hesitantly, though reciprocatingly, towards the Russian oilfields. We made plans too and built up a fair-sized army, eventually named the 14th Army. It became known as the Forgotten Army and I've subscribed to that view, I'm afraid, by not following their progress.

Eventually the Jap advanced. He crossed the Indian border and advanced on Arakan. We checked him and the silly ass held to his intention and spent valuable time in trying to reduce Arakan, the garrison of which held out stubbornly. Relief was sent, the Jap had outstripped his supplies which were also cut by the behind-the-line parachute landings by the Chindits under Wingate.

It was the turning-point. The poor old Jap started to withdraw, the withdrawal turned to rout and he's been retreating ever since. Right down Burma he was driven and soon Mandalay was outflanked, cut off, and attacked successfully. One or two coast leapfrog landings were made and just before the present monsoon broke Rangoon was taken.

Most of Burma is now in our hands and speculation is prominent about the next move, whether it will be towards Singapore. The terrain is bad and amphibious attacks will have to be made. We are sending troops out by Lancaster and other planes and are assembling again no doubt.

SUNDAY 15 JULY
The lights were on last night. Street lamps I mean. Officially street lamps start tonight because the clocks go back from two hours DBST advance to one hour today, and the lamps were lit last evening as a try-out. We had been out and came along Woodbridge Road on top of the tram and the kiddies were thrilled to see them in brilliant clusters as we looked along the straight parts of the road. So was I. It's quite a landmark in the war.

President Truman has crossed the Atlantic in a cruiser, was escorted by our destroyers when in our waters and today landed at Antwerp. Churchill left England a week ago for a week's holiday at Hendaye near the Spanish frontier in southern France and is on his way to Potsdam. There's a meeting of the Big Three there soon, possibly the details for the peace conference will be decided.

SUNDAY 22 JULY
The Potsdam Conference opened last Thursday and is still sitting even today, Sunday. There's great secrecy over their cogitations, so

great that no one knows even the subjects, and the hall is guarded to such an extent that when one day the place was shaken by demolition explosions nearby it took an hour for someone to get past the Russian guards to find the cause and another hour to go back with the message to stop it.

Churchill got away yesterday to inspect a march past of the famous Desert Rats, a nickname bestowed on the 11th Hussars who have made the greatest march in history, from El Alamein to mid-Italy to Normandy, Belgium, Holland and Berlin.

Those damn Jerries are amazing. When Churchill went out in his car the other day they actually cheered him. There were slightly sardonic references to it on the wireless news suggesting they possibly really were relieved to get away from the Nazi tyranny and might have regarded Churchill as a deliverer.

In Burma there have been about 9,000 survivors of the Jap 28th Army surrounded by our advance for some time. They are now trying to break out and there is some brisk fighting as the Japs try to reach the Sittoung river, which is flooded, in bad monsoon weather.

American warships have been inside Tokio Bay looking unsuccessfully for enemy ships. Loss of face with a vengeance for the Sons of Heaven. They must be feeling rather shaky about things by now.

FRIDAY 27 JULY
Election results were announced yesterday and there was a violent swing to the left. The Labour Party have 395 seats and the Conservatives 190, a huge majority. The immediate result is that Churchill does not go back to Potsdam. Attlee will go instead and I'm afraid history will decide that Attlee is no statesman. He looks too weak.

An interesting development in the Jap war: England and America issued from Potsdam yesterday a surrender ultimatum to Japan. Japan has rejected it and says it will fight to the bitter end and the American reply today was to tell Japan which are the next eleven towns on the list for aerial attack. Four of them will be burnt out in the next four days. That speaks eloquently of the relative powers of the two aerial sides.

THURSDAY 2 AUGUST
The Potsdam Conference ended early today and President Truman came to Plymouth where he met the King on *Renown*. He

returns to America in his own cruiser *Augusta*. All the subjects discussed at the conference were kept very secret, just nothing was divulged. Tonight, however, a statement was made at 2230 hr and I'm sitting up to hear it.

2245. Quite a long statement. It dealt in a general manner with what it was intended to do with Germany but details are to be left to the peace conferences to which France and China are to be invited. The high spots which I picked up are that Germany is to be completely demilitarised and all factories which could be employed on arms production are to be scrapped. Reparations will be taken in kind. Russian from her zone of occupation and British from the western zone of occupation, but reparations taken will not be such that they interfere with Germany's capacity to recover. Russia will have a strip of East Prussia and Poland and a strip of Germany west of existing Poland. All Germans in Poland, Hungary and Czecho-Slovakia must go but their departure will be regulated.

There will probably be full reports and criticisms in the paper tomorrow.

TUESDAY 7 AUGUST

Big news today. Bigger than any other item of all the war, or possibly, of all time so far. The Atomic Bomb has been used for the first time in Japan. The size used has an explosive power equivalent to 20,000 tons of HE and yet is only the size of a 400-lb bomb. Twenty thousand tons!!!! As one report puts it four of them will equal the total which Jerry dropped here during the war.

The imagination boggles at it at first then becomes very, very serious as one realises the possibilities, finally breathing a very deep prayer of thanks that Jerry didn't get hold of it first. The escapes we have had in this war are really sobering.

It appears that research was first started seriously into splitting the atom before the war and in 1939 it was realised that 'atomic fission' was a possibility. Research became government supported and progress was made until arrangements were made to work with America. In 1942 cooperation was such that it was agreed that America was the only possible venue of development in view of the Jerry threat to England, and they started work with four camps, two of them employing colossal numbers of workers who knew nothing of what they were doing. As one would expect uranium is the active element.

Jerry was working on the same lines and was using heavy water in conjunction with uranium, chiefly in Norway. Unfortunately for him we sent saboteurs over who blew up his research stations but we don't know what results he achieved. As a scale of the power of the new explosive it has been stated that a piece the size of a pea blew a hole in the desert in which a 'large house' could be placed. At a test of a bomb, men over 10,000 yd away were knocked over by the blast.

The Japs say the sample was dropped on a parachute and wide damage was done. The town chosen was Hiroshima and there is a security silence on news from America over the results.

Now what??? Will it mean the end of the war or the end of the human race? It might be as serious as that. Uranium may not be the only usable unstable element and with the hate the Jerries must have for us it is to be hoped there will be a really effective control on their scientists.

WEDNESDAY 8 AUGUST
Russia has declared war on Japan. It comes into effect tomorrow the 9th but due to the global nature of the conflict it is already the 9th out there so the new phase of the war is on. The reason is a bit naive. Stalin recalled that Japan had rejected the offer to surrender just recently and the Allies had asked Russia to intervene and so save time and lives and she has done so. Just that.

Re the new bomb, recce photos reveal that 60 per cent of Hiroshima is devastated. Over four square miles is in ruins. The reports speak of clouds of dust from pulverised bricks rising eight miles, of the pilot of the plane which dropped it racing away until at 10,000 yd range the crew felt the heat and the noise sounded like close heavy ack-ack. Another plane 170 miles away saw the explosion flash and it was in broad daylight. The Japs say people outside were burned to death by the heat and those in shelter were killed by blast. Corpses are too numerous to count, they say, but it is an outside broadcast and not intended for home consumption, so may be exaggerated.

Fresh data includes that the actual weight of the explosive was 8 lb, and that only 0.1 per cent of the available energy of the material was used. Amazing stuff.

THURSDAY 9 AUGUST
The Russians have started fighting in Manchuria. They have taken the offensive on the east and west borders of that squarish-shaped

country and have advanced in places up to fourteen miles. The Japs are reported to have 700,000 men there with a little armour so I guess it won't be long before the more numerous and better equipped Russians have succeeded in their well-practised pincer movement. The two forces are at the moment about 800 miles apart. The Japs have mobilised to meet 'this illegal invasion'. Perhaps they've forgotten Pearl Harbour.

A second atomic bomb has been dropped. This time it's on Nagasaki. No details or news of any sort have been issued.

It's all stage managed to get the best results. We issued the invitation to Japan to surrender on 26 July which they rejected. It was followed by an atomic bomb attack two days ago, to show them why we had issued the surrender invitation, then Russia declared war to make them wish they had surrendered and now a second atomic bomb is dropped to drive the lesson home. Possibly there will be another peace ultimatum soon; indeed it's probable.

FRIDAY 10 AUGUST

Whoops today. Japan has offered to surrender under the terms issued from the Potsdam Conference of 26 July which embraced unconditional surrender, with one 'if' – 'if the said declaration does not comprise any demand which prejudices the prerogatives of His Majesty as a sovereign ruler'. In other words if they can keep their Mikado unaffected and undamaged and without loss of too much face.

That atomic bomb business has eclipsed the more normal methods of attack. I haven't even bothered to report they are continuing. Yesterday for instance we sent in 1,200 carrier-borne planes.

Disquieting news about the food situation. An UNRRA official has given a very grave warning about the coming winter. He says that unless something is done and soon it will be the most serious in history. The European harvest is mostly 10 per cent to 15 per cent under last year and the transport which has been supplied is much under requirements. I can see our belts being tighter still this winter but I suppose we can't see the liberated countries starve. Don't see why Germany should be helped though, unless she gets to such a state she starts epidemics. We have stated we won't send her food unless that state is reached and I just hope we keep to it. She wouldn't have cared about us if she had won.

Incidentally her plans for captured England were released recently, to be used if she had won. They included one item that

<u>all</u> males of between seventeen and, I believe, sixty-five were to be exported to labour camps on the continent. Wonder if the jolly old Pope would have protested about that?

Went to see a pictorial exhibition yesterday about 'The war and Japan'. Quite good, gave a good photographic survey of the war, the conditions, the Jap services and the campaigns. One photo was of those ruddy yellow baskets using live Chinese prisoners as targets for bayonet practice.

Well, well, diary, looks as though I won't be writing you as a war diary much longer. I shall miss you.

MONDAY 13 AUGUST

No reply from Japan yet.

Carrier plane attacks have been resumed on Japan, on the Tokio area, and a battle fleet is cruising off the Tokio seas. Suggests we have a pretty good counter to the kamikaze suicide plane attacks.

Naturally rumours have been flying around, chiefly in America. One rumour is that the Japs had surrendered completely, another that they had been given a time limit, otherwise more atomic attacks would be made. An observer says if the suspense is kept up at this level, when peace does come, the Americans will celebrate a 'weary ritual'. In Canada a recorded speech by MacKenzie King, the Premier, greeting the end of the war and naming next Sunday as a day of thanksgiving, was broadcast in error. Naturally celebration was great but unfortunately a little premature. In Sydney celebration was at such a level that arson, looting and sacrilege of last war's memorials took place. The Sydneysians are asking what they are to expect when real peace comes.

Wonder if my forecast or prophecy made some years ago of 23 August '45 as peace day will come off after all? Naturally I had the European war in mind but I shall be tickled if it becomes correct for the whole war. Hope it does in a way. It's only ten days ahead and we are told that VJ day will not be named immediately until they accept our last terms.

Fred came home last week after four and a half years in the Middle East and Italy. He doesn't seem a scrap different from when he left but he's seen quite a bit.

TUESDAY 14 AUGUST

0815 hr. Have just heard on the 8 o'clock news that just before 7 o'clock a message was picked up from Japan saying acceptance of the Potsdam terms was on its way to the Allies. At about 6 o'clock we had picked up the beginning of a long coded message to Switzerland so presumably it will be all over soon.

Am starting work today after the second August week's holiday. Looks as if I shall be back again on the VJ holiday soon.

The news I recorded this morning set off some Americans celebrating again over in America, in spite of the hour at which it came. Then at 1700 hr the Japs sent another Morse message in English that the acceptance was really then being sent to Switzerland. They also broadcast to their own people to stand by for 'a really important announcement' at noon tomorrow which will be about 0400 hr here. It seemed significant to me this morning that the message being sent to Switzerland around 2000 hr was a long one. Surrender only necessitated two words. It would almost seem that they are playing for time somehow. Their own radio today has been giving only news and talks – no music or entertainment.

The Russians are going well ahead in Manchuria and in Sakhalin too.

WEDNESDAY 15 AUGUST
0115 hr. Was awakened a little while ago by a row. Japan has surrendered and people had started to celebrate. Hooters from the dock, ship sirens and then railway locos, all tapped out · · · —. Fireworks, a few, went up and people started to get about. Oerlikons from the ships in the docks tapped it out too in streams of crimson tracer. Hope it falls harmlessly.

It's all over. I've just picked up an American news service which relayed Attlee's announcement. Today, Wednesday, and tomorrow will be the public holidays and we will all be rejoicing. Peace again, thank goodness. That Oerlikon and the sirens are still sounding the V for Victory outside.

2200 hr. Have only just really realised the war is over. It was when the radio announcer said the King, in his speech just now, had asked us to think of those who had laid down their lives in the war and that he would play Walford Davies's 'Solemn Melody'. Somehow with thoughts of Den and Win and Mother it became very close and yet that doesn't express it. Yes, it's over now, there should be no more of the Supreme Sacrifice. We lost only one from that cause but five altogether who were with us in 1939 are gone now. Dora's mother and father who should have been with us are passed on too.

There are occasional entries in the diary until 2 December, reporting the return of prisoners of war from the Far East, the trials of war criminals and the true horrors of the Holocaust. Mr Brown also wrote at length about the secret weapons employed by both sides and those still on the drawing board. The economic distress of the formerly occupied countries, and the British Isles as Lease Lend is called in, and the potential problems with Russia are matters for concern. He was reluctant to bring the diaries to a close but finally does so on Victory Day 8 June 1946.

VICTORY DAY, SATURDAY 8 JUNE 1946

Yes, we are celebrating today so I suppose it's a suitable day on which to close this diary. I've enjoyed it; it's run to nearly 3,000 pages, readable possibly only to myself, but I hope it will provide a little relaxation, if not interesting reading in its recorded experiences and impressions, some future period, years hence. I hope I am spared to read it in the years ahead when all this is a faint memory. I'm disappointed in one or two things, chiefly in that I obeyed official instructions too literally. We were told to be careful in what we wrote and said, that the merest trifle, if found in the hand of the enemy, might be of supreme importance to them. Accordingly I kept to myself lots I would have recorded for after all it was a very real possibility that Jerry would come here.

We expected it and yet we didn't but it was certain that if he came Suffolk would see him. I wonder if I did record one of the vivid experiences in that regard? It was summer of 1940 and things were looking bad and invasion was being prepared for. From the west came the blackest, biggest, most enveloping menacing thundercloud I've ever seen. It came on remorselessly, it seemed, and I went round seeing if anything was open to the effects and if things were left out in the garden. The blackest prospect we've ever had – and it turned northward and we didn't get a drop of rain! I literally dare not think it was an omen of the expected invasion but the thought did occur as I stood at the front door watching it. We were serious minded then in our inmost thoughts and sure enough it proved itself to be an omen.

Here in Ipswich our chief contacts with the war, our chief aspects, were aerial and invasional. And nobody jibbed. I know one chap who vowed, early in the affair, he was keeping a tank full of petrol and if Jerry came he would be off like a shot taking his family to safety. He didn't do anything of the sort beyond arranging for his girl to go into the country in June '41 and was a keen Home Guard and tackled a bad fire single-handed when Jerry dropped incendiaries.

Yes, it was chiefly aerial. Our biggest care was for the night's events and it coloured my records I'm afraid, but they were genuine and I can honestly say nothing was entered for effect. I suppose I was a blithering idiot in some ways but my views helped me in some ways. I decided early to 'enjoy' the war as far as I could. Nothing I could do would change events in the slightest and if one takes an interest in having a tooth removed the shock is diminished. I remember, for instance, when Greenwood mentioned apologetically that we were doing long night duties I replied that they gave me a chance of seeing the stars. He thought I was loopy but I'll guarantee that no one else in the sector noticed that Jupiter had a retrograde movement that summer and autumn so I won there. Poor old Jupiter! He was accused by many people of being a landing light for Martlesham aerodrome. By the nature of things he was very bright and reasonably in the same part of the sky every night.

Many memories come crowding along directly one starts to think but they are mostly recorded. One thing, however, has emerged and that is the way we British stood head and shoulders above the other countries. Radio-location in its many forms, the Spitfire and Hurricane, the big bomber, the big bombs, atomic research, Fido, Pluto, the Merlin, Centaurus, Whittle's jet, the planned iceberg aerodrome, the frogmen, the receptions planned, if not used, for Jerry's invasion reception, the petrol pipeline in England, and all the many, many other achievements. If war comes again (and heaven forbid but many think it will) it's a comforting thought that we have brains on our side.

The position at the moment is this. From a food point of view we are worse off than at any time in the war. Through drought or mismanagement, probably both, the wheat position is bad and so is rice. There is a big probability that bread will be rationed here soon. The flour is back to 85 per cent extraction, feeding stuffs for stock and poultry will be cut by 40 per cent, 60 per cent and more in some cases next October. Canada and America are exporting all they can, as far as the many strikes in America will permit them, and we ourselves are cutting to the bone to feed Europe. Russia is doing nothing beyond keeping grain to herself. She may not have any to spare but she doesn't even make any offers. The Labour government is nationalising everything it can – mines, railways, gas, steel and some of the road transport. Probably more when they think of it and that is the background for the trade revival which is not so evident as it should be.

Export comes first for we must build up trade to pay for the many imports we need. The American loan is not yet through in its finality and we need the exports so, although goods are a little more numerous, it's still almost impossible to buy a cycle cover. Clothes are still rationed and will be for a year, probably two or three, and I still can't go into a shop and buy the chocolate I'd like to. Cars are almost impossible too and second-hand prices are enormous, about 150 per cent of their original price pre-war. Houses are a national joke. There was a big brick shortage which is a little easier now but seeing that there are few houses it won't matter much. Prefabricated houses are being put up but the declared policy is to insist that councils erect most of the permanent houses and private builders are not to be encouraged.

Politically things are bad and Russia is the chief stumbling block. She occupied Azerbaijan, the northern province of Persia, and refused Persian entry to the district. There's oil there. Persia reported the matter to the United Nations Organisation and Russia pettishly replied that Britain was endangering peace by having troops in Greece (in accordance with agreement until the elections took place) and in Indonesia. Both charges were rejected unanimously by the Council of the UNO and Russia was ordered to get out of Persia. She has now done so but with bad grace. There was a conference of foreign ministers in Paris to frame peace treaties but Russia torpedoed it by disagreeing with most things. She has now accused Britain and America of combining against Russia and our two Foreign Secretaries have replied in definite terms. Russia will be a headache.

Italy has had her elections and has also rejected the monarchy and voted for a republic by a small majority. King Emmanuel abdicated a month ago as he promised and his son Umberto took over. Now he goes in a day or two. Belgium is not too keen to have her King Leopold back again. France has had elections and has also lost de Gaulle who resigned after about ten threats to do so. He never was a statesman.

And in Nuremburg the trial of the Jerry criminals still goes on. A little while ago four Jerries who burnt four of our women who were caught when dropped over France, and burnt them alive, were sentenced to imprisonment; and our rations are being cut to feed them with. The food ration is pretty low in Germany but people are saying, 'Would Jerry have cared about us if she had won?' Still I suppose we must be as Christian as possible.

Today is Victory Day. There was a big parade in London, rounded off by a big aerial fly-past which was led by a single Hurricane, bless it, but slightly spoilt by the rain which is often present in such functions, but everyone seems happy. It's Victory Day and we deserve to celebrate. We won, just, but we won well and are rightly proud of our achievements. We've escaped something.

So I take leave of you, Diary, hoping that if ever I resume you it won't be for another war.

Select Bibliography

Calder, Angus, *The People's War 1939–1945* (London, Jonathan Cape, 1969)

Churchill, Winston S., *The Second World War*, 6 vols (London, Cassell, 1948–54)

Goralski, Robert, *World War II Almanac 1931–1945* (London, Hamish Hamilton, 1981)

Haines, Gregory & Coward, Cdr B.R., RN, *Battleship, Cruiser, Destroyer* (Leicester, 1994 edn)

Harrisson, Tom, *Living Through the Blitz* (London, Collins, 1976)

Jane's Fighting Ships of World War II (London, Random House, 1989)

Longmate, Norman, *How We Lived Then* (London, Hutchinson, 1971)

Middlebrook, M. & Everitt, C., *The Bomber Command Diaries 1939–1945* (Harmondsworth, Penguin Books, 1985)

Nicolson, Harold, *Diaries and Letters 1939–45* (London, Collins, 1968)

Taylor, A.J.P., *English History 1914–1945* (Oxford University Press, 1965)

Ramsey, Winston G., *Blitz Then and Now*, 3 vols (London, Battle of Britain Prints Int., 1990)

Richards, D. & Saunders, Hilary St G., *Royal Air Force 1939–1945* (London, HMSO, 1954)

Roskill, S., *The War at Sea* (London, HMSO, 1961)

Smith, Graham, *Suffolk Airfields in the Second World War* (Newbury, Countryside Books, 1997)

Woodman, Richard, *Arctic Convoys* (London, John Murray, 1994)

Index

Note: RB refers to Richard Brown, the diarist; maps are indicated by *italicised* page numbers